STRENGTH-BASED PRACTICE WITH CHILDREN AND FAMILIES

A HOPE-INSPIRING AND EMPOWERING APPROACH

ANGELA HODGKINS AND ALISON PROWLE

To order our books please go to our website www.criticalpublishing.com or contact our distributor Ingram Publisher Services, telephone 01752 202301 or email IPSUK.orders@ ingramcontent.com. Details of bulk order discounts can be found at www.criticalpublishing. com/delivery-information.

Our titles are also available in electronic format: for individual use via our website and for libraries and other institutions from all the major ebook platforms.

CRITICAL
PUBLISHING

STRENGTH-BASED PRACTICE WITH CHILDREN AND FAMILIES

A HOPE-INSPIRING AND EMPOWERING APPROACH

ANGELA HODGKINS AND ALISON PROWLE

First published in 2023 by Critical Publishing Ltd

British Library Cataloguing in Publication Data
A CIP record for this book is available from the British Library

ISBN: 978-1-915080-26-4

This book is also available in the following ebook formats:

EPUB ISBN: 978-1-915080-27-1
Adobe ebook ISBN: 978-1-915080-28-8

Text design by Greensplash
Cover design by Out of House Limited
Project management by Newgen Publishing UK

Critical Publishing
3 Connaught Road
St Albans
AL3 5RX

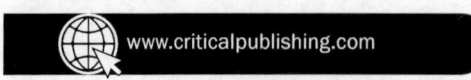 www.criticalpublishing.com

Printed on FSC accredited paper

Contents

Dedication

We would like to dedicate this book to our mothers, Joan Lillian Farley and Susan Harriet Williams, who showed strength and resilience in the face of adversity.

Angela Hodgkins and Alison Prowle

It takes courage to be gentle and kind when everyone expects boldness and anger.

Maya Angelou

List of figures and tables

Figures

Tables

About the authors

Angela Hodgkins

Angela Hodgkins has worked with children and families for 20 years in a range of settings and roles. She is now a senior lecturer at the University of Worcester and Course Leader for the BA (Hons) Integrated Working with Children and Families. Angela's main research interests are empathy, emotional intelligence and children's rights. She is currently conducting research for a PhD, looking at early childhood practitioners' perceptions of empathy within their role.

Alison Prowle

Alison Prowle began her career as a primary school teacher where she first witnessed the effects of multiple disadvantages on outcomes for children. This sparked a passion for early intervention with families and young children, working within schools, children's centres, the voluntary sector and local government. Most recently Alison has been teaching, researching and writing in the area of adverse childhood experiences, integrated working, parenting, and families at the University of Worcester.

About the contributors

Luiza Bivolaru is a senior practitioner with 20 years' experience of social work. Originally from Romania, Luiza moved to Wales with her husband in 2005 and started work as a social worker in a local authority adoption team. She believes people and relationships are the greatest resource in workplaces as well as personal life. Nurturing both ensures growth and tapping into strengths otherwise concealed.

Helen Coleman qualified as a speech and language therapist in 2003. After 10 years working in the NHS in a variety of settings, she now runs her own independent practice. She specialises in working with children with speech sound disorders and Development Language Disorder (DLD). She lives in Hampshire with her husband and teenaged daughter.

Gilda Davies originally trained as an enrolled nurse in South Wales before training as a children's nurse in London. She became interested in working with children with complex care needs when working in Romania with HIV+ children and spent the next 24 years in children's hospice care. Gilda is now a senior lecturer in children's nursing.

Poppie Ephgrave has worked in early years settings for seven years and trained at the University of Hertfordshire where she completed her BA in early childhood education. She is currently studying for her Master's degree and developing her research skills. She is passionate about critical pedagogy, philosophy and child-centred approaches, and about building relationships with children and seeing their smiles every day.

Mark Escott's (MBE) own troubled childhood led him to co-found the Life Chance Group, an award-winning therapeutic education, training and care provider, specialising in supporting young people and families who have experienced trauma. A best-selling author, in 2023 he was awarded the British Empire Medal for services to education.

Anisha Furaha qualified as a nursery nurse many years ago and worked in a variety of settings. The case study she has written in this book is based on memories of an incident when she worked in a primary school.

Ahzan Ghalib is a lecturer of academic skills at Birmingham City University. He is also a passionate advocate for equality, diversity and inclusion within the education sector. *'It is important to remember that lots of different flowers create a bouquet.'*

Michelle Griffiths is a team manager with 15 years' experience in social work. Originally from Birmingham, Michelle moved to Wales with her husband in 2009 and was employed as a social worker in the Local Authority Children with Disabilities Team, before being employed as a senior practitioner in a Locality Social Work Team. In 2017, Michelle secured a team manager post in the Supporting Change team in Blaenau Gwent. Michelle believes relationship building is the key to effective social work practice and by adopting a strength-based, outcome focused approach, positive working relationships are formed and change is achievable.

Nisha Kapoor is the mother of two children of mixed heritage. Her case study is about when her son's class were learning about Diwali. She hopes it will help people to think about involving parents when planning lessons about diverse cultures.

Phillipa Mason is a teaching assistant (TA) in a primary school and has a particular interest in SEND. Philippa returned to education after taking a job as a TA and has enjoyed the combination of academic study and work-based practice and the impact this has had on her ability to support all children to achieve their potential.

Cory Philips is a band 6 registered midwife and has been working in a large hospital for almost two years now, after completing three years' training. She sees herself as an advocate for women in labour and she works with women to make their own choices, always striving to create a positive birthing experience.

Sarah Savage is a qualified and experienced social worker who lives and works in Wales. She is currently team manager for a 0–25 disability service, where she has led her team through a series of service changes using a strength-based approach.

Charlotte Selvey has recently completed an Early Years Foundation Degree. Her place of work is a rural setting in a deprived area with families from all walks of life. This has given her the opportunity to support children and families in finding solutions to everyday issues.

Megan Smart was until recently working as an early years educator with ages 0–2 years in a private day nursery. She has since moved to a teaching assistant position in a primary school, but remains passionate about building close attachments with young children.

Gemma Southall spent many years working within the early years sector, before training to be a primary school teacher. She has now been at Wollescote Primary School for 11 years and is the assistant headteacher. She feels strongly about celebrating diversity and says she wouldn't want to work anywhere else.

Julia Swallow Edwards began her youth and community work career in 1996, raising awareness of HIV and Aids with Youthlink Wales. For the last 26 years, Julia has worked in open access and targeted provision. Her experience includes youth centre management, youth justice and managing a schools linked youth work programme. Julia is a qualified humanistic existential counsellor, youth and community worker, manager and teacher, with her research focused on partnership working and Wales New Curriculum. She has recently joined Cardiff Metropolitan University leading their Foundation Programme and lecturing on the undergraduate Youth and Community Work Degree.

Samuel Taylor is a music and drama student at the Guildford School of Acting. He is a passionate advocate for young people's participation both within the arts and in public life in general. Samuel has previously represented young people as a member of Youth Parliament and a Youth Mayor. He has spoken at the Senedd (Welsh Parliament) Westminster and the United Nations.

Caitlin Teague's professional career is in antenatal and post-natal care. She is now working alongside health visitors as a '*healthy child*' programme practitioner for the NHS. She works with families holistically and always manages to find strengths in order to promote resilience and self-efficacy.

Sarah Watkins was a primary teacher for many years and then head of school at her old primary school. Sarah is the author of two other books and is an associate lecturer at the University of Worcester, as well as running her own outdoor play company, Dandy Lions.

Olivia and Alex Storey are proud parents of a four and a half year-old girl. They will always remember and be eternally grateful for the support the National Health Service and early years practitioners provided their family through a particularly challenging time (and value their continued support).

Zoe Wright has worked in early years education in many roles and developed her practice and ethos through many books and experiences. But ultimately the children have been her biggest teacher. Montessori trained, she taught Reception in the private, voluntary and independent (PVI) sector for many years before moving into nursery management and ultimately now operational management and training and development. She is an instinctive practitioner and trusts the children to show her the way.

Acknowledgements

The idea for this book came from an ex-student of ours, Joe Groom, a nursery manager who asked Angela if she could recommend a book on strength-based practice with young children. Searching for such a book indicated that there was no such thing, so we decided to write it! Thank you, Joe, for starting this process.

We had both been advocates of the approach for some time and, as senior lecturers, we had instilled in our students the importance of a hope-inspiring, empowering approach to working with children and families. Through our teaching and collaborations with fellow educators, we came to meet many inspirational practitioners who had great stories to tell about the strength-based approaches to their work. We felt that the voices of these inspiring professionals should be heard by a wider audience, so we invited them to write case studies for our book. We would like to extend our heartfelt gratitude to all of you, your stories have humbled us and made us so proud.

We would also like to extend our thanks to Julia Morris and Lily Harrison from Critical Publishing for their support and guidance. We have been so impressed with Critical Publishing at every stage of the process.

We would like to thank our husbands, Shaun and Malcolm, and our families for their patience while this book has taken up so much of our time.

Finally, we would like to thank each other. Our collaborations are always enjoyable, and we value the strengths in each other; from Alison's great ideas and creativity to Angela's organisation and love of detail! We have loved the process and are already planning our next book.

1 A glass half full: introducing our strength-based philosophy

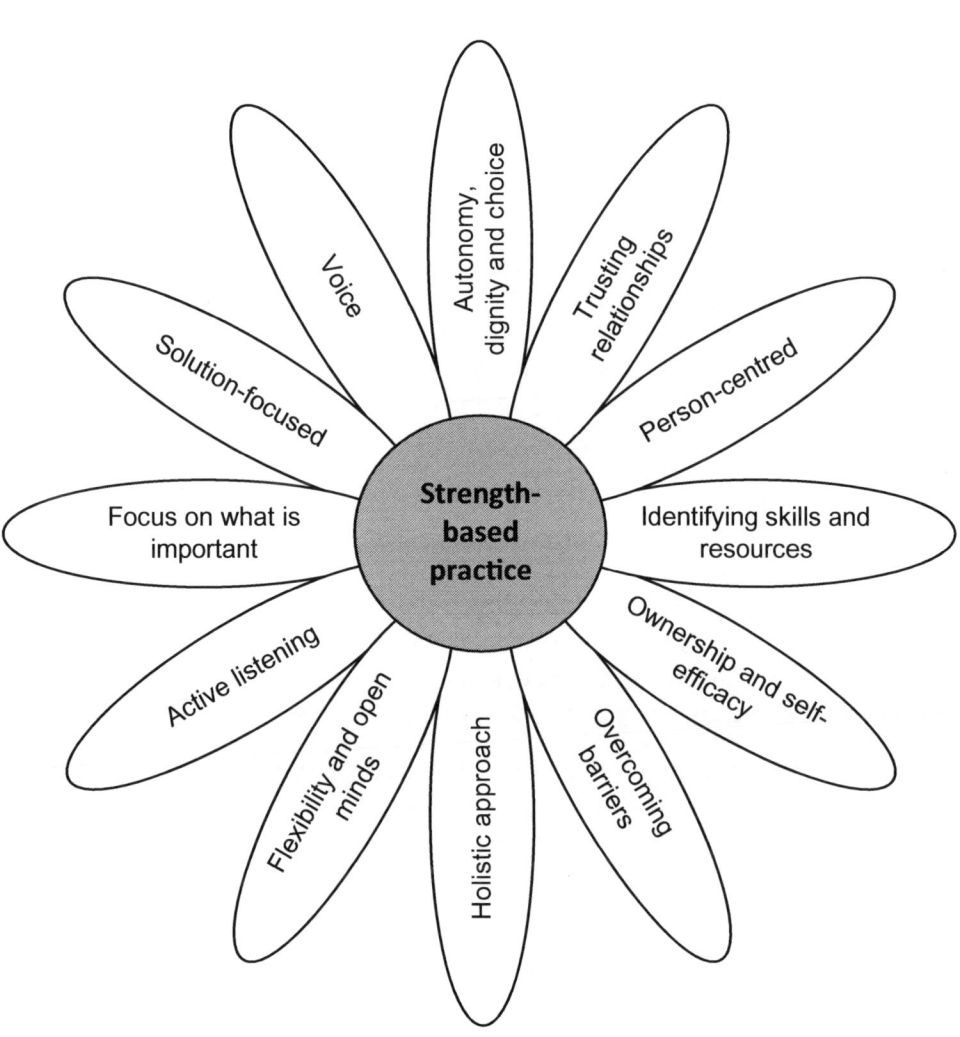

Chapter objectives ◎

This chapter:

*   identifies the elements of a strength-based approach;
*   outlines some theoretical perspectives on strength-based approaches;
*   introduces our personal strength-based philosophy;
*   introduces the chapters of this book.

Introduction

In this chapter the authors set out the strength-based approach taken throughout this book. We decided to write this book because we are passionate about strength-based practice, which informs our interactions with children, young people and families. This book is an optimistic and hopeful one, underpinned by a belief that practitioners can identify strengths within the most challenging of situations. Hammond (2010) explains, '*every person, family, group and community holds the key to their own transformation and meaningful change process*'. Where there are adverse life experiences within families, there will always be strengths within a family and identifying these can empower families to help themselves. Where there are challenges for a child in relation to special educational needs and disabilities (SEND) or health conditions, there will always be strengths in other areas, and identifying these empowers children and improves barrier-esteem and resilience. The problem with a deficit model where the focus is on '*what is wrong*' is that people rely on experts to solve the problem. However, when people are seen as experts in their own lives and are encouraged to resolve their own problems, they then take control and learn (Hammond, 2010). This is important in the development of resilience. Resilient people are able to set realistic goals for themselves and they view obstacles as challenges to confront. They have a strong sense of optimism and hope and an ability to '*bounce back*' in the face of adversity.

The following short fable (Figure 1.1) explains our philosophy of looking for opportunities and strengths, rather than problems and difficulties. The view of the second salesman is much more positive and, therefore, likely to succeed.

Many years ago two salesman were sent abroad by a shoe manufacturer to investigate and report back on market potential.

The first salesman reported back, 'There is no potential here – nobody wears shoes.'

The second salesman reported back, 'There is massive potential here – nobody wears shoes.'

Figure 1.1 *A fable summarising our approach (author unknown)*

Strength-based approaches

The idea of a strength-based philosophy is not a new one, in fact Dewey (1938, in Lopez and Louis, 2009) believed that '*the purpose of education is to allow each individual to come into full possession of his or her personal power*'. Encouraging independence and teaching people the skills they need to help themselves are cornerstones of working with people. The strength-based approach is concerned with helping people to identify and acknowledge their own strengths and enabling them to flourish.

Strength-based practice as we understand it today originated in the health sector where it is widely used in health and social care services (DHSC, 2019). The approach has since been adopted in the social work profession and is growing in popularity within the early years and education sectors, with Australia at the forefront of the approach. In education, the strength-based view is that '*potential exists in all students and that educators do well to discover and implement the kinds of learning experiences that can help their students realize this potential*' (Lopez and Louis, 2009, p 2). Table 1.1 outlines the principles of some strength-based approaches. The next stage was to identify which principles were important to us and to the professionals in our case studies. This enabled us to build a philosophy that makes sense to us and our experiences of working with people.

Table 1.1 *Principles within strength-based approaches*

Source	Definition of strength-based approach
Health & Social Care standards (DHSC, 2019) UK	Holistic and disciplinary
	Collaborative
	Proportionate
	Appropriate to the individual/flexible
	Aligned with risk enablement and positive risk taking
	A focus on what matters to you and what is strong
	Identifying personal, family and community strengths
	Supporting community development
	Applicable to any intervention, setting, type or level of need and profession
Principles of strength-based education (Lopez and Louis, 2009)	Measurements and data must include strengths
	Individualised support
	Networking and relationships
	Deliberate application of strengths
	Intentional development of strength
Care and Support Regulations (SCIE, 2015)	Consider the person's own strengths and capabilities
	Identify support from wider support network or within the community
	Looks at a person's life holistically, considering their needs in the context of their skills, ambitions, and priorities
	Identify the individual's strengths – personal, community and social networks – and maximise those strengths to enable them to achieve their desired outcomes
	Identify personal resources, abilities, skills, knowledge, potential, etc
	Identify social network and its resources, abilities, skills, etc
	Identify community resources, also known as 'social capital' and/or 'universal resources'

Table 1.1 (Cont.)

Source	Definition of strength-based approach
Principles of strength-based nursing (Gottlieb, 2013; Gottlieb et al, 2022)	Person/family-centred care
	Health promotion and healing
	Empowerment
	Collaborative partnership
	Innate capacities for health and healing
	Working with the whole, while appreciating interrelationships
	Recognising the uniqueness of people and organisations
	Environments that promote health and facilitate development
	Understanding the significance of subjective reality and created meaning
	Valuing self-determination
	Recognising that person and environment are integral
	Collaborative partnerships
Department of Early Education Care and Development (2012) Australia	The opposite of a deficit model
	Understanding differences in learning
	Starting with what is present
	Focus on what learning and development could look like in the future
	Everyone has strengths and abilities
	Children grow and develop from their strengths and abilities
	Problem is the problem – the person is not the problem
	Valuing everyone equally
	Acknowledging that people experience difficulties and challenges that need support
	Identifying what is going well
	Relationships and communication are key
	Honesty and transparency

Reflective questions ⑦

» Choose the five principles from Table 1.1 that most stand out as being important to you.

» For each principle, identify how you might ensure that the principle could be demonstrated in your own work setting, for example:

1. Person/family-centred care	Taking time to get to know parents by setting up activity days with opportunities for conversation.
	Home visits before child starts nursery, getting to know the family in their own space.
	Adopting a keyworker system.

Social pedagogy

Another approach about which the authors of this book are passionate is social pedagogy, the principles of which align closely with the strength-based approach (see Figure 1.2). The overarching themes of equality, empowerment and relationships are represented, along with the essential personal skills of empathy and positive regard. We have incorporated some of these standards into our strength-based philosophy.

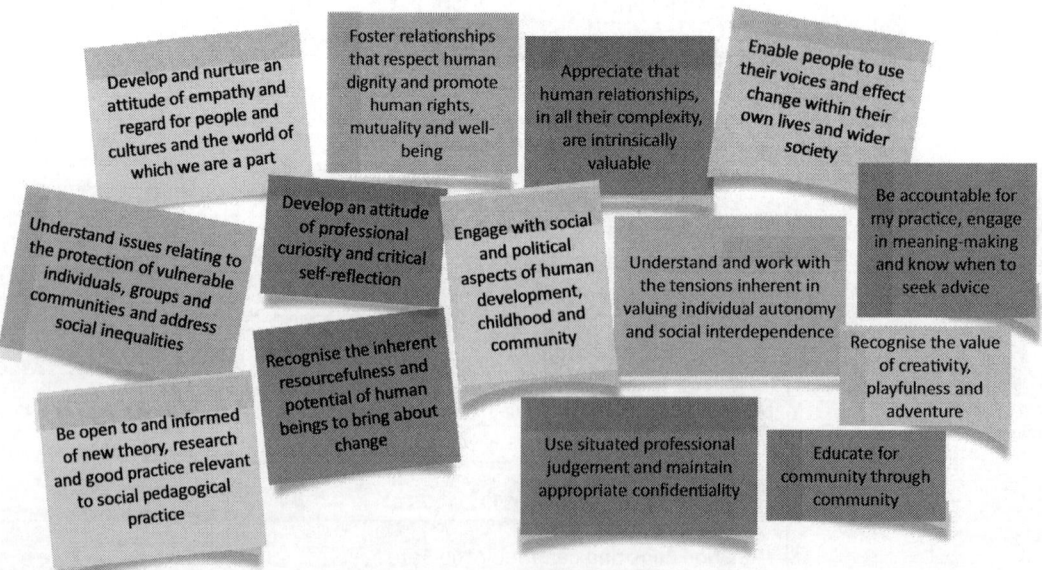

Figure 1.2 *Diagram based on ThemPra (2021) social pedagogy standards*

Our strength-based philosophy

We have drawn together aspects of our strength-based philosophy in Figure 1.3 below (also shown at the start of this chapter). The following section explores each of these facets in more detail.

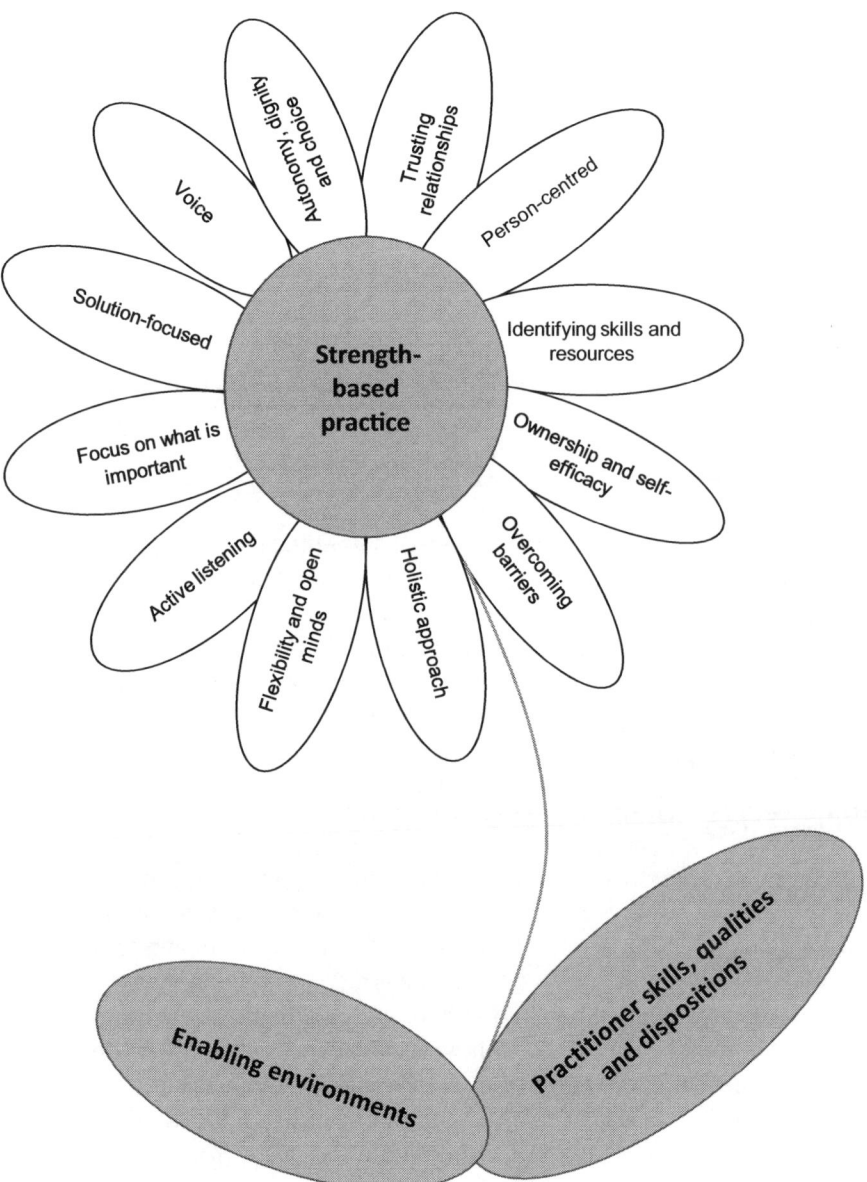

Figure 1.3 *The flower: our understanding of strength-based practice with children and families*

The flower

There were many symbols that could have been chosen to represent our philosophy, but the daisy seemed most fitting. This simple flower blooms for most of the year, brightening up lawns, verges and grassland everywhere. With its many petals, this flower provided a useful motif for reflecting a multi-faceted understanding of strength-based practice. However, each '*petal*' is actually an individual flower as common daisies have composite flower heads, made up of lots of tiny flowers (The Wildlife Trusts, nd). Often associated with simplicity and transformation, the flower, with its yellow sun-like centre, provides a positive and hopeful image for exploring a practice of focusing on strengths. The daisy is persistent and widespread and reflects the way in which a focus on strengths can be contagious in spreading more positive ways of thinking and being.

The leaves

At the base of a single daisy stem are the leaves, crucial for feeding the plant and allowing it to make the most of the sunlight. It is here that we have located the importance of an enabling environment and also how practitioners' own skills, qualities and attributes can become a resource for the family.

Enabling environments

The concept of an enabling environment is well documented in early years practice. The Early Years Alliance defines an enabling environment as '*a rich and varied space where risks are minimised and well managed, and children are protected from harm and abuse*' (Early Years Alliance, nd). Hence the concept of an enabling environment applies as much to the emotional environment as to the physical environment. However, the construct of an enabling environment has resonance beyond early childhood, with a recognition of its importance in education, health and youth work.

Practitioner skills, qualities and attributes

The role of the practitioner in supporting strength-based approaches is of paramount importance. In our previous book, we conceptualised the practitioner as an '*architect of hope-inspiring relationships*' (Prowle and Hodgkins, 2020, p 139), helping families to envisage and work towards positive outcomes, even in challenging circumstances. This requires building an authentic and trustful relationship with families. While there are many skills and attributes that can contribute positively to your work with families, perhaps the most important at the point of establishing the relationship include being open, friendly, approachable and non-judgemental in your approach. As the relationship moves on reliability, commitment and resilience become ever more important. Throughout the book, the role of the practitioner is explored in more detail.

The petals

The petals of the flower diagram represent the many facets of strength-based practice. These are explored in more detail throughout the book, but an overview is provided here.

Trusting relationships

Merriam-Webster defines trust as '*assured reliance on the character, ability, strength, or truth of someone or something*'. It is worth remembering that some of the people you are working with (particularly those who have experienced trauma) may have difficulties with relationships and trust. Recognising that trust is not automatic and will need to be nurtured is a crucial starting point in building a positive relationship. For Hohman (2021), practitioners need to engage in mindful and purposeful action to engage families and help restore trust, prior to beginning any other work. Key to this is the creation of a safe space where individuals or families feel supported and listened to. Reliability, consistency and transparency are all fundamental to helping to develop trustful and productive working relationships.

Solution-focused

While it can sometimes be helpful to explore and analyse '*the problem*' and its underlying causes and consequences, often a focus on solutions can help individuals move forward more quickly. Thinking about solutions enables a focus on imagining possibilities and the future rather than re-rehearsing the difficulties of the past. For McKergow (2021) this facilitates positive change by helping to '*stretch the world*' for individuals we are working with, allowing them to envision and then work towards new possibilities and goals. Hence this approach can be very empowering and help to support increased confidence and self-efficacy.

A focus on what is important

For families or individuals struggling with feeling overwhelmed, it can sometimes be very difficult to prioritise. Helping families identify what is most important can be very helpful in enabling them to move on. This is particularly important in situations which are very complex and where there are a number of issues affecting the family. It is impossible to tackle everything at once, so identifying priorities and then approaching these in a strength-based manner can be very helpful in enabling the family to see that they are making progress.

Voice

It is crucially important that the people we are working with have a say in what is going on. This is equally important for parents and for children. When we think of the '*child's voice*' we are referring not only to what children may say to us directly, but also to the multiplicity of ways that they may express themselves. This is summarised beautifully in Malaguzzi's one hundred languages of children. It means more than seeking their views, which could just mean the child saying what they want, rather than really being involved in what happens. For the practitioner this means being attuned to the child, picking up on their non-verbal cues and advocating for their views.

Autonomy, dignity and choice

Autonomy is about having control and choice over one's life and decisions. It is important to recognise that personal dignity and autonomy are the very foundation of human rights and are closely aligned to the principles of equality and non-discrimination. Marginalised groups may find it difficult (because of structural and societal issues) to fully access their rights and exercise autonomy and hence may need support to do so. The practitioner can help by prioritising individuals' choice and autonomy in all aspects of their practice and working hard to reduce stigmatisation and marginalisation within wider communities.

Person-centred approach

A person-centred approach (PCA) is about focusing caring work on the needs and aspirations of the individual. It includes a focus on not judging others, trying to understand the experiences of others from their own point of view, and treating people with compassion and respect. A PCA recognises that people are individuals, and that support needs to be bespoke and personalised in order to achieve the best outcomes.

Identifying strengths, skills and assets

Everyone has strengths, skills and abilities. However, some individuals may find it hard to identify or articulate their own strengths, and some skills may be subtle and less noticeable than others. Chapter 3 talks about strength-spotting, helping children to recognise their own strengths. This approach can be very effective in supporting children's confidence and learning. Young people, adults, families and communities can all benefit from strength and asset spotting. Strengths and assets in this context refer to different elements that may help or enable the individual to deal with challenges and achieve their desired outcomes. These elements may include their personal resources, abilities, skills, knowledge and potential; and their social network and its resources, abilities, skills, community resources and networks (also known as social capital). Identifying these strengths and assets can provide individuals with a greater understanding of all the resources that they have in their corner to help them achieve positive outcomes (SCIE, 2015).

Ownership and self-efficacy

According to Bandura (1977, p 2) self-efficacy is *'the belief in one's capabilities to organise and execute the courses of action required to manage prospective situations'*. People with high self-efficacy can develop deep interests in the activities they enjoy, show commitment to meeting their goals and recover more quickly from setbacks. Conversely, lower self-efficacy can result in avoidance of challenge, a focus on personal failure and loss of self-confidence. When supporting individuals or families to make positive change, understanding self-efficacy can be very important. Like resilience, self-efficacy is something that can be learned and coached, and providing the people we work with opportunities to develop their self-efficacy can be helpful in enabling them to maximise their strengths.

Resilience and overcoming barriers

Resilience refers to both the process and the outcome of successfully adapting to difficult or challenging life experiences (American Psychological Association, 2023). It entails an ability to cope in spite of setbacks, barriers or limited resources. Miles (2015) identifies many reasons why resilience is a helpful trait to develop, including enhanced health and longevity, improved education and employment outcomes and increased community involvement. There is much that practitioners can do to support both their own resilience and that of the people they work with (Hart and Heaver, 2015) but there is evidence that a systematic and whole systems approach (involving all who work with the child/family) can be most effective. There is also a recognition that working with children, young people and families is challenging and often emotionally demanding. Therefore, practitioners themselves need the time and support to develop their own resilience, not least so that they can model resilient moves to others.

Holistic approach

An holistic approach means to provide support that looks at the whole person. This means that practitioners sometimes need to step outside their primary role (for example as educators or healthcare workers) and view the entire person. Hence, support should also consider their physical, emotional, social and spiritual well-being. Multi-agency responses can be helpful in helping us to view the person holistically, as can listening to the person, getting to know them as an individual and knowing what is important to them.

Flexibility and open-mindedness

Open-mindedness can be defined as the willingness to consider experiences, beliefs, values and perspectives that differ from one's own (Bautista et al, 2018). This is important for practitioners who may encounter a wide range of different circumstances, individuals and value systems in the course of their work. Being able to put aside their own assumptions and biases to tune into the realities and perspectives of others is a key skill for practice.

Active and empathetic listening

Richard Nelson-Jones (2014) says we should recognise the difference between hearing and listening. While hearing involves decoding sounds, listening involves tuning in to the individual in an attempt to accurately understand the meaning that they are communicating. Listening in this way involves giving our whole attention, being comfortable with silence and focusing on understanding not replying (Engel, 2018). Listening in this way can be extremely powerful, especially for those who may not have felt heard in the past.

Unconditional positive regard

The term unconditional regard was first used by Rogers (1951). He described it as 'caring for the client as a separate person, with permission to have his own feelings, his own experiences' (Rogers, 1957, p 98). It entails support and acceptance of a person regardless of what that person says or does. Myers (2007) sees this as an attitude of grace, which allows individuals to open up, drop pretences and experience growth.

Optimism and hope

Optimism is an attitude of mind characterised by hope and confidence in success and a positive outcome. As such, optimists tend to view difficulties as temporary setbacks or an opportunity for learning. An optimistic attitude can have many benefits and has even been associated with a better immune system (Segerstrom and Sephton, 2010) and an increased life-expectancy (Buigues et al, 2021). Optimism is not so much about ignoring the realities of a situation as it is about finding positives to work with and making the most of situations. Crucially, optimism is not simply an innate character trait, but something that can be practised and learned (Seligman, 2007). The practitioner can help by modelling optimism, focusing on efforts not results and helping individuals to remember happier and more successful times.

Can too much positivity be problematic?

While there is much evidence for the benefits of adopting a strength-based approach, practitioners need to be cognisant of the need to avoid a '*positivity at all costs*' approach. Strength-based practice does not negate the need to recognise that some experiences are incredibly difficult, or even tragic. Trying to put a positive slant on such situations may come across as inauthentic, disingenuous or even dismissive of the very real struggles of others. In turn, this can silence those we are working with, deterring them from seeking help and invalidating their experience. In turn, this can lead to enhanced feelings of isolation and helplessness. Often termed '*toxic positivity*' an unrelenting and exclusive focus on strengths can result in negative outcomes for the people with whom we are working (Campbell-Sills et al, 2006) despite the best intentions of the practitioner. This sort of positivity often surfaces when practitioners are struggling to know how to respond to a difficult situation. Sometimes, just acknowledging that something is really hard or really painful and that you are glad they shared it with you can be the very best response you can offer.

Another criticism of a strength-based approach is that in focusing exclusively on strengths we can ignore or underestimate the risks that can be present in a situation. This is important from a safeguarding perspective as the Care Act 2014 places a duty on us to identify potential harm, to protect those who have experienced it and to prevent harm from reoccurring. However, it is possible to balance our accountability with a strength-based lens through fostering their engagement and involving people proactively in all aspects of their support. This is explored more fully in the safeguarding chapter.

While the foregoing urges caution in taking an exclusively strength-based approach, a focus on strengths can provide a useful tool in your practitioner toolbox. It helps practitioners to move beyond the traditional deficit models which focus solely upon the problem, and hence upon what is *not* going well, and enables us to identify those areas of success that can be used as a springboard for positive change. In doing so, it can help those we work with to recognise, celebrate and further develop their talents, abilities and social connections.

The authors reflect on their own philosophy of strength-based practice

Alison

I first became an advocate of strength-based practice after years of working with families who had been told that they were failing. In many cases, they had given up and really did not believe that positive change was possible for them. I started to think that there must be a better way of doing things. Now, focusing on strengths has become a core principle of my practice, and makes such a difference. I think I apply it in many aspects of life, including my parenting and my relationships. It's not a cure-all, but it provides us with a great starting point.

Angela

I think that in my role today, trusting relationships are key. My students need to be able to trust me so I am honest, and I do my very best to support them in any way I can. Another really important aspect of SBP (strength-based practice) is 'flexibility and open minds'. No one approach suits everyone, every person is an individual, so I need to be flexible in my approach. Some students need reassurance and gentleness, others need to be directed and challenged. It is up to me to get to know them as individuals and to decipher what they need from me. As a teacher, I never feel that I am the expert with all the answers; I am open to listening to their experiences and learning from them. I also encourage them to be open and to listen to each other's perspectives. Each person in the classroom comes to the group with their own experiences, so it is important to encourage ownership of their own skills and knowledge. All of my students have had work experience and they all have valuable knowledge and skills to share, to the benefit of the whole group.

Reflective questions ⑦

» Think of an example where you adopted a strength-based approach.

- What were the circumstances?

- How did you identify and build upon strengths?

- What were the benefits of this approach?

- Were there any challenges and how did you overcome them?

» Think of an example where you did not adopt a strength-based approach.

- What were the circumstances?

- What approaches did you take?

→

> – What were the benefits of this approach?
>
> – Were there any challenges and how did you overcome them?
>
> – Would there have been merit in adopting a strength-based approach in this example?
>
> – How would you go about working to identify and build on strengths?
>
> » Reflect upon your own strengths as a practitioner. You may also want to ask those around you about how they perceive your strengths. Make a record of your strengths – this could take the form of a list, a journal entry or something more creative. Store your strengths somewhere safe as there will be an opportunity to use this reflection later in the book.

Chapter summary 📖

This chapter has introduced the concept of strength-based practice and explored why this might be a useful tool for our practitioner toolbox. Strength-based practice encourages us to focus on what is strong and going well rather than on the deficits and problems. As such, it can be a game-changer in helping children and families to celebrate their successes and move forward with confidence. The remainder of the book explores how you can apply strength-based practice to different situations and in different work contexts.

Further reading 📚

• Prowle, A and Hodgkins, A (2020) *Making a Difference with Children and Families – Re-imagining the Role of the Practitioner.* London: Red Globe Books, Bloomsbury.

This is our first book, where the ideas influencing this book originated. The book is a hopeful positive one which incorporates all aspects of work with children and families.

• Malaguzzi, L (1996) *The Hundred Languages of Children: The Reggio Emilia Approach to Early Childhood Education.* New Jersey: Ablex Publishing Corporation.

The Reggio Emilia approach shares many ideas with the strength-based approach, particularly in relation to understanding others as individuals and appreciating the voice of the child.

• Plotinsky, M (2021) How to Resist Toxic Positivity. [online] Available at: www.educationworld.com/teachers/how-resist-toxic-positivity (accessed 19 June 2023).

Useful summary of '*toxic positivity*', particularly in an education context – a positive psychology approach.

References

American Psychological Association (2014) *The Road to Resilience*. [online] Available at: www.apa.org/helpcenter/road-resilience.aspx (accessed 24 July 2023).

American Psychological Association (2023) *APA Dictionary of Psychology: Resilience*. [online] Available at: https://dictionary.apa.org (accessed 29 June 2023).

Bandura, A (1977) Self-efficacy: Toward a Unifying Theory of Behavioral Change. *Psychology Review*, 84(2): 191–215.

Bautista, N, Misco, T and Quaye, S (2018) Early Childhood Open-Mindedness: An Investigation into Preservice Teachers' Capacity to Address Controversial Issues. *Journal of Teacher Education*, 69(2): 154–68.

Buigues, C, Queralt, A, De Velasco, J, Salvador-Sanz, A, Jennings, C, Wood, D and Trapero, I (2021) Psycho-social Factors in Patients with Cardiovascular Disease Attending a Family-centred Prevention and Rehabilitation Programme: Euroaction Model in Spain. *Life*, 11(2): 89.

Campbell-Sills, L, Barlow, D, Brown, T and Hofmann, S (2006) Effects of Suppression and Acceptance on Emotional Responses of Individuals with Anxiety and Mood Disorders. *Behaviour Research and Therapy*, 44(9): 1251–63.

Department of Education and Early Childhood Development (2012) *Strength-based Approach*. [online] Available at: www.education.vic.gov.au/documents/childhood/professionals/learning/strengthbappr.pdf (accessed 19 June 2023).

Department of Health and Social Care (2019) *Strengths-based Approach: Practice Framework and Practice Handbook*. [online] Available at: https://assets.publishing.service.gov.uk/government/uploads/system/uploads/attachment_data/file/778134/stengths-based-approach-practice-framework-and-handbook.pdf (accessed 19 June 2023).

Early Years Alliance (nd) *Enabling Environments*. [online] Available at: www.eyalliance.org.uk/enabling-environments (accessed 29 June 2023).

Engel, J (2018) How Empathic and Active Listening Can Improve Workplace Communication. *Forbes*. [online] Available at: www.forbes.com/sites/forbescoachescouncil/2018/12/19/how-empathic-and-active-listening-can-improve-workplace-communication (accessed 19 June 2023).

Gottlieb, L (2013). *Strengths-based Nursing Care: Health and Healing for Person and Family*. New York: Springer Publishing.

Gottlieb, R L, Vaca, C E, Paredes, R, Mera, J, Webb, B J, Perez, G et al (2022) Early Remdesivir to Prevent Progression to Severe Covid-19 in Outpatients. *New England Journal of Medicine*, 386(4): 305–15.

Hammond, W (2010) *Principles of Strength-based Practice*. Resiliency Initiatives, Calgary: Alberta. [online] Available at: https://greaterfallsconnections.org/wp-content/uploads/2014/07/Principles-of-Strength-2.pdf (accessed 19 June 2023).

Hart, A and Heaver, R (2015) *Resilience Approaches to Supporting Young People's Mental Health: Appraising the Evidence Base for Schools and Communities*. Brighton: University of Brighton. [online] Available at: www.boingboing.org.uk/resilience-approaches-guide/ (accessed 19 June 2023).

Hohman, M (2021) *Motivational Interviewing In Social Work Practice*. London: Guilford Publications.

Lopez, S J and Louis, M C (2009) The Principles of Strengths-Based Education. *Journal of College and Character*, 10: 1–8.

McKergow, M (2021) *The Next Generation of Solution Focused Practice: Stretching the World for New Opportunities and Progress*. Oxford: Routledge.

Miles, J (2015) *The Importance of Building Resilience*, Counselling Directory. [online] Available at: www.counselling-directory.org.uk/counsellor-articles/the-importance-of-building-resilience (accessed 19 June 2023).

Myers, D (2007) *Psychology*. New York: Worth Publishers.

Nelson-Jones, R (2014) *Practical Counselling and Helping Skills*. London: Sage.

Prowle, A and Hodgkins, A (2020) *Making a Difference with Children and Families – Re-imagining the Role of the Practitioner*. London: Red Globe Books, Bloomsbury.

Rogers, C (1951) *Client-centered Therapy: Its Current Practice, Implications and Theory*. London: Constable.

Rogers, C (1957) The Necessary and Sufficient Conditions of Therapeutic Personality Change. *Journal of Consulting Psychology*, 21(2): 95–103.

Segerstrom, S and Sephton, S (2010) Optimistic Expectancies and Cell-mediated Immunity: The Role of Positive Affect. *Psychological Science*, 21(3): 448–55.

Seligman, M (2007) *The Optimistic Child: A Proven Program to Safeguard Children Against Depression and Build Lifelong Resilience*. London: Houghton Mifflin Harcourt.

Social Care Institute for Excellence (SCIE) (2015) *Care Act: Guidance on Strengths-based Approaches*. [online] Available at: www.scie.org.uk/strength-based-approaches (accessed 19 June 2023).

The Wildlife Trusts (nd) *Common Daisy*. [online] Available at: www.wildlifetrusts.org/wildlife-explorer/wildflowers/common-daisy (accessed 29 June 2023).

ThemPra (2021) *Social Pedagogy*. [online] Available at: www.thempra.org.uk/social-pedagogy/ (accessed 19 June 2023).

2 From conception to the first months

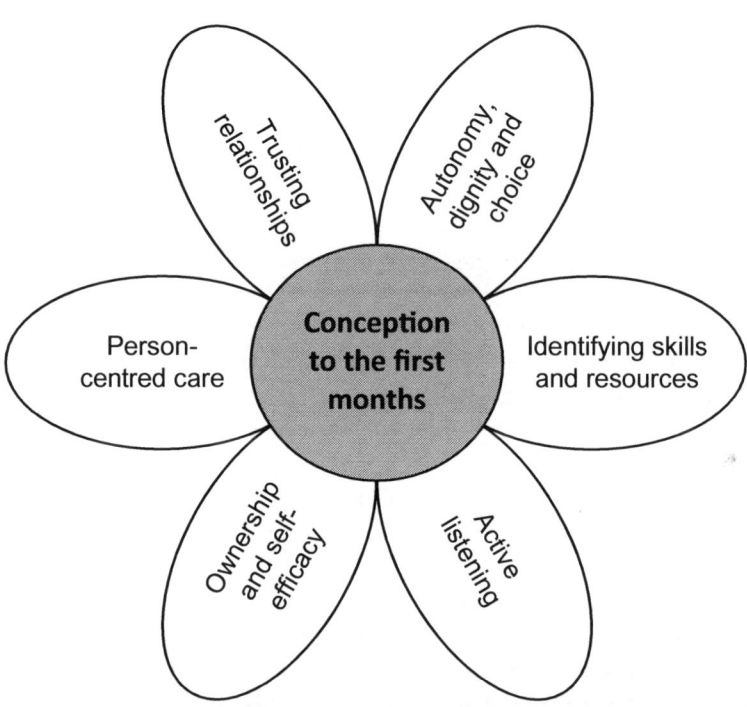

Chapter objectives ◎

This chapter:

- outlines the principles of strength-based practice in antenatal care, labour and birth;
- discusses strength-based approaches to supporting a positive transition to parenthood;
- illustrates child-centred, strength-based care of the baby.

Introduction

This chapter focuses on antenatal care, birth and the care of babies and their families. The chapter begins with a section on antenatal care, with a focus on listening to the mother (and other family members) and providing person-centred care. The identification of strengths and potential is discussed with professionals as advocates for women during pregnancy and birth are examined through a case study written by a qualified midwife.

The transition to parenthood can be difficult for some, so ways of making transitions positive and hopeful are important. Attachment between mother and baby and the building of relationships with caregivers are crucial, so ways of supporting new parents and babies are explored, while retaining the principle that people are experts in their own lives. When caring for babies, a holistic view with the child at the centre is paramount. Parenting which is based on the parent–child relationship and which is baby-led are explored. Case studies from professionals working as midwives, and with new parents, provide examples from their strength-based practice.

Antenatal care, labour and birth

Pregnancy and birth, although natural processes, are major transitions in the lives of women and their families. They bring more profound changes and demand more adjustment than any other life event (Deave, Johnson and Ingram, 2008). Supportive antenatal care which utilises families' strengths is therefore crucial. Heinonen (2021) recommends a *salutogenic* approach – one that focuses on health and well-being, rather than focusing on illness, and one which fully involves partners. For the majority of women, pregnancy is '*a low risk process*' (Villarmea and Kelly, 2020, p 156), therefore women should be able to control what happens to them throughout this process. The latest guidance from the National Institute for Health and Care Excellence (NICE, 2021) is very much strength-based, focused on '*placing women at the centre of their own care*' (RCM, 2021). A '*one size fits all*' approach is not applicable, as every woman and family is different in culture, background, values and past experiences. Parents' needs should be respected, along with '*non-judgemental, strengths-based support from facilitators*' (Stewart-Brown and Schrader-McMillan, 2010).

Reflective questions ⑦

» Examine each of the assumptions in Figure 2.1, which are common beliefs about pregnancy and birth. Reflect on the realities and the spectrum of experiences that women may actually experience. How damaging can these statements be to women?

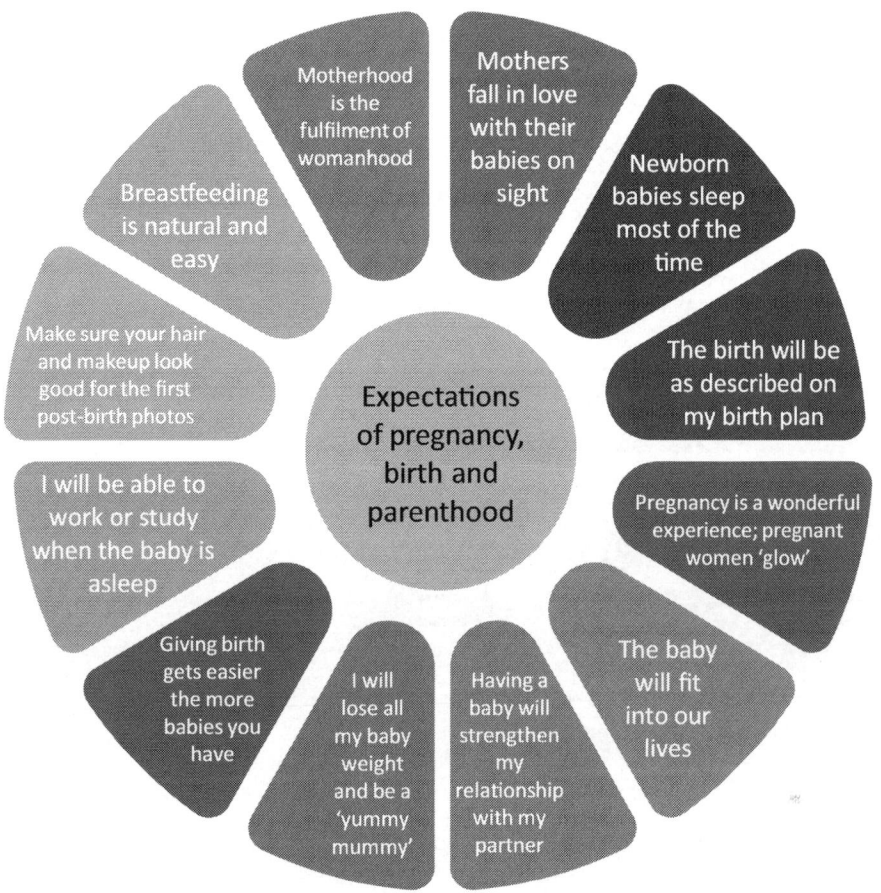

Figure 2.1 *Expectations of pregnancy, birth and parenthood*

A DoH and NHS resource document (2011) states that *'from pregnancy onwards, the relationship between a baby and his or her primary caregiver has a lasting impact on that child's future, including on his or her health as an adult'*. It is important, then, to minimise anxiety and create a feeling of competence in parents-to-be while they build this relationship. One way that practitioners can do this is by reframing any perceived weaknesses or worries into positive strengths. Figure 2.2 below provides some examples of negative perceptions of people, reframed into positive characteristics. Identifying people's skills and resources and voicing these characteristics makes people feel capable and positive.

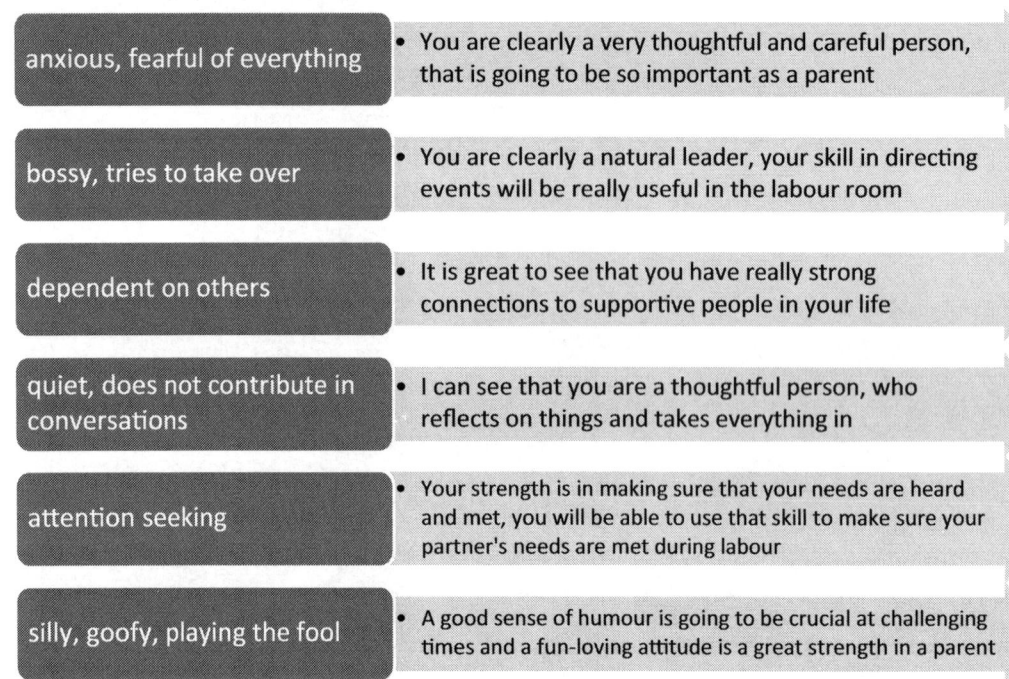

Figure 2.2 Reframing negative perceptions

Using empathy and tuning into the people we work with enables us to build supportive relationships with people (Hodgkins, 2019). This initiates person-centred care that empowers and supports. The Royal College of Midwives (RCM, 2021) claim that this personalised approach improves outcomes for mothers and babies. However, the ꞌ ꞌ˾ ꞌvidence that this isn't always the case. A study by Villarmea and Kelly (2020) suggest˸ ꞌ ꞏꞏ˸ when women are in labour and are experiencing pain and fear with contractions, this affects their ability to retain information or make decisions, and it is then that clinicians may take over and make decisions about what is '*for the best*'. This can disempower women and make them feel that they have no power over what happens to them.

Self-efficacy, the belief that one is capable of one's own ability, is a concept first proposed by Bandura (1977) and this is a powerful tool. Tanglakmankhong, Perrin and Lowe (2010, p 193) write that '*women who have greater confidence in their ability to cope with labour report having less fear in childbirth*'. Building self-efficacy, then, can improve outcomes for women in labour. But not everyone has high self-efficacy. Bandura (1977) suggested four sources of self-efficacy beliefs (see Table 2.1).

Table 2.1 *Four sources of self-efficacy*

• Mastery experiences	having had success in the past builds self-belief
• Vicarious experiences	observing people we see as similar to ourselves succeeding
• Verbal persuasion	being persuaded that we are capable by influential people in our lives
• Emotional and physiological states	good mental health, positive emotions boost our self-confidence
A fifth source was later suggested by Maddux (2005).	
• Imaginal experiences	visualising ourselves succeeding

These self-efficacy resources are useful in identifying strategies for working with people. If we use the example of a woman giving birth and feeling fearful, then there are five things we can try. We can point out how well she coped with a previous birth (mastery experience), we can talk about others who have been through the same thing successfully (vicarious experience), we can get loved ones to give positive messages (verbal persuasion) and we can try to enhance positive emotions like the anticipation of meeting the new baby (emotional state). We can even use visualisation techniques to help women feel more relaxed, less frightened and more confident in their own ability.

In a strength-based approach, care must be taken to listen to the woman, using emotional intelligence to interpret both verbal and non-verbal communication and to ask questions to ascertain what is going on for her, rather than expecting her to either make a decision alone or surrender control to professionals. Villarmea and Kelly (2020, p 518) suggest that asking these questions is helpful:

1.   What is your understanding of the current situation?

2.   What is most important to you?

3.   What else matters to you?

4.   What are you afraid of?

It can help to discover gaps in understanding, identify the woman's values and detect fears. In this way, her voice can be heard in the most challenging of situations. Much has been written about shared decision making in childbirth, the Villarmea and Kelly (2020) study being just one. In the case study below, Cory gives an account of the importance of shared decision making within a large NHS hospital. Midwives strive to provide high quality, safe care for women in a relationship based on trust and a genuine desire to meet women's needs (Feeley, Thompson and Downe, 2020). This mutually trusting relationship is a cornerstone of midwifery practice.

NICE guidelines (2021) state that in labour and birth, *'women's decisions should be respected, even when this is contrary to the views of the healthcare professional'*. The guidelines state that the advantages and risks of all interventions and procedures must be fully explained, but that the woman must ultimately be able to make her own decisions. This, then, could potentially lead to an ethical dilemma, for example, if professionals view a woman's decision as one that creates heightened risk.

Reflective questions ⑦

Breech birth

A woman is in the early stages of labour, and she arrives at the hospital. On examination, it is apparent that the baby is in a breech position. The midwife explains this to the woman and then clarifies that it is hospital policy to organise a caesarean delivery. The woman, however, does not want a caesarean and insists that she wants to give birth naturally. This would go against the hospital's normal policy.

» What are the options here?

» What are the important things to consider when talking to the woman and her birth partner?

Midwives today see themselves as advocates for women, as Cory explains in the case study below. In a multi-disciplinary team within a hospital environment, it is the midwife's responsibility to advocate *'to ensure that care always focuses on the needs, views, preferences, and decisions of the woman, and the needs of the newborn infant'* (NMC, 2019). Cory's case study explains the importance of this.

CASE STUDY 🔊

Cory: empowering women in labour

Cory is a midwife, working in a large hospital. She has written this description of the role of the midwife today and what she sees as her responsibilities towards women in labour.

Although the move to hospital births over time has created some life-saving advances, obstetrics has also degraded women's natural human ability for childbearing and birth. In many cases, women are limited in their choices due to being 'high-risk' and under obstetric-led care, but it is the duty of midwives who care for women during labour to provide them with freedom and choice to promote ownership and competence. Midwives are advocates for women; educating them about their bodies' natural capabilities and empowering them to make their own choices. All women I care for have the right to be fully aware of their choices and how important that is to ensure positive birthing experiences. In early pregnancy, women should be educated on birth and normal processes that happen in labour, so they feel in control of their bodies.

'High-risk' women are not offered home births as a choice, as they may potentially need interventions by an obstetrician. The concept of home births has been discouraged and the perspective of hospital births being safer has led to women fearing birth at home. However, a hospital environment can be alienating for women, the unfamiliar surroundings causing fear and anxiety, contributing to the feeling of loss of control (RCM, 2008). Physical objects in the birth setting such as technical machinery, specifically in an obstetric unit, make a real difference to how women feel. Hospital spaces are generally constructed to manage sickness and disease; however, the birth space should reflect healthy women to promote normality and positive outcomes (Shah and Setola, 2019). It is essential that the birthplace facilitates a sense of privacy and safety, otherwise women's sense of feeling monitored increases neocortical activity and the subsequent release of adrenaline, which hinders the release of oxytocin that is necessary for the progress of labour (Dooris and Rocca-Ihenacho, 2019). I encourage women in labour to bring home comforts into the hospital setting, as this can make a real difference to how women feel and perceive the birth environment in hospitals. I like to inform women in labour of potential processes or events that may or may not occur in order to prepare women and ensure they are not startled if any of these things were to follow. An example of this is informing women of professionals who may enter the birthing room, such as other midwives for 'fresh eyes', obstetricians on ward rounds, clinical support workers for support and potentially anaesthetists if the emergency buzzer was ever pulled. In the chaos of an emergency, it is especially important to inform women of what is happening around them and why, so they still feel somewhat mindful and confident in their surroundings.

Women who birth in hospitals tend to respond passively to events suggested by healthcare professionals, but women who birth in midwife-led units or at home take control of the space by moving freely, doing as they wish (Cheyne and Duff, 2019). Therefore, birth settings should balance and facilitate aspects of friendliness and freedom to promote women's ownership over the environment (Dooris and Rocca-Ihenacho, 2019). Women's privacy must always be protected, otherwise this can significantly hinder the natural processes of labour by making women feel observed and vulnerable. I always acknowledge and consider the degree of privacy in birthing environments, to respect this basic human right. I do this by knocking on the door and announcing myself before entering the room, ensuring the privacy curtain is always drawn to reduce the risk of intrusions, ensuring that women are asked permission for other professionals to enter the room, structuring minimal and appropriate lighting and also covering women's dignity with blankets and bed sheets.

Reflective questions ⑦

»   Considering what Cory says about women's experiences of giving birth in hospital, reflect on your own experiences of hospitals and list words to describe the feelings.

»   If you were in hospital and in labour, what would you want, in an ideal situation? Do you think this would be possible in a UK hospital?

»   In your own practice with families, how can you promote feelings of competence?

The transition to parenthood

Whatever the situation, it is important not to underestimate the impact that having a baby has on individuals, but also on relationships. Differences in hopes, expectations and values can become magnified and exaggerated, particularly when new parents are worried and exhausted. It is easy then for couples to become tense, resentful and argumentative, without having the time alone together to sort out these differences. Sometimes parents can be faced with deciding whether their relationship is good for them and safe for their baby (NCT, 2022), and, of course, for single mothers facing these challenges alone, the situation can be even more difficult.

The transition to parenthood brings with it many changes. Being accountable for a new life can be both fulfilling and disquieting; the responsibility can be overwhelming in the early days. Daily routines change as new parents prioritise the baby's needs, and balancing work and parenting can be difficult. There may be unrealistic expectations on new parents to be happy and fulfilled, when in reality they may be exhausted and stressed. Hormone imbalances in new mothers may cause depression and, in rare cases, severe mental health issues. It is important, therefore, to ensure that new parents are aware of the signs to look out for and of ways to access support. The identification of skills and resources available to the new parents is an important characteristic of strength-based care. The NCT call the first three months after the birth the fourth trimester, which they see as a useful concept:

> *it reminds them that it is OK to find the early days with a baby hard. It is a period of transition, where women become mums, men become dads, and babies adjust to life outside the womb.*

(NCT, 2022)

The fourth trimester is a time to recover from the birth, to adjust to the responsibility, to become accustomed to their new role as parent and to get know the baby.

Supporting parents

Some parents may be more in need of support than others, for example, very young mothers, single and isolated mothers, homeless, mentally ill or imprisoned mothers, and those living in poverty or with abusive partners. Everyone has their own particular needs, and when providing support for new mothers it is important to remember that we must keep an open mind and respect parents as experts in their own lives. What may be unacceptable to us may be perfectly acceptable to someone else; acceptance and tolerance of other people's life-styles is important in raising the confidence of new parents. If parents are focusing on their baby and not tidying the house, for example, that is their choice; they are putting their child first. If children are put outside in a pram on the coldest of days, this is fine as long as they are wrapped up warmly. If children stay up till midnight and go to bed when their parents do, that is completely their choice, as long as they are not exposed to adult TV programmes. Cultural differences in parenting must be respected, so choices must be made by families themselves, and intervention by professionals should be necessary only if there is a safeguarding concern.

CASE STUDY ☻

Caitlin: working with new mums

Caitlin is a healthy child programme practitioner working in the NHS with health visitors in Leicestershire. She says that her passion is in working with mums. She has worked in the past for the NCT who, she says, have a very strength-based approach and work with new parents on resilience and self-efficacy. In her current organisation, she looks at the child's developmental needs, the family's needs and environmental factors, when working with families.

The area Caitlin works in is very deprived and she stresses the need to try and find the positives and to be very strength-based, otherwise, it could be quite depressing, although she admits that, sometimes, it can be harder to find those strengths. Caitlin says that when she is working with families, she naturally looks for ways to work with them which suit them. She doesn't like the feeling of going into someone's home and telling them what they should be doing, so she tries hard not to come across like that. She worries about offending people, so she looks for something, however small, that she can reframe as a strength. She provides this example from one of the families she works with.

I was talking to a mother about her toddler, about eating, and she said she worried about not having any sort of routine in their lives. So, we talked about the fact you don't have to have the same routine as the next door neighbour. I said, 'I'm not going to tell you that you all have to get up at 7am to all have breakfast together; if there's no reason to be up at 7am, don't do that, just find something that works for you and create a routine for you and the family just to give the child a bit more structure but in a way that fits into your actual lifestyle'. There is always something people can use to their advantage.

When she first rang us, this lady had quite a lot of mental health issues; she was very anxious, and she's being looked after for OCD. She's very funny about her child touching his food and using his hands and she's trying hard not to transfer her anxieties onto him. She was worried about that and worried about holding him back from doing things because she couldn't let go enough. That's the sort of work I enjoy, so I went round to her house, and I sat on the floor

→

(she gave me a mat to sit on because I couldn't take my shoes off). I sat on her floor for about 40 minutes, and we just chatted, so it wasn't like I was the expert coming in to tell her what to do. We just talked; we talked about what she can do, what she can cope with, what she can't cope with. She said she worried about her carpets, so I said 'well, can he eat in the kitchen? Could you get him a little table and chair in the kitchen? Then he could eat in there and you don't have to worry about your carpets', and she said, 'oh yeah, I could'. I came out of that visit thinking 'she feels better now she has a plan' and the next time I saw her she said she felt so much better.

It gave her a boost and she was able to think of little things she could do herself that could make a difference. She's the one doing it every day, so she needs to instigate things now and make the changes to feel better about it. She just needed someone to highlight to her what she could do and to think about what could work for her as an individual. I would talk to someone else differently because they are different person with different problems, so the solutions would be different. I like to think I'm not there with a set of rules everyone should follow, I'm there to talk to you and think about what could work for your family. I like to leave feeling like people are more confident. I'm sure that lady would love it if I went to see her every month and said, 'come on, you can do it', but I can't afford the time to do that, so I've got to get them to a situation where they feel confident. I feel like it's important to just be real with people and say things like 'oh I know, I've three kids and my youngest is like this' and then you're more like a human being to them and that helps if they can see that other people have found it difficult, it's not just them. It gives people a bit more confidence.

Reflective questions ⑦

» Consider what Caitlin says about not wanting to appear as an expert telling people what to do. What is your view on this balance of personal and professional stances?

» Think of a person that you know, or work with, who has many problems and difficulties. List as many strengths and positives as you can. Does this change the way you see the person?

» Caitlin shares some of her own experiences with the mothers she works with; is this appropriate to do in your own role? What are the advantages and disadvantages of sharing personal experiences?

Strength-based approaches with vulnerable parents and babies

In Caitlin's case study, she talks about the fact that with some families, it is harder to find strengths, but in a strength-based approach, we believe that there are *always* positives somewhere. When working with vulnerable new parents, especially those living in disadvantaged areas, it is important to remember that the outcome should be to increase self-efficacy, to reduce stress and, consequently, to reduce the risk of toxic stress in children. Toxic stress is defined as '*the strong, frequent, or prolonged activation of the body's stress response systems in infants while not being buffered by protection from a supportive adult*' (McCrae et al, 2021, p 2). Table 2.2 shows some of the causes of toxic stress. Can you add more?

Table 2.2 *Causes of toxic stress*

Previous personal trauma	Unpredictable or absent partners	Family conflict
Childcare inaccessibility	Poverty	Inability to meet basic needs
Social isolation	Unemployment	Discrimination, eg racism
Acculturative stress*	Caring responsibilities	Abuse or neglect
Mental illness	Exposure to violence	Poor or limited access to healthcare
Ill health, disability or accident	Relationship break-up	Victim of crime
High number of children	Unsafe neighbourhoods	Substance abuse
Stigma and bullying	Lack of safe, adequate housing	Bereavement

* The stress associated with being an immigrant or ethnic minority going through the process of adapting to another culture.

The stresses detailed in Table 2.2 are significant, and families may experience one or many of these factors. It is also important to remember that people experience these stressors differently. For example, if a member of a family is abusing drugs, others in the family may follow suit, whereas there may be other family members who, seeing the adverse effects, will make the decision never to go down that path. Some people, following a serious accident, will sink into a deep depression, others will be determined to recover and will work hard to achieve this. The story of Christopher Reeve in Chapter 6 illustrates the significance of attitude and the impact of positivity and hope in adversity. Table 2.3 below outlines some of the strengths that people may have in their lives, which can help to counteract the negatives. You may be able to add more.

Table 2.3 *Strengths and protective factors*

Personal attributes	Partner support	Service providers
Social networks	Family support	Self-efficacy
Bonding/attachment	Parenting knowledge	Connections to faith and culture

Strength-based care of the newborn

Much of this chapter has been about person-centred care for pregnant women and the importance of ascertaining the strengths of new mothers. Newborn babies are completely dependent on adults to keep them safe and healthy and to meet their needs, but babies also have their own voice and are able to articulate this through crying. A trusting relationship is crucial for newborn babies as the baby learns to feel safe and secure in the fact that their cries will be answered, and their needs met.

For most parents, learning to read their baby's cues comes naturally through spending time together. During the first six months of life, the baby learns that their parents will come when they communicate with a cry or a yell. Research by Wolpert (in Pitman, 2005) suggests that babies appreciate being responded to, even if the parent is unable to identify what the baby wants. Having someone respond by holding the baby and talking to the baby makes them feel better.

Attachment parenting

There are many parenting styles; authoritative, authoritarian, passive, uninvolved, parent led. A style that is relatively new, originating with the work of Sears and Sears (2001) and growing in popularity, is attachment parenting, sometimes called baby-led parenting. Figure 2.3 below outlines the principles of the approach.

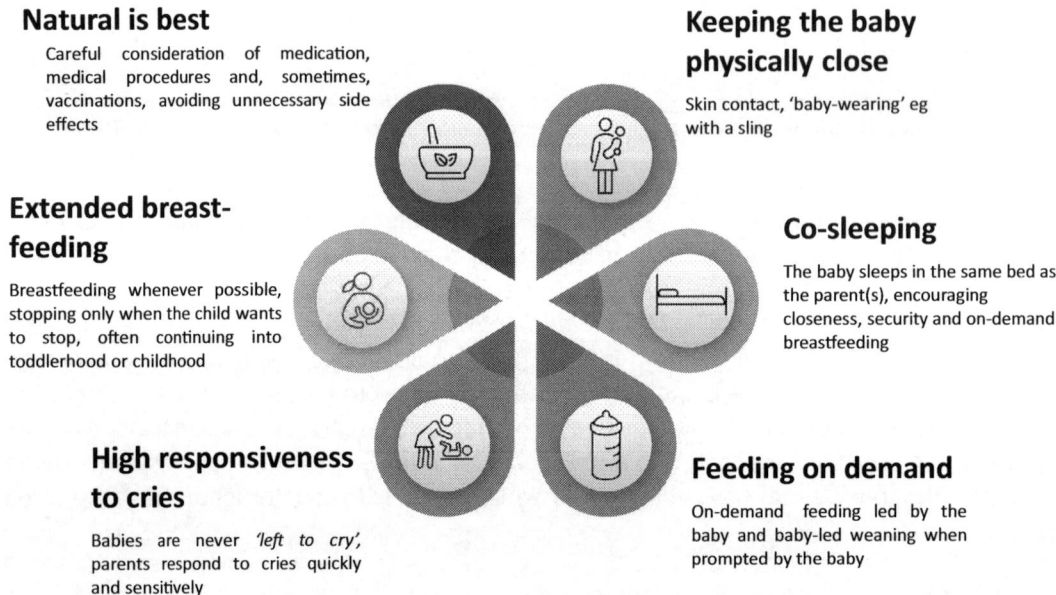

Natural is best
Careful consideration of medication, medical procedures and, sometimes, vaccinations, avoiding unnecessary side effects

Keeping the baby physically close
Skin contact, 'baby-wearing' eg with a sling

Extended breast-feeding
Breastfeeding whenever possible, stopping only when the child wants to stop, often continuing into toddlerhood or childhood

Co-sleeping
The baby sleeps in the same bed as the parent(s), encouraging closeness, security and on-demand breastfeeding

High responsiveness to cries
Babies are never 'left to cry', parents respond to cries quickly and sensitively

Feeding on demand
On-demand feeding led by the baby and baby-led weaning when prompted by the baby

Figure 2.3 Attachment parenting

Some of the principles of attachment parenting are more controversial than others. Many people today agree with the principle of baby-led weaning, for example, but the public has more negative views of breastfeeding a three year-old child, for example. However, there is a lot of evidence (Miller and Commons, 2010) that attachment parenting, which is led by the needs of the baby, and which centres around the relationship between parents and baby, has real physical and psychological benefits. Miller and Commons' research shows that the biggest benefit is '*the mitigation of potentially overwhelming negative emotional states*' (2010, p 1) from practices such as leaving babies to cry. They also identify increased emotion regulation and increased resilience in children brought up in this way. Loton and Waters (2017) have also reported benefits from attachment parenting, such as higher life satisfaction, positive emotional well-being and lower stress during childhood. Although this type of parenting seems ideally suited to a strength-based philosophy, it is important to be flexible. If parents want to embrace aspects of the approach but not others, then this is their choice.

Parenting self-efficacy

Bandura (1977) originally proposed the concept of self-efficacy to describe a person's belief in their own ability. Parenting self-efficacy (PSE) is the belief that a parent holds as to how effectively she/he can carry out the necessary tasks in order to parent a child. We have looked at sources of self-efficacy during labour earlier in this chapter (see Figure 2.1), and the theory is equally applicable to self-efficacy in parenting, for example:

- mastery experiences – having looked after children before;
- vicarious experiences – observing similar parents succeeding;
- verbal persuasion – being persuaded by others that we are capable;
- emotional and physiological states – good mental health.

Belsky (1984) took Bandura's idea of self-efficacy and connected it to parenting, identifying three influences on parenting which affect PSE (see Figure 2.4).

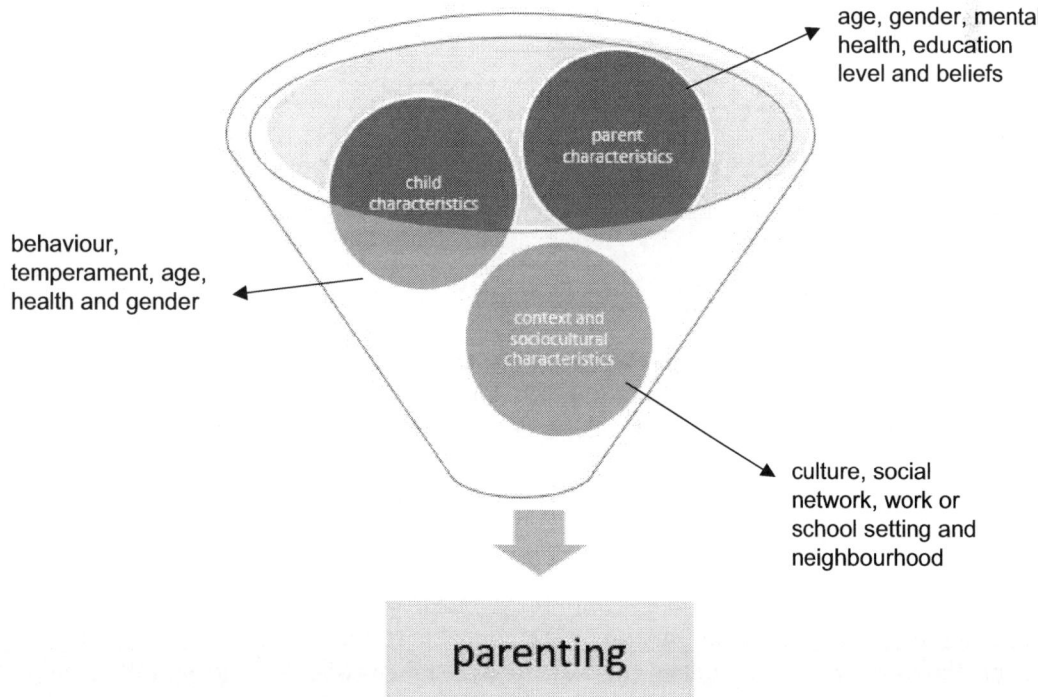

Figure 2.4 *Belsky's (1984) influences on parenting*

There are, of course, other influences on parents, and not all of the factors identified by Bensky are applicable to all parents. Consider Hamza's story below.

CASE STUDY ⊖

Hamza's story

I am Hamza, a Syrian woman forced to leave my country in 2012 because of the civil war. I am now living as a refugee in the UK with my husband. We have recently become parents, but I have been feeling lost without the support of the women in my family, who are all displaced in different places in Europe. At times, I feel like I am not coping at all, my baby cries a lot at night time, and I don't always know what's wrong with her. In the daytime it is okay – I talk to her all the time and sing to her and tell her the stories I remember my mother telling me and she seems quite calm during the day, but at night it's so difficult. I don't think I am a good mother; there are no women in my family to help me and I don't know what to do.

Reflective questions ⑦

» Which of Bandura's four sources of self-efficacy are missing in Hamza's life?

» How do each of Bensky's three influences impact Hamza?

» Which level of PSE can you identify in Hamza's case?

» What could you say to Hamza to help her feel like she is capable of being a good mother?

Chapter summary ⑧

In this chapter, strength-based approaches have been explored in relation to antenatal care, labour and birth and the transition to parenthood. Pregnancy, giving birth and becoming a parent are major transitions in life, so supportive care which utilises the family's strengths is crucial. Self-efficacy is the key to confidence at all stages, and Cory's case study effectively describes the midwife's role in empowering and advocating for women to make their own decisions. Women in labour must be listened to and their choices respected and valued. Relationships between professionals and families should be trusting and positive, which allows for the development of self-efficacy and confidence. This is important in the transition to parenthood; parents can be helped to identify their strengths, skills and resources and to find their own way of managing the transition. Caitlin's case study gives real examples of building trusting relationships with parents and providing person-centred support and empowerment.

Lastly, strength-based approaches with parents and babies were discussed, with attachment parenting seen as a positive baby-centred approach to caring for a newborn. Increasing self-efficacy in parents, particularly with vulnerable parents, is the best preparation for long-lasting child-centred care.

Further reading 📚

- Villarmea, S and Kelly, B (2020) Barriers to Establishing Shared Decision-making in Childbirth: Unveiling Epistemic Stereotypes about Women in Labour. *Journal of Evaluation in Clinical Practice*, 26(2): 515–19.

  This journal article gives lots of examples of the benefits of fully involving women in their own care during labour and childbirth.

- www.nct.org.uk/

  This is a comprehensive website by the National Childbirth Trust, with lots of information on a wide variety of matters relating to pregnancy, birth, babies and parenthood.

References 📚

Bandura, A (1977) Self-efficacy: Toward a Unifying Theory of Behavioral Change. *Psychological Review*, 84(2): 191–215.

Belsky, J (1984) Determinants of Parenting: A Process Model. *Child Development*, 55(1): 83–96.

Cheyne, H and Duff, E (2019) Chapter 3: Anatomy and Physiology of Labour and Associated Behavioural Clues. In Downe, S and Byron, S (eds) *Squaring the Circle* (pp 32–46). London: Pinter and Martin Printers.

Deave, T, Johnson, D and Ingram, J (2008) Transition to Parenthood: The Needs of Parents in Pregnancy and Early Parenthood. *BMC Pregnancy and Childbirth*, 8(1): 30–6.

Department of Health (2011) *Preparation for Birth and Beyond: A Resource Pack for Leaders of Community Groups and Activities*. [online] Available at: www.gov.uk/government/publications/preparation-for-birth-and-beyond-a-resorce-pack-for-leaders-of-community-groups-and-activities (accessed 30 June 2023).

Dooris, M and Rocca-Ihenacho, L (2019). Chapter 20: Healthy Settings and Birth. In Downe, S and Byron, S (eds) *Squaring the Circle* (pp 241–52). London: Pinter and Martin Printers.

Feeley, C, Thomson, G and Downe, S (2020) Understanding how Midwives Employed by the National Health Service Facilitate Women's Alternative Birthing Choices: Findings from a Feminist Pragmatist Study. *PLoS ONE*, 15(11): 1–23.

Heinonen, K (2021) Strengthening Antenatal Care towards a Salutogenic Approach: A Meta-Ethnography. *International Journal of Environmental Research and Public Health*, 18(10): 51–68.

Hodgkins, A (2019) Advanced Empathy in the Early Years – A Risky Strength? *NZ International Research in Early Childhood Education Journal*, 22(1): 46–58.

Loton, D and Waters, L (2017) The Mediating Effect of Self-Efficacy in the Connections between Strength-Based Parenting, Happiness and Psychological Distress in Teens. *Frontiers in Psychology*, 8: 1–13.

Maddux, J E (2005) Self-efficacy: The Power of Believing You Can. In Snyder, C R and Lopez, S J (eds) *Handbook of Positive Psychology* (pp 227–87). New York: Oxford University Press.

McCrae, J S, Robinson, J A L, Spain, A K, Byers, K and Axelrod, J L (2021) The Mitigating Toxic Stress Study Design: Approaches to Developmental Evaluation of Pediatric Health Care Innovations Addressing Social Determinants of Health and Toxic Stress. *BMC Health Services Research*, 21(1): 1–14.

Miller, P and Commons, M (2010) The Benefits of Attachment Parenting for Infants and Children: A Behavioral Developmental View. *Behavioral Development Bulletin*, 10: 1–14.

National Institute for Health and Care Excellence (NICE) (2021) *Antenatal Care: NICE Guideline.* [online] Available at: www.nice.org.uk/guidance/NG201 (accessed 19 June 2023).

National Midwifery Council (2019) *Standards of Proficiency for Midwives.* [online] Available at: www.nmc.org.uk/globalassets/sitedocuments/standards/standards-of-proficiency-for-midwives.pdf (accessed 28 July 2023).

NCT (2022) *What Is the Fourth Trimester?* [online] Available at: www.nct.org.uk/baby-toddler/emotional-and-social-development/what-fourth-trimester (accessed 19 June 2023).

Pitman, T (2005) Reading Baby's Cues. *Today's Parent, Baby & Toddler*, 6(1): 43–4.

Royal College of Midwives (RCM) (2008) Birth Environment. *Evidence-based Guidelines for Midwifery-led Care in Labour* (p 2). London: Royal College of Midwives.

Royal College of Midwives (2021) *New NICE Guideline Rightly Focused on Women Centred Care Says RCM.* [online] Available at: www.rcm.org.uk/media-releases/2021/august/new-nice-guideline-rightly-focused-on-women-centred-care-says-rcm/ (accessed 19 June 2023).

Sears, B and Sears, M (2001) *The Attachment Parenting Book: A Commonsense Guide to Understanding and Nurturing Your Baby.* New York: Little, Brown and Company.

Shah, N and Setola, N (2019) Chapter 18: Designing Space and Place of Birth. In Downe, S and Byron, S (eds) *Squaring the Circle* (pp 219–30). London: Pinter and Martin Printers.

Stewart-Brown, S and Schrader-McMillan, A (2010) Home and Community Based Parenting Support Programmes and Interventions. University of Warwick. [online] Available at: http://go.warwick.ac.uk/wrap (accessed 19 June 2023).

Tanglakmankhong, K, Perrin, N and Lowe, N (2010) Childbirth Self-Efficacy Inventory and Childbirth Attitudes. *Journal of Advanced Nursing*, 67(1): 193–203.

3 Strength-based practice within the early years

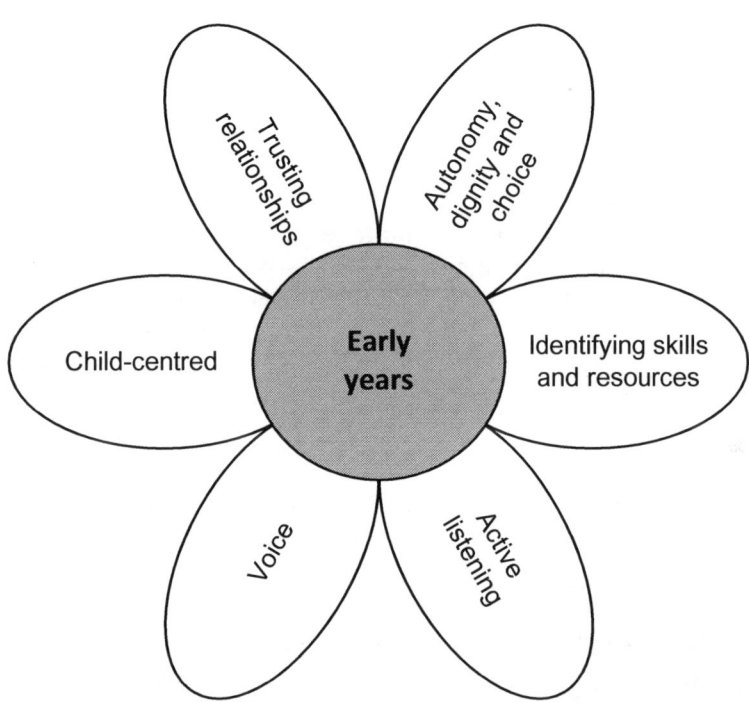

Chapter objectives ◎

This chapter:

- discusses the importance of building secure, trusting relationships and attachments with young children;

- analyses ways of focusing on individuality – identifying children's strengths, interests and fascinations and encouraging choice and voice;

- evaluates ways of supporting young children to develop independence, self-control and other key social/emotional skills.

Introduction

This chapter focuses on strength-based approaches in early years settings, for those practitioners working in nurseries, in preschools or as home care providers with children up to school age. Many strength-based approaches are already embedded within early years practice, for example, the importance of key worker relationships and the encouragement of independent self-care skills. However, there are occasions when a subtle change can enrich a strength-based approach. In this chapter, the focus is on three main areas as outlined in the chapter objectives. A case study describing the practice of an early years educator working in a private day nursery details how the approach works through a practical application.

Relationships

A secure relationship built on trust is one of the cornerstones of a strength-based approach. Within an early years setting, the relationship between practitioner and child is probably the most crucial aspect of practice, hence the significance of having a named key person for each child (DfE, 2021). When a child receives a warm, empathic response from a person they are attached to, they learn to trust that their needs will be met and thus feel a sense of security and belonging. As Maslow (1943) maintained, the basic need for psychological safety, or security, must be met before any further development can take place. If a child does not feel secure, then they cannot learn, so attachment must be a priority in the early years.

Attachment

Much of the seminal work on attachment theory is by Bowlby (1952) who believed that the early bonds formed by a child and their caregivers have a significant impact on the child's life. Bowlby (1969, p 194) defined attachment as a '*lasting psychological connectedness between human beings*'. Some of Bowlby's work has been questioned in recent years, particularly his now widely discredited experimental work on maternal deprivation, which claimed that mothers and babies must not be separated in the first three years of the child's life if serious emotional problems are to be avoided. However, the stages of attachment identified by Bowlby still influence practice today, as do the types of attachment defined by Ainsworth and Bell (1970), who also identified early attachments as being pivotal in early social and emotional development. In the twenty-first century, we now understand more about attachment, thanks to advances in medical technology and our contemporary knowledge of brain development (Jarvis, 2020). Experiments measuring the stress hormone cortisol in babies and toddlers show that, in general, being cared for at home causes a decrease in levels of cortisol, and those attending full daycare show an increase in cortisol levels (Watamura et al, 2010). However, this does vary according to the quality of daycare provision and, crucially, good quality daycare is better for young children's stress levels than poor quality care at home (Shpancer, 2002). Persistently high cortisol levels can lead to poor *executive functioning,* a term which refers to mental processes such as working memory (the capacity to hold and manipulate information over short periods of time), the ability to pause and think before acting, and '*cognitive or mental flexibility such as the ability to shift attention between tasks*' (Scorza et al, 2016, p 314). Two areas of executive functioning which are particularly important for development of young children in the early years are self-control and self-regulation. The implication of this research is that young children need affectionate, trusting relationships with '*well-trained, well-managed and supported professional adults*' (Shonkoff and Meisels, 2000, p 508). Such a relationship is likely to develop children's self-regulation skills and increase resilience. The strength-based approach places trusting relationships at the heart of practice, and this is more important than ever for the youngest members of society. Adults working with young children in the early years, then, need to have the skills to build this important attachment.

Person-centred skills

For practitioners, a strength-based approach is about providing a secure and enabling environment in which young children can grow and develop in their own way. Practitioners using person-centred skills create an ideal environment in which children can flourish. The basis of person-centred care is use of the '*core conditions*' first described by Carl Rogers (1957) (Figure 3.1).

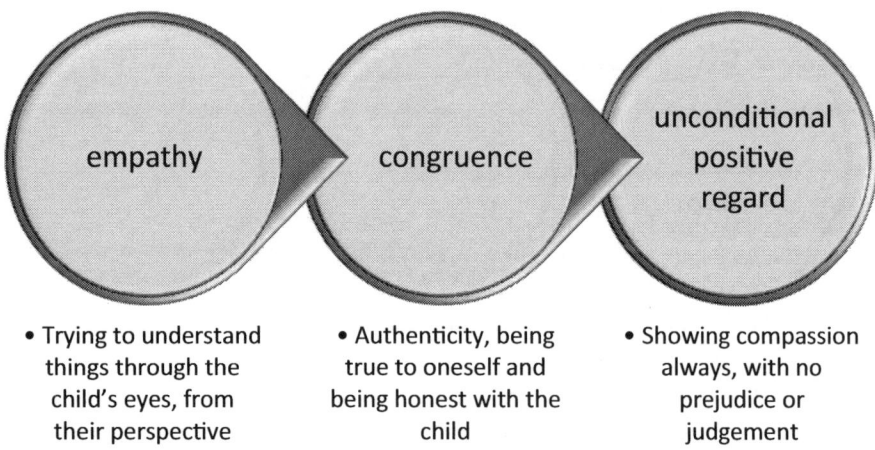

Figure 3.1 *Rogers' (1957) core conditions*

Of the three core conditions, empathy is one of the most important emotional competencies required to build this close attachment (Hodgkins, 2019), along with compassion and affection. Empathy helps us to understand how situations appear to another person, looking at a situation '*through their eyes*', or trying '*walk in their shoes*', therefore it is essential for anyone working with people, particularly young children who may not be able to voice their emotions. The second core condition, congruence, describes the authenticity of relationships, with practitioners being consistent in their communication and willing to show emotion themselves. If early years practitioners are encouraging children to express and talk about their feelings, then the adults around them should do the same, for example, saying things like '*I'm disappointed that we can't go outside today because of the bad weather too*'. This helps children to identify emotions. Unconditional positive regard is the third core condition, and it refers to caring for someone and respecting them without prejudice. Hammond (2010, p 5) says that children '*need to know someone cares and will be there unconditionally for them*'. This describes the feeling of being accepted and liked for who they are.

Love and affection

Concepts of affection and '*love*' within early years practice have, in recent years, been examined and theorised, a leading example being the idea of '*professional love*' presented by Page (2018) who describes the term as '*the secure attachment and emotional intimacy of the relationship between child and practitioner*' (p 134). Professional love is not a replacement for parental love but is an important substitution within the early years setting. It will vary from child to child, with some children being confident and self-sufficient, and others '*looking to professionals as a secure base where they can receive cuddles and reassurance*' (Davis, 2021). Davis' view that children need to receive cuddles is an important one, as there is much evidence to support the idea that children's emotional well-being is dependent on physical touch (Svinth, 2018). However, there is some reluctance on the part of some settings, particularly in schools, due to anxieties around safeguarding (Goddard, 2020). This reluctance has resulted in some no-touch policies in schools, which the authors of this book believe to be very damaging.

Reflective questions ⑦

» What do you consider to be an appropriate and authentic way of showing affection with young children?

» Why is this important?

» How might this help to develop a strength-based approach?

Individuality

Another key belief in strength-based practice is that everyone has strengths and abilities and that children grow from these strengths and abilities (DEECD, 2012). The approach sees children as experts in their own lives (Clark, 2017) with their own personality, likes, dislikes and fascinations. The adult role within the approach is one of supporting and enabling, without making decisions on the child's behalf. The concept of the unique child is a guiding theme of the EYFS (DfE, 2021) and this appreciation of the child as being the only one of their kind, being remarkable in their own way, lays the foundation for a strength-based approach. To discover a person's uniqueness, we have to spend time with them, observe, listen and learn.

The voice of the child

Children have a right to be heard, throughout their childhood. Listening to children is the best way to understand them in order to provide individualised care, and there is evidence supporting the fact that being listened to at a young age provides children with a sense of well-being, raises children's self-esteem and means less chance of developing anxiety (Roberts, 2006). Therefore, the voice of the child should be a priority in all early years settings. Listening to young children should be an active, two-way process. The challenge is to listen and interpret without making assumptions or putting your own meaning on what you are '*hearing*'. '*The adult's role is to interpret children's voices, as long as care is taken to hear the child's authentic voice, without conjecture*' (Prowle and Hodgkins, 2020, p 52). This can sometimes seem challenging with very young children. We can ask a three year-old what they would like to do and listen to their answer, but we cannot do that verbally with a baby. However, even the youngest babies are skilful communicators (Clark, 2017) and the adult's role is to tune in to the way the child communicates. This is where observation is important; through careful and continual observation, we can get to know the individual child well and begin to interpret expressions, body language, sounds and movements, using observation alongside our empathy skills to tune into what they are feeling (Nergaard, 2019).

Routines

Planning positive child-centred care routines is at the foundation of early years practice. Feeding, dressing, nappy-changing and sleeping are all important parts of the day, offering opportunities for interaction and for the development of self-efficacy. Self-efficacy develops in the first few years of life and is the belief that one is capable of completing a task or managing a situation. Bandura (1977, p 192) first described the concept as *'the core belief that one has the power to affect changes by one's actions'*. Developing self-efficacy in childhood promotes resilience, confidence in handling difficult situations and a life-course which is both active and self-determined (Schwarzer, 2014).

help children to plan	*It's time to get changed, what will you need?*	
praise efforts	*Well done, you undid your own shoes*	
teach them how to handle frustration	*Ah never mind, everyone spills drinks sometimes. I did that last week. Let's get another one*	
listen to the child	*You're hot? Do you want to take your hat off?*	
spark their interest	*You could cut the fruit yourself today, if you like*	
set realistic goals	*Can you wipe your own table today?*	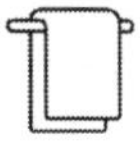
use language with babies	Saying *'all gone!'* when feeding, and *'let's get you changed'*	
name their strengths	*You dried your hands all by yourself!*	
let babies have a go	*Do you want to hold the spoon?*	

Figure 3.2 *Self-efficacy activities*

Care routines should always be child-centred, and care must be taken to ensure that routines are not things that are '*done to*' the children (Figure 3.2). Imagine someone coming and wiping your face with a wet cloth without warning; this would be unpleasant and unsettling, but it is what can happen in early years settings, without empathy and consideration of the child's point of view. Care routines should always be about identifying and encouraging strengths.

Strength-spotting

Even the youngest children can demonstrate a flair or talent, and the practitioner who spends time getting to know them can spot these and encourage the development of the child's natural abilities. A child may demonstrate extreme curiosity, exceptional memory, good reasoning, problem solving or a vivid imagination, all of which are signs of a flair in a particular field. Look at the first example in Table 3.1 below. Here a child, Atef, is described as having an obsession with toy cars and as being reluctant to take part in any other activity. Most practitioners will have come across this situation and may have responded by trying to get Atef to try other activities. However, when a child is in a state of *flow*, highly engaged in what they are doing (Peterson, 2013), this is when deep learning takes place. In the most watched TED talk of all time, educationalist Ken Robinson (2007) famously tells the story of a little girl, Gillian, whose nursery teachers said she had ADHD and needed to be medicated as she could not keep still. When the child's parents took her to see a doctor, the doctor listened to what they had to say and then left the child in a room with a radio playing. Immediately, they saw Gillian get up and start to move to the music. In the story, the doctor said to the child's mother, '*Gillian isn't sick, she's a dancer*'. In this true story, Gillian's parents started to encourage their child's flair for dance, and she grew up to be a very successful and famous dancer. This very powerful story demonstrates the way that an optimistic, strength-based approach to a child's uniqueness can make the difference between seeing the child as a problem and seeing the child as a unique person with a talent. We cannot always see the child's talents at an early age, but we can encourage the fascinations they have and nurture them to grow to be their best selves.

Reflective questions ⑦

» Look at the scenarios in Table 3.1 and consider what your reaction would be to each scenario.

» What might be the benefit of a strength-based approach for each child?

Table 3.1 *Scenarios, reactions and strength-based suggestions*

Scenario	Common reaction	Strength-based approach
Atef, age three, wants to play with the cars on the mat every day.	He must be redirected to other activities so that he gets the most out of the opportunities at nursery.	Atef is fascinated by cars, let him be immersed in this interest, it is important to him. We don't know what he is gaining from it, but it is his choice.

Table 3.1 (*Cont.*)

Scenario	Common reaction	Strength-based approach
Carmen, age 18 months, is always throwing things. Everything the staff give her is thrown, usually back at them!	Staff should use distraction techniques to get Carmen to do other, less destructive, things.	Carmen enjoys the trajectory schema. This is obviously important to her. Staff could provide appropriate resources (eg soft balls) so that she can continue safely.
Bobby, age two, will not sit and eat his food at snack times. He picks at it but then wanders off.	Adults could sit with Bobby and praise him when he stays in his seat and eats all of his food.	Bobby should be able to choose when he eats. If he is a child who prefers to eat little and often, then this is his choice. A café-style approach to snack time would suit Bobby better than set times for eating.

Personal, social and emotional development

This prime area of learning in the EYFS is crucial in helping children to understand their emotions and the emotions of others (DfE, 2021). It encompasses building self-confidence and self-awareness and helping children to manage their feelings and behaviour. One of the best ways to do this, of course, is by creating a strong, secure relationship between practitioners and children. Children who feel secure and supported will be ready to start building relationships and friendships of their own. Demonstrating ways of relating to others with respect and care will provide a good model for young children.

Role modelling

It is well established through social learning theory that children learn by watching others (Bandura, Ross and Ross, 1961), so the adults that a child spends time with should model positive behaviour. This means more than just holding the door open for someone and saying please and thank you. Adults should also model life skills such as working hard and learning new skills. An example of harnessing children's tendency to imitate others comes from a principle of Steiner education (Gelitz, 2017). In lots of Reception classes in the UK, young children are supported in reading simple books from a reading scheme. In a Steiner school, however, in a reading session, you may see the teacher sitting reading her own novel, while the children have a selection of all sorts of picture books to explore. The idea is that role modelling an enjoyment of books is more important than the mechanics of phonics at this age.

In addition to modelling positive behaviours, adults can also model making mistakes and dealing with these in a positive way. This helps children to understand that mistakes are a normal part of life, and this will help them to develop resilience, learning to '*bounce back*' when things go wrong. For example, if a practitioner tries to draw a horse and fails, it is good for the children to see her admit that she hasn't done well and to try again. Resilience is not always about '*powering through*' when things are tough; it is sometimes about identifying tools that can help in those times and being honest about when we are not succeeding at it (Abaza and Nelson, 2018). By saying to a child '*I'm feeling tired today because I didn't sleep well, so I'm sitting down for a bit*', you are identifying your limitations and ways of dealing with them positively.

Positive and respectful behaviour strategies

'*Behaviour management*' is a term widely used in early years settings, but this is a rather a negative term which suggests that children's behaviour is likely to be unacceptable and will need to be managed by adults. The rewarding of '*good*' behaviour and punishment of '*inappropriate*' behaviour is an approach with its foundations in classical conditioning theory (Skinner, 1938) and many strategies used in early years settings are still based on this outdated theory, for example behaviour charts. In an article suggesting that behaviour charts are ineffective, Davis (2022) suggests that strategies like these assume that all the children in the setting have control over their behaviour, which is very unlikely.

There is a higher than ever emphasis on emotional health today, and in the early years you understand more about the brain development of young children and the links between the brain and emotions (Conkbayir, 2021). Additionally, there are increasing demands for early years settings to include more children with diverse needs and/or vulnerable backgrounds (Fenton et al, 2015), so it is more important than ever that you work *with* children as they learn to regulate their own emotions. This can be achieved by creating a safe, secure environment that is emotionally literate (Allingham, 2020). Emotional literacy is the understanding that someone has of their own emotions. The term originated from psychologist Claude Steiner (1997, p 11) who maintained that '*emotional literacy improves relationships, creates loving possibilities between people, makes co-operative work possible, and facilitates the feeling of community*'. Consequently, nurturing emotional literacy in young children is one of the most beneficial things we can do for them and their future. Emotion coaching is a method of doing this that is used in many early years settings today.

Emotion coaching

A nurturing and supportive environment is one that will encourage emotional literacy and build resilience in young children. When children learn to understand their emotions through an emotionally literate environment, the next step is to learn how to handle them. The overarching principles of emotion coaching are that emotions (anger, fear, sadness, joy and disgust) are innate and there are valid reasons for them to occur (Gus, Rose and Gilbert, 2015). Within a trusting, secure relationship, the adult can help the child to understand their emotions and learn ways of dealing with difficult situations. Figure 3.3 illustrates an example of emotion coaching in action.

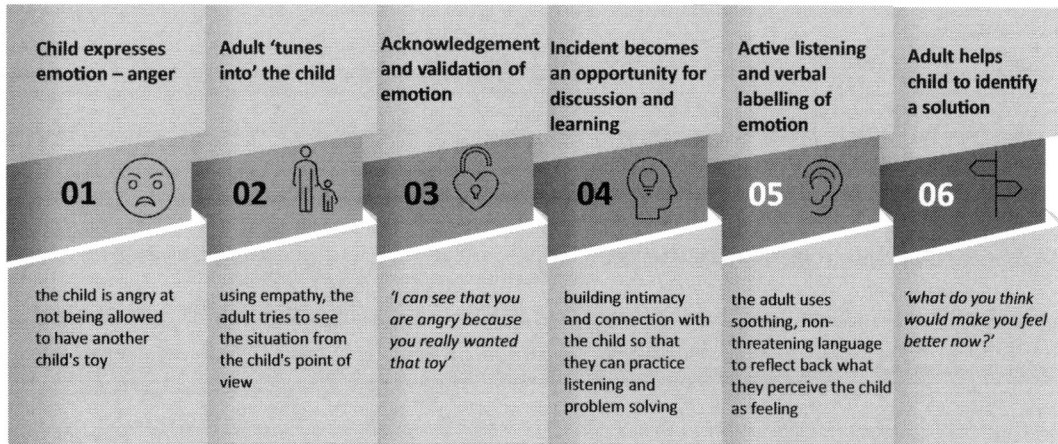

Figure 3.3 *Emotion coaching in action (adapted from Gottman's five steps, 1998)*

Emotion coaching is not only useful in supporting children to develop emotion regulation, it also impacts positively on the adult, promoting understanding of the child, helping to cement the relationship between them and so making interactions less stressful.

Risk, challenge and protection

One of the principles of the strength-based approach in the health sector is that risk is not seen as a barrier, but as an enabler (DHSC, 2019). In a healthcare setting, the professional's role is to support people in managing their own risk, rather than reducing risks. This is a little more complex in the early years. Practitioners know the importance of not *'wrapping children in cotton wool'*, of allowing children to take risks to challenge their physical capabilities (Johnston et al, 2018) but we are also responsible for protecting them from harm. An effective way of maintaining a strength-based approach and enabling children to feel capable and confident is to create an environment where children can challenge themselves safely. Letting a toddler use a hand trowel to do some gardening will make them feel competent and useful; supervising the activity and the subsequent hand washing maintains safety.

Reflective questions ?

My perfect day

Think of a young child you know well; close your eyes and picture the child in your mind. Now think about what would make tomorrow the best day possible for that child. Write a list of things that would enable that child to have the perfect day at your setting.

» What would they be doing?

» Which children would they be with?

→

> » Which adults, if any, would they like to be with?
>
> » Where would they be?
>
> » What would they be wearing?
>
> » What would they eat/drink?
>
> » What would they choose to play with?
>
> Now reflect on how useful the activity has been and whether this might be a helpful thing to do with other children in your setting. Would it help you to plan for children's individual needs and interests?

CASE STUDY ☺

Meg is an early years educator, working in the 0–2 year olds' room of a private day nursery. Here, she talks about how she sees her role in building attachments with, and getting to know, new children.

When new children start, we have three settling in sessions. At the first one, the parent(s) and baby meet the staff and see the room and they spend an hour with us. We ask lots of questions to find out as much as we can about the child; information about illnesses, allergies, the birth, but also about what they like to do at home, favourite toys, special people in their lives and any comforters they use. Cultural capital is important too, so we need to know what the child knows and has experienced. We don't want to talk to the child about the seaside if he has never been; we wouldn't plan to discuss the child's garden if he lives in a high rise flat. We need to know as much as possible about the child's world. At the second session, parents stay with their child for half an hour and then leave their child for an hour. It's always the parent's choice how long they stay; we are led by them. We tell the parents that we will phone them if their child is upset, but that we will try several things first to settle them, for example, walking around the outside of the nursery, or distracting them with a toy or a snack. At the third session, parents usually leave their child for the whole hour and a half. We try to make sure the same member of staff is there for all three days and most parents want to 'rip the plaster off' straight away and leave their child from the second session.

For the first four weeks, the settling in period, we have no assessment, and the child doesn't have a named key worker. After the four weeks, the key worker is chosen, and it will be the person the child has bonded with. That attachment is really important. We build a relationship with the child, first of all, through in-depth discussions with parents. We talk to them regularly about the child's interests, what the child has been doing, days out they have had, etc and this helps us to get to know the child really well. We use an online system, and parents can post messages and photos to us, so we can see what they have been doing at the weekend. This two-way process is really valuable; we send messages and photos back to the parents too. As well as the online system, we always tell parents that they can phone us and ask about their child at any time. If a child is unsettled when the parent leaves them in the morning, we can take a photo of them later when they are happy and engaged in an activity and we'll post that to the parents. We always put a positive spin on things, so if a child has been crying when their parent leaves, we will say things like 'she was a little bit unsettled in the morning, but she really enjoyed playing in the sand and she ate all of her lunch today'. We do 'snapshot' observations too and send these to parents. These are always about things the child does alone so, for example, we'll note that today the child found his own wellies, and we'll send that straight to the parents.

I think it's important to build an attachment with the child, but you have to be careful and make sure this is a professional attachment. We had a little boy who started with us and he was really confident and happy. Then a new student came to work in the room, and it was clear that this little boy was her favourite. She kept picking him up and carrying him around and then he developed an inappropriate attachment to her. It made things very difficult because he was always looking for her and wanting to be picked up and he wouldn't play on his own any more. So, I think that an attachment is important, but it needs to be a professional one that benefits the child and encourages independence, rather than over-reliance on one particular person in a nursery setting.

As well as partnership with parents, listening to the voice of the child him- or herself is important. Most of the children in our room are non-verbal, so it's about observing them and interacting with them regularly. That is important for our planning. We do 'in the moment' planning, which is solely based on the child's personal interests. The role of the adult is to look for a spark of interest and to build on that. We call this a 'teachable moment'. For example, a child was recently trying to scoop sand with a spoon, and he was concentrating for a long time, he was totally focused on scooping, so I built on this, by setting up a water activity with lots of spoons and containers for scooping. Another thing we do is talk to other practitioners if we haven't been there. If I am not in on one day, then I ask the practitioners who were in what my key children did, so I can build on anything they showed an interest in. It is all part of knowing the child as much as possible and understanding the child's world.

Reflective questions ⑦

» What are your immediate thoughts on reading the case study?

» What are the strength-based aspects of Meg's work with babies and their families?

» What do you think about Meg's view of professional attachment?

» What can you learn from this case study for your own practice?

Chapter summary 📖

In this chapter, strength-based approaches have been explored in relation to early years practice. Relationships with young children are an aspect of the strength-based approach which is at the heart of early years practice. Building a secure attachment and getting to know the individual child is fundamental and Meg's case study illustrates the way that this happens in a private day nursery. Learning about each child's unique self, their interests, skills and fascinations, is essential if practitioners are to plan suitable activities that encourage and enthuse young children. Meg's explanation of how she creates '*teachable moments*' from a child's '*spark of interest*' explains this process well. In this way, even the youngest children and babies are making choices and enabling their non-verbal '*voices*' to be heard. The chapter has also investigated ways of encouraging independence, self-control and resilience in young children. A strength-based approach in the early years is empowering for children and encourages a child-centred environment where children are inspired to develop into the best version of themselves that they can be.

Further reading 📚

- Prowle, A and Hodgkins, A (2020) *Making a Difference with Children and Families – Re-imagining the Role of the Practitioner*. London: Red Globe Books, Bloomsbury.

  This book is useful for anyone working with children and families. It considers the essential skills and qualities for working with children and families today. Importantly, it provides practitioners and students with opportunities to reflect upon what it means to be an effective practitioner, through the exploration of theoretical material and practice case studies from a range of professional disciplines.

- Robinson, K and Robinson, K (2022) *Imagine If ...: Creating a Future for Us All.* London: Penguin.

  This book summarises Sir Ken Robinson's influential work; his daughter Kate continued writing the book after her father's death in 2020. The book sets out his view for creating new systems of education that are based on diversity, creativity and collaboration.

References 📚

Abaza, M and Nelson, K (2018) Leading by Example: Role Modeling Resilience Helps Our Learners and Ourselves. *Academic Medicine*, 93(2): 157–8.

Ainsworth, M and Bell, S (1970) Attachment, Exploration, and Separation: Illustrated by the Behaviour of One-year-olds in a Strange Situation. *Child Development*, 41(1): 49–67.

Allingham, S (2020) *Emotional Literacy in the Early Years: Helping Children Balance Body and Mind.* London: Mark Allen Group.

Bandura, A (1977) Self-efficacy: Toward a Unifying Theory of Behavioral Change. *Psychological Review*, 84: 191–215.

Bandura, A, Ross, D and Ross, S (1961) Transmission of Aggression through Imitation of Aggressive Models. *Journal of Abnormal and Social Psychology*, 63: 575–82.

Bowlby, J (1952) *Maternal Care and Mental Health.* Geneva: The World Health Organization. [online] Available at: https://apps.who.int/iris/handle/10665/40724 (accessed 19 June 2023).

Bowlby, J (1969) *Attachment and Loss.* Vol. 1. New York: Basic Books.

Clark, A (2017) *Listening to Young Children, Expanded Third Edition: A Guide to Understanding and Using the Mosaic Approach.* London: Jessica Kingsley.

Conkbayir, M (2021) *Early Childhood and Neuroscience: Theory, Research and Implications for Practice,* 2nd ed. London: Bloomsbury Academic.

Davis, E (2021) *Why Children Need Professional Love.* Famly. [online] Available at: www.famly.co/blog/professional-love-early-years (accessed 19 June 2023).

Davis, E (2022) Good or Bad? *Nursery World,* March.

Department for Education (DfE) (2021) Early Years Foundation Stage (EYFS) Statutory Framework. [online] Available at: www.gov.uk/government/publications/early-years-foundation-stage-framework--2 (accessed 19 June 2023).

Department of Education and Early Childhood Development (2012) *Strength-Based Approach. A Guide to Writing Transition Learning and Development Statements.* [online] Available at: https://wrap2fasd.org/2022/12/16/strength-based-approach-a-guide-to-writing-transition-learning-and-development-statements/ (accessed 30 June 23).

Department for Health and Social Care (DHSC) (2019) *Strengths-based Social Work: Practice Framework and Handbook.* [online] Available at: www.gov.uk/government/publications/strengths-based-social-work-practice-framework-and-handbook (accessed 30 June 2023).

Fenton, A, Walsh, K, Wong, S and Cumming, T (2015) Using Strengths-Based Approaches in Early Years Practice and Research. *International Journal of Early Childhood,* 47: 27–52.

Gelitz, P (2017). *Role Model and Imitation.* [online] Available at: www.erziehungskunst.de/en/article/early-childhood/role-model-and-imitation/ (accessed 19 June 2023).

Goddard, C (2020) EYFS Best Practice in Schools – Be in Touch. *Nursery World,* 16 March. [online] Available at: www.nurseryworld.co.uk/features/article/eyfs-best-practice-in-schools-be-in-touch (accessed 30 June 2023).

Gottman, J (1998) *Raising an Emotionally Intelligent Child.* New York: Simon and Schuster.

Gus, L, Rose, J and Gilbert, L (2015) Emotion Coaching: A Universal Strategy for Supporting and Promoting Sustainable Emotional and Behavioural Well-being. *Educational & Child Psychology,* 32(1): 31–41.

Hammond, W (2010) Principles of Strength-Based Practice. *Resiliency Initiatives,* 1–7.

Hodgkins, A (2019) Advanced Empathy in the Early Years – a Risky Strength? *NZ International Research in Early Childhood Education,* 22 (1): 46–58.

Jarvis, P (2020) Attachment theory, Cortisol and Care for the Under-threes in the Twenty-first Century: Constructing Evidence-informed Policy. *Early Years,* 42: 4–5.

Johnston, J, Nahmad-Williams, L, Oates, R and Wood, V (2018) *Early Childhood Studies: Principles and Practice,* 2nd ed. London: Routledge.

Maslow, A (1943) A Theory of Human Motivation. *Psychological Review,* 50(4): 370–96.

Nergaard, K (2019) Empathic Expressions among Three-year-olds in Play and Interaction in ECEC Institutions in Norway: Bodily Empathic Expressions Purposed for Peers' Well-being and Confirming Relationships. *Early Child Development and Care,* 189(9): 1444–56.

Page, J (2018) Characterising the Principles of Professional Love in Early Childhood Care and Education. *International Journal of Early Years Education*, 26(2): 125–41.

Peterson, C (2013) The Strengths Revolution: A Positive Psychology Perspective. *Reclaiming Children and Youth*, 21(4): 7–14.

Prowle, A and Hodgkins, A (2020) *Making a Difference with Children and Families: Re-imagining the Role of the Practitioner*. London: Red Globe Books, Bloomsbury.

Roberts, R (2006) *Self-esteem and Early Learning: Key People from Birth to School (Zero to Eight)*, 3rd ed. London: Sage.

Robinson, K (2007) Do Schools Kill Creativity? TED talk, 7 January 2007. [online] Available at: www. youtube.com/watch?v=iG9CE55wbtY (accessed 19 June 2023).

Rogers, C (1957) The Necessary and Sufficient Conditions of Therapeutic Personality Change. *Journal of Consulting Psychology*, 21(2): 95–103.

Schwarzer, R (2014) *Self-efficacy: Thought Control of Action*. Hoboken: Taylor and Francis.

Scorza, P, Arayad, R, Wuermlib, A and Betancourt, T (2016) Towards Clarity in Research on 'Noncognitive' Skills: Linking Executive Functions, Self-Regulation, and Economic Development to Advance Life Outcomes for Children, Adolescents and Youth Globally. *Human Development*, 58(6): 313–17.

Shonkoff, J and Meisels, S (2000) *Handbook of Child Intervention*, 2nd ed. New York: Cambridge University Press.

Shpancer, N (2002) The Home-daycare Link: Mapping Children's New World Order. *Early Childhood Research Quarterly*, 17(3): 374–92.

Skinner, B F (1938) *The Behavior of Organisms: An Experimental Analysis*. New York: Appleton-Century.

Steiner, C with Perry, P (1997) *Achieving Emotional Literacy*. London: Bloomsbury.

Svinth (2018) Being Touched – the Transformative Potential of Nurturing Touch Practices in Relation to Toddlers' Learning and Emotional Well-being. *Early Child Development and Care*, 188(7): 924–36.

Watamura, S, Coe, C, Laudenslager, M and Robertson, S (2010) Child Care Setting Affects Salivary Cortisol and Antibody Secretion in Young Children. *Psychoneuroendocrinology*, 35(8): 1156–66.

4 Strength-based practice in middle childhood

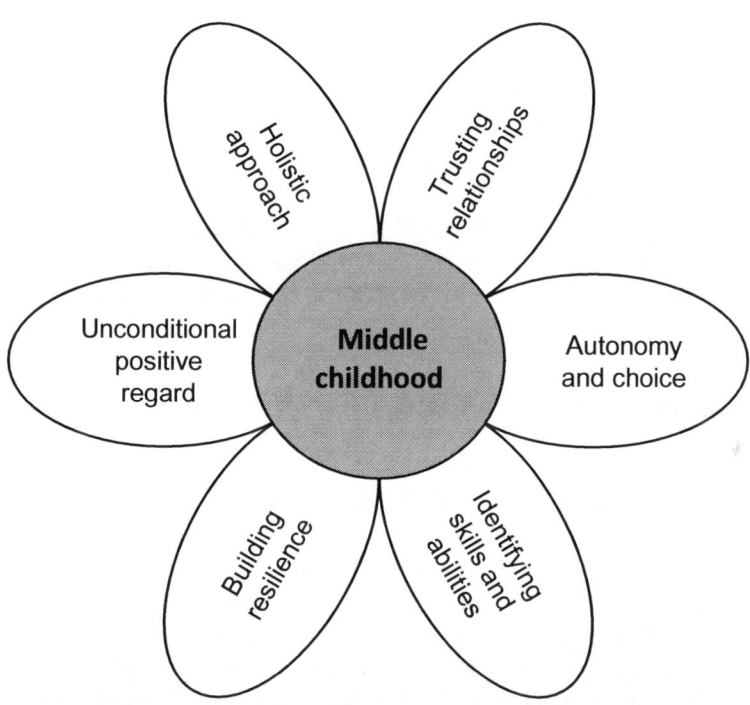

Chapter objectives

This chapter:

- explains why middle childhood is such an important time for a child's developing sense of self;

- stresses the importance of family relationships and peer friendships;

- outlines how freely chosen play and children's interests can be used as strengths;

- identifies opportunities in middle childhood for children to journey towards self-efficacy.

Introduction

Picture the scene. It is a glorious day in autumn half term, and I (Alison) am on Poppit Sands beach in West Wales. My granddaughter, Izzy (eight), and my nephew Logan (seven) are engaged in a very complicated game whereby they are building a memorial to a deceased seabird that we passed on our way here. They have called him Sammy Seagull. As I watch, they are negotiating, compromising, building on one another's ideas, and showing empathy towards the deceased bird. Their creativity and engagement astound me as I sip my coffee and just watch their interactions. They are fully absorbed right up until I say that it is time to head home, and over the next few days they keep returning to the topic of Sammy the Seagull in their conversation, their artwork and their play.

I reflect on the incredible phase of the life-course that is middle childhood, and all the wonderful opportunities it presents for children to explore ideas, extend their understanding of the world and develop their sense of self. Yet this phase of childhood is often forgotten and perhaps overshadowed by the emphasis we place on early years and adolescence. In this chapter, we want to celebrate middle childhood and explore some of the key issues and opportunities that present during this unique time. We also reflect upon how practitioners, especially those working in schools, can model strength-based approaches which enhance children's lives in the present and help to set them up for positive and successful futures.

What do we mean by middle childhood?

While definitions of middle childhood vary, the term generally refers to the developmental period between early childhood and adolescence, covering the ages between six and 11. This broadly aligns to the ages when children are in primary school. Traditionally, this middle period of childhood has received less emphasis than the phases that precede and follow it. Sigmund Freud, for example, saw middle childhood as a period of dormant development and latency (Jacobs, 2004), arguing that there are no significant contributions to a child's personality that take place at this time. Hence, compared to early childhood and adolescence, the period of middle childhood is relatively under-researched. Indeed, Mah and Ford-Jones (2012) refer to middle childhood as the *'forgotten years'*. However, since the 1980s there has been a renewed interest in middle childhood as a time which consolidates and extends development from early childhood (Montemayor, Adams and Gullotta, 1990) and allows children to begin to make sense of their place in the world, imbibing social values and developing identities that are separate from their parents (Greenspan and Pollock, 1991). It is becoming evident that middle childhood is an important time for children's development, as they begin to grapple with more complex learning, develop and maintain friendships, acquire abilities in self-regulation and extend their understanding of themselves and the world around them (Cincotta, 2008).

Understanding development in middle childhood

One of the most comprehensive articulations of children's development in middle childhood is Piaget's exploration of the concrete operational stage (Sullivan, 2009). Piaget's theory of cognitive development suggests that children typically move through four different stages of learning, which are broadly aligned to children's ages. His theory focuses not only on understanding how children acquire knowledge, but also on understanding the nature of intelligence. Table 4.1 below summarises Piaget's four stages.

Table 4.1 *Stages of learning, adapted from Piaget (1964)*

Piaget's stage of development	Age	Description of stage	Developmental changes
Sensorimotor stage	Birth to two years	During the earliest stage of cognitive development, infants and toddlers acquire knowledge through sensory experiences and manipulating objects. Initially a child's experience is governed by reflexes, senses and motor responses. This is a time of rapid growth and development.	• Children understand the world through movements and sensations. • Children learn about the world through basic actions (eg sucking, grasping, looking, listening). • They learn that things continue to exist when they cannot be seen (object permanence). • Children begin to recognise that they are separate from the people and objects around them. • In a basic sense they understand that their actions can cause effects in the world around them.
Pre-operational stage	Ages two to seven	The foundations of language development may have been laid during the previous stage, but the emergence of language is one of the major hallmarks of the pre-operational stage. Children learn through play but will struggle to understand the perspectives of others.	• Children begin to think symbolically and learn to use words and pictures to represent objects. • Children tend to be egocentric and struggle to see things from the perspective of others. • Children are becoming more proficient with language and thinking, but still tend to think in very concrete terms.
Concrete operational stage	Ages seven to 11	While children are still very concrete and literal in their thinking, they become more adept at using logic. Children become better at thinking about how other people might view a situation and hence less egocentric.	• Children begin to think logically. • They understand the concept of conservation (eg the amount of liquid in a short, wide cup is equal to that in a tall, thin glass). • Thinking becomes more logical and organised, but still quite concrete. • They begin using inductive logic, or reasoning from specific information to a general principle.

$\longrightarrow$

Table 4.1 (Cont.)

Piaget's stage of development	Age	Description of stage	Developmental changes
Formal operational stage	Ages 12 and up	The final stage involves an increase in logic, the ability to use deductive reasoning, and an understanding of abstract ideas. At this point, young people become capable of seeing multiple perspectives and think more logically about the world around them.	• Begin to think abstractly and reason about hypothetical problems. • Begin to think more about moral, philosophical, ethical, social and political issues that require theoretical and abstract reasoning. • Begin to use deductive logic, or reasoning from a general principle to specific information.

While there are number of criticisms levelled against Piaget's theory, such as the non-representative nature of his sample (Lourenço and Machado, 1996), the lack of scientific controls and the possibility that he may have underestimated children's abilities, Piaget's theory does help shine a light on the important phase of middle childhood. Far from being a period of development latency as Freud suggested, it is an important time for the consolidation of previously acquired skills and providing the foundations for logical thinking, ethical awareness and social competence. Figure 4.1 below highlights, in more detail, some of the developmental changes that children go through during middle childhood.

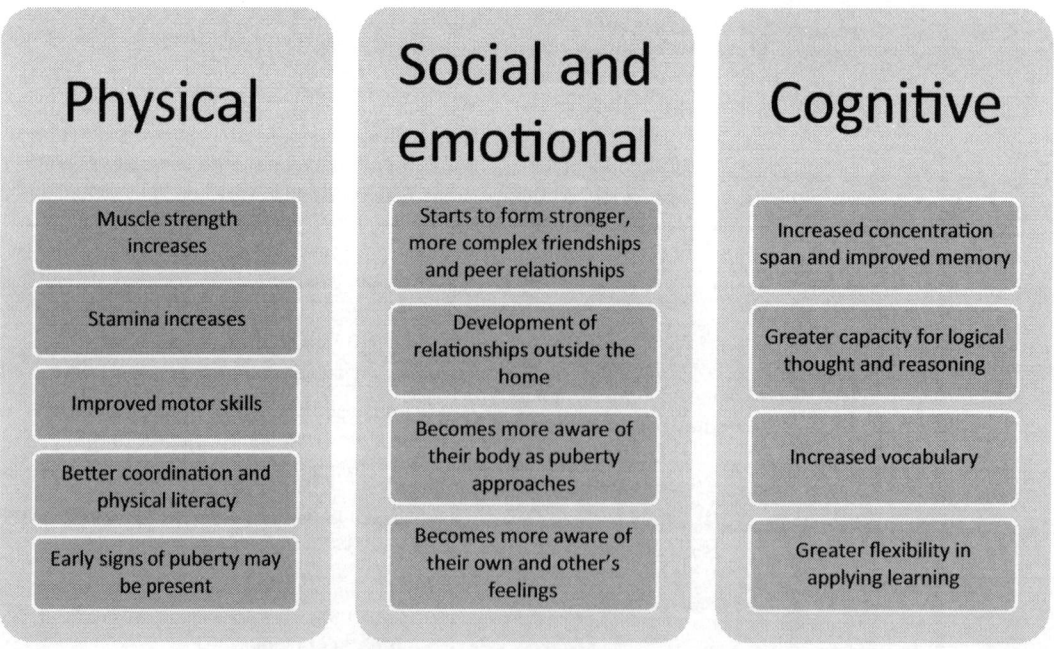

Figure 4.1 *Developmental changes in middle childhood*

Reflective questions ⑦

In early childhood, we can learn so much from observing children naturalistically. However, observation in middle childhood seems to be a lost art, and those observations that do occur tend to be focused around specific areas of learning.

If your context allows, ethically observe a small group of children in middle childhood for 10–15 minutes. Carefully record exactly what the children are doing and saying. After your observation find a quiet place to sit and read what you have written.

»   What did you observe?

»   What have you learned about children in middle childhood from your observation?

»   How will you use these insights in practice?

Parent–child relationships: the Circle of Security

Middle childhood is a time when children's relationships outside the home begin to become more important. Having a secure attachment to parents and carers (see Chapter 2) will provide that secure base from which children can explore their wider social world with confidence and ease. In a study by Abtahi and Kerns (2017), more securely attached children showed better emotion regulation when facing challenges in other relationships. They were better equipped to cope with setbacks and more skilled in resolving conflicts. Supporting parents to create and sustain positive attachments with their children is an important strength-based approach to enabling children's social and emotional development in middle childhood and beyond.

There are numerous approaches to supporting positive parenting (see Chapter 7), but one approach that has particular resonance when thinking about supporting secure parent–child attachments in middle childhood is the Circle of Security (COS). The Circle of Security provides a framework (represented graphically) for understanding attachment relationships, as well as a strength-based intervention approach (Powell et al, 2014). These attachments will subsequently provide a foundation from which the child can go away from the parent to develop meaningful and fulfilling relationships with others. There are also times when the parent needs to welcome the child coming back to them, and provide warmth, comfort and emotional support when needed. The role of the parent is to be consistently '*bigger, stronger, wiser and kind*', taking charge when necessary and helping the child to organise their feelings. The circle graphic (see Further reading below) provides a useful and easy to understand visual map of how an attuned parent/carer can attend to a child's needs and thereby promote secure attachments.

Shemmings (2018) makes the point that when discussing attachment with parents, it is better to avoid the word attachment altogether and use the word '*relationships*' instead. This is because attachment is often misunderstood and can be used pejoratively, causing the parent to feel inadequate or judged. Hence, the emphasis needs to be on helping to create strong and supportive relationships between parent and child, in order to facilitate that secure base from which the child can explore their world. According to Meins (2017), there is a link between secure attachment and the carer's capacity to treat their child as an individual with a mind of their own, often described as '*mind-mindedness*' or '*mindfulness*'. Figure 4.2 below shows some examples of how parents/carers (not to mention practitioners) may be seen to be mind-minded and acknowledge the autonomy of children.

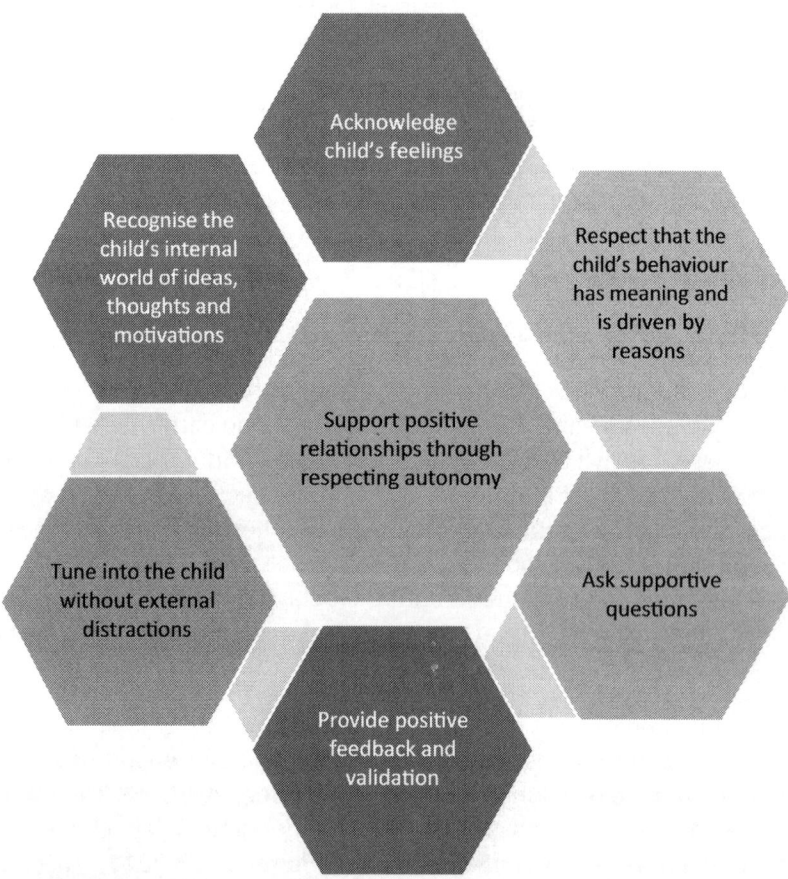

Figure 4.2 *Mind-mindedness*

Other relationships

Middle childhood is a time when other relationships, outside the parent–child relationship, become increasingly important. These relationships can provide enriching experiences for children and can be an important part of their strength-based assets. Relationships with school-based staff, siblings, other children and members of extended family can all play an important role in middle childhood, as the child begins to create unique relationships with key people, independently from their parents.

The importance of siblings

Sibling relationships are often the longest lasting relationships that people have over their life-course. There is much evidence to suggest that having siblings can positively affect a child's development, particularly a child's social skills, regardless of birth order (Marano, 2010). Some research indicates that having a sibling in adulthood helps alleviate depression and anxiety. The strengths of sibling relationships are easy to spot and include having someone to play with, talk to and share ideas and belongings with. Moreover, siblings have grown up in a similar environment and therefore have the same terms of reference. It is for this reason that Hartup (1979) states that sibling-to-sibling relationships influence children independently and also as part of an overall family dynamic. Sibling relationships differ from other relationships in terms of frequency (and amount) of interaction, durability of relations, accessibility and common experiences (Cicirelli, 1976). However, these relationships are not without challenges. Sibling rivalry is a common experience and may begin in early childhood or often with the birth of a new baby. Some sibling conflicts can be useful, helping children to develop problem-solving skills and understand different perspectives. In turn, finding a way through sibling conflict can help children develop skills to manage other relationships, particularly peer friendships. Sibling rivalry can manifest itself in the following ways (Figure 4.3).

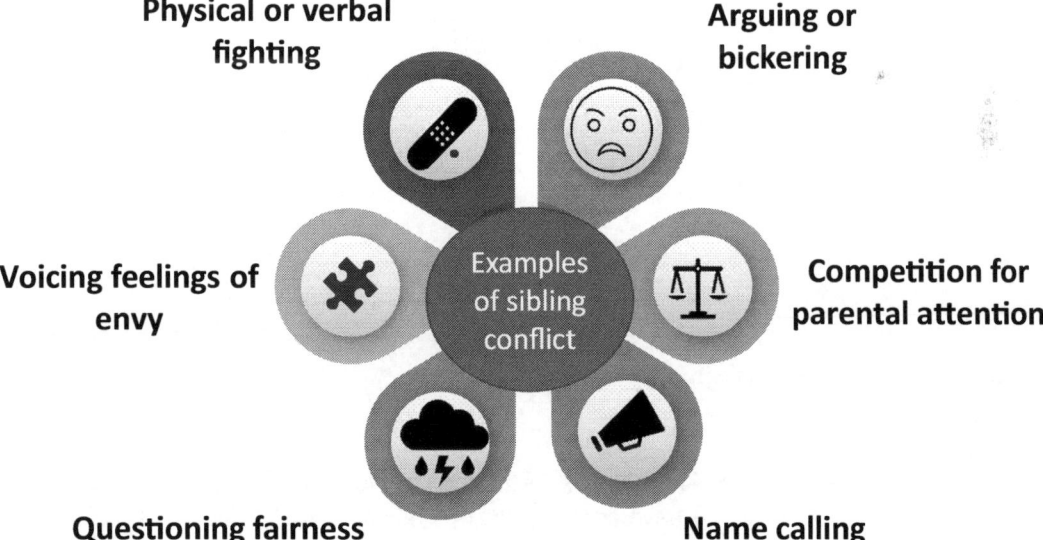

Figure 4.3 *Examples of sibling conflict*

While sibling conflict is a universal experience in family life, it can generate additional stress for families, particularly when compounded by other factors such as major life experiences, family adversity and a lack of conflict resolution skills within the family. The attuned practitioner can assist in such situations by supporting parents to recognise that conflict is a normal part of a sibling relationship. They can also model effective conflict management, fairness and empathy, and encourage boundary setting.

Grandparents

Relationships with grandparents (and other members of the extended family) can be a great source of strength for children in middle childhood. The individual relationship will, of course, be affected by a range of factors such as proximity, age and health status of the grandparent, and the extent to which they are involved in the child's life. Some grandparents may be actively involved in childcare on a weekly basis. Others may be working themselves and their role is restricted to high days and holidays. Figure 4.4 shows some of the strengths a strong relationship with a relative other than parents and siblings can afford a child in middle childhood.

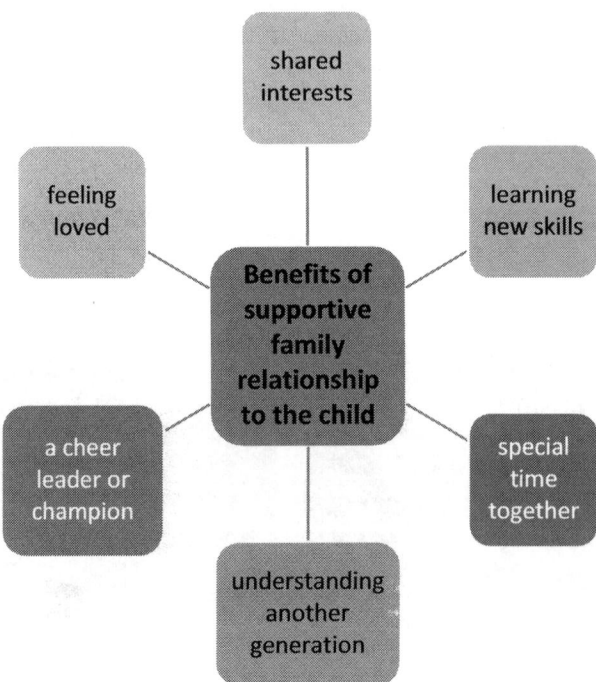

Figure 4.4 *Benefits of a supportive relationship*

It is important, here, to recognise that such relationships work best when a principle of reciprocity is embedded. While we have considered the specific value to the child arising from relationships with grandparents, the grandparents will reap benefits too. It is useful for practitioners working with children to understand who is important to the child and to find ways to support and celebrate these relationships through the work that they do.

Peer friendships

Hutchinson (2015) states that during middle childhood, the child's social world expands exponentially, and while parents and siblings continue to have a strong influence, middle childhood marks a growing peer orientation where children begin to demonstrate enhanced competence in managing their social relationships.

There is much research that identifies the importance of peer friendships. Holder and Coleman (2015) highlight that peer friendships are closely linked to well-being. Maunder and Monks (2019) noted that the quality of friendships was closely related to self-esteem, with children who had a reciprocated best friend displaying significantly higher sense of self-worth than those children without a best friend. Moreover, the children with a best friend showed stronger identification with their wider peer groups. It appears, then, that having at least one reciprocated friendship is of enormous benefit to children of this age. Figure 4.5 shows just some of the benefits of high quality, reciprocated friendship.

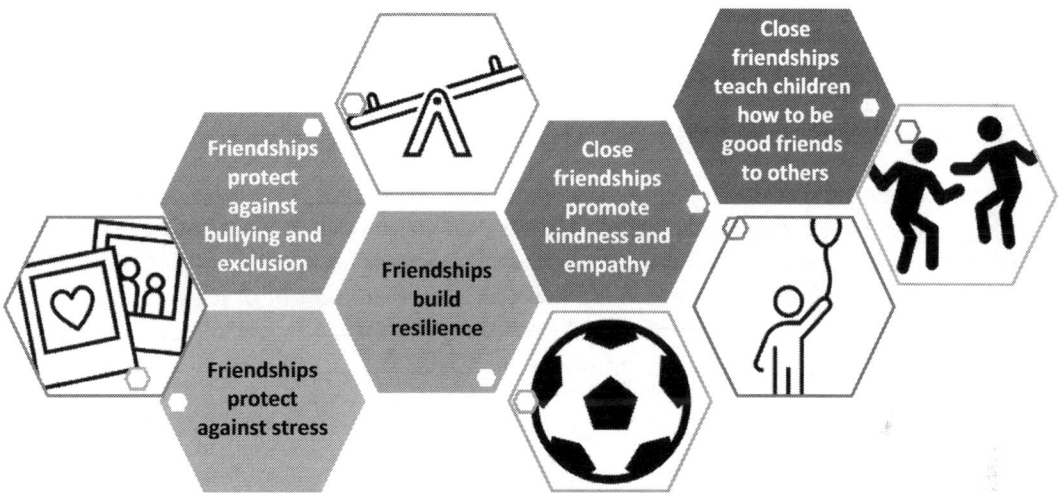

Figure 4.5 Benefits of reciprocated friendships

When children start school, they begin spending an increasing amount of time with their peer group. In turn, this begins to influence their preferences and their understanding of peer group norms. During this period, children tend to move away from imaginative play with peers and spend more time in deep conversation and structured games (Fink and Hughes, 2019). Gender segregation also becomes more prevalent at this time, with some notable differences in the way children of different genders form friendships, with girls congregating in smaller more intimate groups. At this point peers may discourage cross-gender friendships. This presents challenges for practitioners in relation to how they promote inclusion in an era when there is a growing recognition of issues surrounding children's gender identification.

Many researchers have distinguished between having strong reciprocal friendships and having wider popularity within the peer group. It may be possible to enjoy popularity without having close friendships or indeed to have a close reciprocal friendship but not be popular with the other children. However, an absence of reciprocal friendships in middle childhood has been associated with feelings of loneliness, lack of self-worth, depression and anxiety in adolescence and beyond (Parker and Asher, 1993). In discussing children's friendships,

Fink and Hughes (2019) identify the importance of children's *'theory of mind'* for negotiating friendships, showing empathy and conflict resolution. Theory of mind is:

> the understanding that others have intentions, desires, beliefs, perceptions, and emotions different from one's own, and that such intentions, desires, and so forth affect people's actions and behaviours.
>
> (APA Dictionary, 2023)

Children able to establish lasting and reciprocal friendships tend to have a more developed theory of mind. Hence, supporting children to understand and articulate their own and other's feelings and points of view and mental states is important in promoting positive peer interactions and setting strong foundations for later relationships.

Reflective questions ⑦

Olivia, Parveen and Zyta are in Year 3. They have been firm friends since Reception class and can often be found playing together and planning sleepovers at each other's houses. However, today Zyta is inconsolable. Through her sobs she tells you that Olivia and Parveen are now best friends and have been leaving her out of their games. Zyta has no one to play with and she wants to go home. She says that no one likes her, and that Olivia has been laughing at her and telling her she is stupid.

» As a practitioner working with the girls in an after school club, how would you address the issue?

» What theories might help guide your response?

Oscar is an independent-minded and intelligent boy of ten. He prefers to play alone, focusing upon his own strong interests. However, his parents are very worried that Oscar does not appear to have any friends. As far as you can tell from your observations, Oscar is perfectly happy with the situation. He will join a group when encouraged to do so but clearly prefers to be alone or to interact with adults.

» How would you proceed in order to support Oscar and his family?

» Thinking about your own practice context, how could you support children to develop healthy peer friendships?

Social media

Over the last several years, the growth of information and communication technology has been exponential. Children today are born into a world of technology. They are, as Prensky (2001) identified, *'digital natives'*, often more competent at using new technologies than their parents. Children and young people may use social media for a range of different purposes and across different platforms. Technology can open up immense opportunities for children.

For example, they can use computers, tablets or smartphones to search for information, to keep in touch with family and friends, to play games and to generate their own creative outputs. However, there are also risks that accompany children's use of technology. It is imperative that children become aware of the risks and that the adults around them are cognisant of the dangers and have strategies to keep them safe. When we think of children and social media, most people will be aware of the risks from predators, the risk of radicalisation and of children's access to unsuitable material. However, there are other dangers too. In particular, children who do not have access to technology may become marginalised, creating a divide in peer groups. Online bullying is a significant problem and can have devastating effects on children's mental health. Children may also overshare material, creating vulnerability for the present and future. Moreover, social media can mould social attitudes and normalise certain maladaptive behaviours, as has been suggested in high-profile cases which have considered the role that social media has played in the lives of children and young people affected by eating disorders, self-harm and suicide.

McDool et al's (2016) research suggests that spending a great deal of time on social networks reduces the satisfaction that children feel with all aspects of their lives, except for their friendships. There is also evidence that girls are more adversely affected by time spent online than boys. One thing that is evident is that social media will not be going away anytime soon. Hence, it is incumbent on parents and staff working with children to be aware of the challenges and to put in place safeguards to support children with their online lives (more about this in Chapter 9).

Identity formation

Middle childhood is a time when children begin to explore identity and self-understanding (Bandura, 1978). It has long been recognised that a child's sense of self is largely mediated by their perception of how others view them (Mead, 1934). The 'others' here include parents, siblings, other close associations and, increasingly, teachers and peers. For this reason, schools play a salient role in shaping children's self-concept (for better or worse), and there are many studies which highlight that perceptions formed in this way can continue into adulthood. Depending on their individual experience during this period, children may develop views of themselves as capable, talented and productive or as inferior and inadequate. Such influences on self-concept can come from anywhere in the child's ecological system (Bronfenbrenner, 1979). However, given the amount of time proportionately spent in school, children's perspectives of self are likely to be shaped strongly by their experiences in education.

It is incumbent, then, upon school-based staff to ensure that the child's experience is a positive one, and that the environment is conducive to the development of healthy self-esteem. As adults, most of us can remember that one teacher who understood, encouraged and inspired us and this gives a real indication of how powerful a force for good the teacher role can be. Figure 4.6 shows just some of the strength-based ways that teachers can help children to create a positive sense of self.

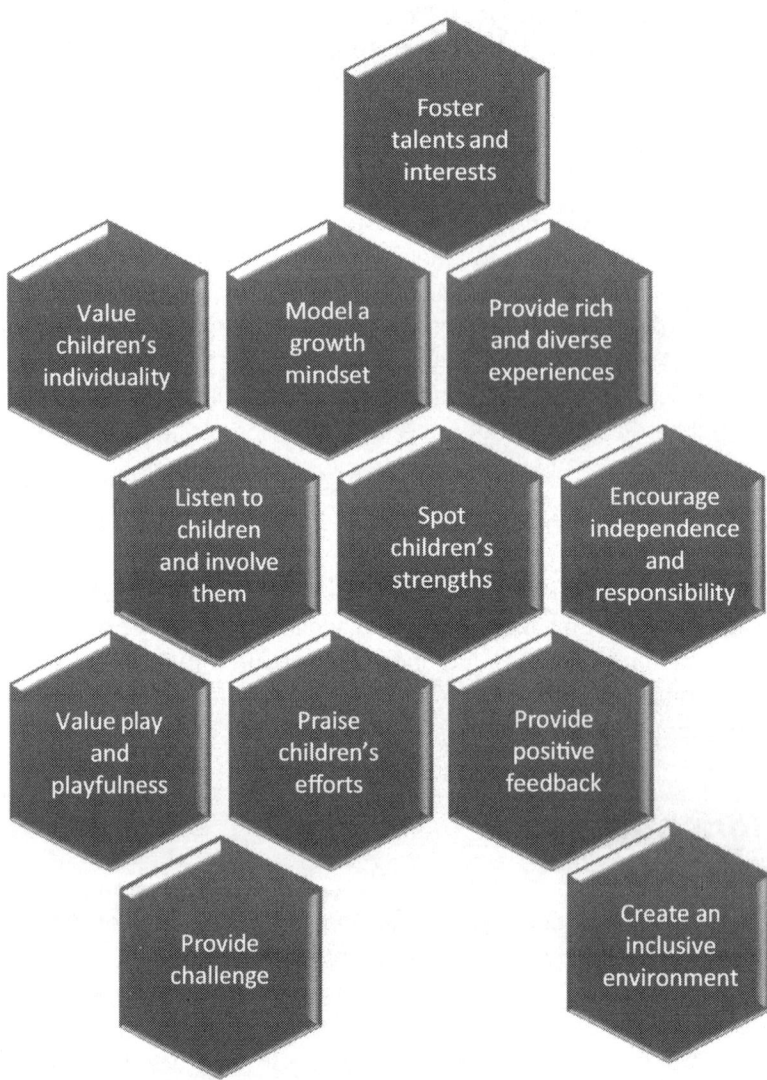

Figure 4.6 *Helping children to create a positive sense of self*

Growth mindsets

A child's mindset has a major influence on how they understand and respond to their world. Carol Dweck (2007) identified two distinct ways in which children understand intelligence and view their learning and potential (Figure 4.7).

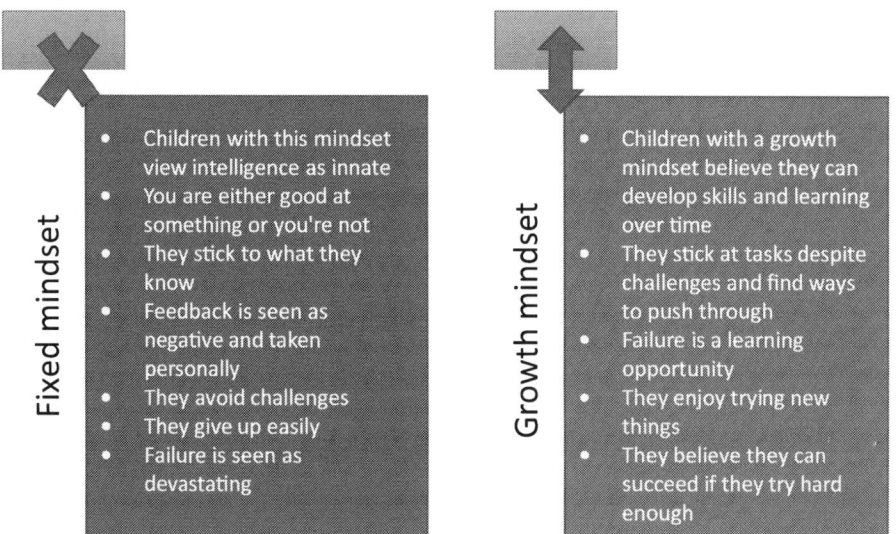

Figure 4.7 *Fixed mindset vs. growth mindset*

In a fixed mindset, children avoid challenges and avoid taking risks if there is a possibility of failure. This can have a significant impact on a child's development at school, on their hobbies and in their friendships. If failure is perceived as a bad thing to be avoided, then the child will make risk-averse decisions and try hard only at what they consider to be those things they are naturally good at. In a growth mindset, however, children understand that overcoming challenges can help them gain new skills and become more intelligent. Working through difficulties and overcoming problems supports the brain's neurological growth.

Many primary schools have adopted a growth mindset approach in order to boost children's learning and development, but also their well-being. Such schools have trained staff and parents to find ways to cultivate children's growth mindsets. They recognise that adults have an important role in encouraging growth mindsets through what they say and how they react.

Some common approaches include the following:

- using the term 'yet', thus opening up the possibility that the skill can be mastered;

- encouraging collaboration and skill sharing to solve problems;

- reframing failure as a rich opportunity for learning;

- praising effort instead of achievement;

- explaining mindset theory to children;

- displaying growth mindset quotes and mantras.

Supporting healthy habits that last a lifetime

During middle childhood, not only are children becoming more independent and more socially adept, but their bodies are growing, and they are becoming more coordinated and physically literate. Hence, middle childhood is a great time to help create interests and habits that will be exciting for children in the present and provide them with a great foundation for later life. Encouraging a growth mindset, positive self-concept and healthy, reciprocal relationships will all support happy childhoods, but also stand children in great stead for the future. It is also crucial to foster interests and talents, providing rich opportunities for children to play and take risks and enjoy their physical landscape.

In the case study below, Sarah, the leader of an exciting outdoor play company, explores how risk and challenge in freely chosen activities can enhance children's autonomy and sense of self.

CASE STUDY ☻

Sarah Watkins: risk as a strength

A child excitedly said to me the other day 'I can't believe you're going to let us use these tools!' 'Yes,' I replied, 'I'm going to help you use these tools.' It's a minor distinction but important. Dandy Lions is a pop-up outdoor play company, and giving children as much autonomy as possible is a strong part of our ethos. I see children of all abilities blossom as they set their own challenges and work to achieve them. Increasingly, children in our society need to experience a greater sense of control.

By supporting a child to use tools, I learn about that child's capability and level of confidence. Dr A Jean Ayres (1972), a pioneering occupational therapist, who carried out ground-breaking research in the area of sensory integration, introduced the term 'just right challenge' to describe the process of ensuring that tasks are difficult enough to provide a challenge but not so difficult that the child gives up in frustration. Through observation and listening to the child, I establish a child's level of competence and the level of support they need. I see extraordinary levels of perseverance and determination from the children because they have devised the challenge themselves and are committed to seeing it through.

Children need time to master skills like drilling holes, sawing wood, starting a fire or constructing a den. We recently worked with a child who suffered significant neglect as a baby. We'd been warned that she frequently showed very challenging behaviour in school. However, she was calm and focused throughout our session because she had the time to execute her very clear plan, devised after exploring the materials available. I worked as a primary teacher for a decade, and it was sometimes difficult in school to enable a child to spend a satisfying amount of time on their task without moving them on. This child has a diagnosed learning delay but, in our session, I was only interested in the type of support she might need to fulfil her plan. As she progressed with her construction, carefully nailing thin wood slices, corks and buttons to a narrow piece of wood, I suggested I could hold the wood steady for her as she nailed pieces in place. This child experienced some manageable frustration but was totally absorbed throughout the session.

Our sessions take place at a wide range of locations. Something I aim to provide in each environment is what I call 'productive uncertainty'. I want children to make progress by engaging with uneven ground, branches, brambles, long grass, mud and puddles. A wild natural space is inclusive and prompts children to choose their own level of challenge. Sensory dysfunction is a rising problem and children need the opportunity to move in different ways, to swing, dig and climb. Landscape architect Helle Nebelong (nd) talks of the 'genius loci', the spirit of a place, the qualities and atmosphere already present. This could be part of a building, a tree with character, or even something that happened there. When we plan for a new space, we consider what it offers the children and how we could enhance their experience. When the children arrive, they interpret the space in ways we couldn't have imagined, putting their own mark on it.

Withdrawal spaces such as dens are crucial so that children can process all the complex things that are going on in their lives. Jimmy was struggling to come to terms with a family bereavement. When he was in a high state of anxiety, he was calmed by swinging in a hammock with the material pulled over his face. During this time, he was more easily able to discuss how the different emotions felt in his body. The process of swinging is also essential for children to develop their vestibular sense, vital for healthy emotional and physical development.

Through Dandy Lions sessions, I find that children, including those with special educational needs (SEN), benefit from working towards shared goals. A group of children might decide to build a bridge, or to transport pinecones to another area without touching the ground. The children identify the strengths that exist in the group and collaborate to achieve the task. There may be an element of conflict, but these discussions are healthy, when they are facilitated by caring, invested adults.

We recently received this comment on social media: 'the two lovely people running the children's activities yesterday were amazing. She clearly loves what she does, and this absolutely shone through. Anyone that knows R knows that getting him to sit still is a mission at the best of times, but he loved it'. *Our spoken language and body language tell a clear story to children. When a child experiences an adult's interest, not just in the outcome of their labours, but in the process, it can be powerful. I appreciate that it is a privilege to enter the child's world and be a co-explorer. I am not there as an expert. I am there to support and enhance the play process. I am there to help children progress from their starting point, whatever that happens to be.*

→

I told a new group the other day that we were going to make a fire. 'Sarah, I can do this', said a child who has just moved here from Ukraine. I gestured for him to come closer. He took the cotton wool and placed it in the centre of the firepit. 'You must stay on there', he said to the other children, pointing at the kneeling pads. He placed the kindling in a neat pile around the cotton wool, leaving gaps, then used the striker to light the cotton wool. He leaned forwards and blew gently on the fire. 'Have you used one of these before?' I asked, pointing at the Dutch Oven. He looked carefully at it, lifting the heavy lid. 'No ... but I'd like to try.'

Reflective questions ⑦

»   Within the case study, Sarah explores the role of the adult. Re-read the case study making notes about the way she supports, helps and co-constructs with the children. What can you learn from her interactions?

»   Sarah is a strong advocate of outdoor play in natural spaces. What benefits can children derive from these opportunities?

»   What does Sarah mean by the term '*productive uncertainty*'? Why is this important for supporting children's holistic development? Could you apply this concept to your own setting?

»   In your own work with children, young people and families how can you provide '*just right challenge*', allowing children to step out of their comfort zone, take risks and learn exciting new skills?

Chapter summary ⓑ

Having read this chapter, we are once more challenged by the amazing opportunities for a strength-based approach. At best, middle childhood can be a unique time for playfulness, learning and connection. It can be a time for adventuring, valuing our uniqueness and discovering where we belong and what we value and enjoy. However, middle childhood also has its risks. There is a growing incidence of anxiety and depression among young children, and middle childhood may also be a time when children face stressors such as friendship difficulties, worries about the future and school. Other children may be facing adverse life experiences (see Chapter 8). It is our desire that by fostering some of the approaches explored in this chapter (and the book as a whole) practitioners can provide an attuned response to children and make the most of opportunities for strength-based practice to support children's well-being in middle childhood and beyond.

Further reading 📖

* The Circle of Security Graphic and many other useful resources about supporting attachment can be found at www.circleofsecurityinternational.com

* Children's play in middle childhood is touched upon only cursorily in this chapter and certainly demands not just a chapter but whole books devoted to it. The national play councils offer a wealth of resources to support an understanding of play, and these can be found on their websites.

    www.playengland.org.uk/

    www.playwales.org.uk/eng/

    www.playscotland.org/

References 📚

Abtahi, M M and Kerns, K A (2017) Attachment and Emotion Regulation in Middle Childhood: Changes in Affect and Vagal Tone during a Social Stress Task. *Attachment & Human Development*, 19(3): 221–42.

American Psychological Association (APA) (2023) *Theory of Mind.* [online] Available at: https://dictionary.apa.org/theory-of-mind (accessed 19 June 2023).

Ayres, A J (1972) *Sensory Integration and Learning Disorders.* Los Angeles: Western Psychological Services.

Bandura, A (1978) Social Learning Theory of Aggression. *Journal of Communication*, 28(3): 12–29.

Bronfenbrenner, U (1979) *The Ecology of Human Development: Experiments by Nature and Design.* Cambridge, MA: Harvard University Press.

Cicirelli, V G (1976) Mother-child and Sibling-sibling Interactions on a Problem-solving Task. *Child Development*, 47: 588–96.

Cincotta, N F (2008) The Journey of Middle Childhood: Who Are 'Latency'-Age Children? In Austrian, S G (ed) *Developmental Theories through the Life Cycle* (pp 79–132). New York: Columbia University Press.

Dweck, C (2007) *Mindset: The New Psychology of Success.* New York: Ballantine Books.

Fink, E and Hughes, C (2019) Children's Friendships. *Psychologist*, 32: 28–31.

Greenspan, S I and Pollock, G H (eds) (1991) *The Course of Life, Vol. 3, Middle and Late Childhood.* New York: International Universities Press.

Hartup, W W (1979) The Social Worlds of Childhood. *American Psychologist*, 34(10): 944.

Holder, M D and Coleman, B (2015) Children's Friendships and Positive Well-being. In Demir, M (ed) *Friendship and Happiness: Across the Lifespan and Cultures* (pp 81–97). New York: Springer.

Hutchinson, E (2015) *Dimensions of Human Behavior – The Changing Life Course*, 6th ed. Virginia, USA: Sage.

Jacobs, M (2004) The Perils of Latency. *Psychodynamic Practice*, 10(4): 500–14.

Lourenço, O and Machado, A (1996) In Defense of Piaget's Theory: A Reply to 10 Common Criticisms. *Psychological Review*, 103(1): 143–64.

Mah, V K and Ford-Jones, E L (2012) Spotlight on Middle Childhood: Rejuvenating the 'forgotten years'. *Paediatrics & Child Health*, 17(2): 81–3.

Marano, H (2010) Oh, Brother! *Psychology Today*. [online] Available at: www.psychologytoday.com/gb/articles/201007/oh-brother (accessed 4 August 2023).

Maunder, R and Monks, C P (2019) Friendships in Middle Childhood: Links to Peer and School Identification, and General Self-worth. *British Journal of Developmental Psychology*, 37(2): 211–29.

McDool, E, Powell, P, Roberts, J and Taylor, K (2016) Social Media Use and Children's Wellbeing. Sheffield Economic Research Paper Series, University of Sheffield. [online] Available at: https://core.ac.uk/download/pdf/78902193.pdf (accessed 19 June 2023).

Mead, G H (1934) *Mind, Self, and Society from the Standpoint of a Social Behaviorist*. Chicago: University of Chicago Press.

Meins, E (2017) Overrated: The Predictive Power of Attachment. *The Psychologist*, 30: 20–4.

Montemayor, R, Adams, G R and Gullotta, T P (eds) (1990) *From Childhood to Adolescence: A Transitional Period? Advances in Adolescent Development*. New York: Sage.

Nebelong, H (nd) *Designs on Play*. [online] Available at: www.freeplaynetwork.org.uk/design/nebelong.htm (accessed 19 June 2023).

Parker, J G and Asher, S R (1993) Friendship and Friendship Quality in Middle Childhood: Links with Peer Group Acceptance and Feelings of Loneliness and Social Dissatisfaction. *Developmental Psychology*, 29: 611–21.

Piaget, J (1964) Cognitive Development in Children: Development and Learning. *Journal of Research in Science Teaching*, 2: 176–86.

Powell, B, Cooper, G, Hoffman, K and Marvin, R (2014) *The Circle of Security Intervention: Enhancing Attachment in Early Parent-child Relationships*. New York: Guilford.

Prensky, M (2001) Digital Natives, Digital Immigrants Part 1. *On the Horizon*, 9: 3–6.

Shemmings, D (2018) Why Social Workers Shouldn't Use 'Attachment' in their Records and Reports. *Community Care*, 28 June. [online] Available at: www.communitycare.co.uk/2018/06/28/social-workers-shouldnt-use-attachment-records-reports/ (accessed 19 June 2023).

Sullivan, L (2009) *The SAGE Glossary of the Social and Behavioral Sciences*. London: Sage.

5 Strength-based practice in services for young people

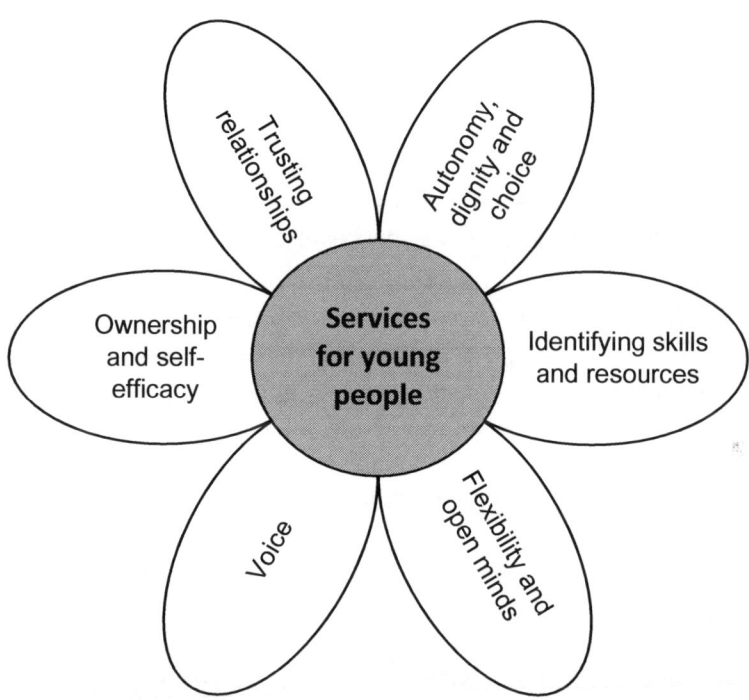

Chapter objectives

This chapter:

- differentiates between adolescence and young adulthood, presenting the challenges and opportunities of this important phase of the life-course;

- considers the importance of young people's participation in decision making, both at an individual level and more generally in public life and civic spaces;

- encourages readers to reflect upon how they can apply strength-based approaches when working with young people.

Introduction

Having considered middle childhood, this chapter now moves on to a further phase of the life-course. The concepts of '*youth*' or '*young people*' are notoriously nebulous and difficult to define. We usually use these terms to denote the period from the beginning of secondary education into young adulthood, in other words from ages 11 to 25. However, this broad definition of young people is fraught with difficulties and inconsistencies. In a technical sense, a young person becomes an adult in the UK when they reach the age of majority at 18. Prior to this, they are considered to be a minor. This is further complicated by the fact that 10 year-olds can be charged with a crime, 13 year-olds can have a social media account, 16 year-olds can enter legal contracts and consent to sexual activity and 17 year-olds can drive a vehicle. Children can have part-time jobs from 14 (or 13 in performance), and 16 year-olds in Scotland and Wales can vote in elections for their devolved parliament but English young people must wait until 18 to vote. With laws like these, it is no wonder that the youth phase of the life-course is highly ambiguous and confusing for young people and services alike. This is exacerbated by the fact that young people develop at different rates, so some of these legal cut-offs can appear very arbitrary. The situation becomes even more complex when considered in a global context, as diverse countries take radically different approaches.

If we consider the phase of youth as encompassing 11–25 year-olds, then this causes further confusion as an 11 year-old minor is very different from a 24 year-old who may be living independently and working full-time. This has caused some theorists (for example Bynnar, 2005) to call for a new stage of the life-course of young adulthood, to reflect the evident differences between adolescents and young adults and to recognise the myriad transitions that young people go through as they become adults.

Adolescence

Adolescence is defined as

> the phase of life between childhood and adulthood, from ages 10 to 19. It is a unique stage of human development and an important time for laying the foundations of good health. Adolescents experience rapid physical, cognitive and psychosocial growth.
>
> (World Health Organization, nd)

At this time, young people also experience many hormonal changes. A great insight into adolescence is provided in the TED talk by neuroscientist Sarah-Jayne Blakemore (see Further resources). Adolescence provides a window of exceptional neuroplasticity, when intervention may be more effective, particularly in the areas of memory, stress and substance use (Fuhrmann, Knoll and Blakemore, 2015). Practitioners can help support young people and parents to navigate their way positively through the turbulence of adolescence, by sharing knowledge about the teenage brain and also signposting to resources that promote body acceptance, a healthy lifestyle and positive mental health and well-being.

Young adulthood

There is a growing body of evidence that young adulthood continues to be a time of rapid brain development. Consequently, an 18 year-old is not the same person they will be at 25

(Giedd, 2004). The MIT Young adult project (Simpson, 2018) has highlighted the following changes (Figure 5.1) which take place in early adulthood (defined here as ages 18–25).

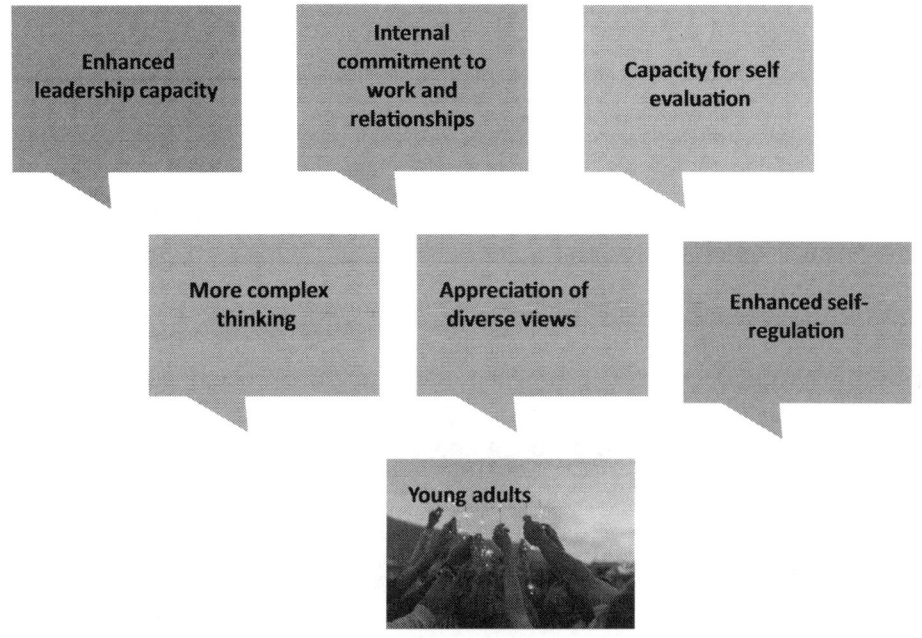

Figure 5.1 *Early adulthood (adapted from Simpson, 2018)*

Simpson (2018) recognises, however, that many young people may never reach some of the milestones associated with young adulthood, owing to a range of individual factors such as disability, illness, poverty of opportunity, neurodiversity, trauma and poor mental health. As a consequence, they may become stuck and therefore not

> *make the kinds of shifts in complexity of thinking that typically occur in young adulthood. They struggle with the expectations and demands of modern life in part because they are handicapped by thinking capacities that are more typical in some ways of adolescence and younger ages.*

(Simpson, 2018, np)

Strength-based approaches to youth work

According to the National Youth Agency (2023), youth work is '*a distinct educational process adapted across a variety of settings to support a young person's personal, social and educational development*'. The purpose of youth work is:

- to explore their values, beliefs, ideas, and issues;

- to enable them to develop their voice, influence and place in society;

- to acquire a set of practical or technical skills and competencies, to realise their full potential.

The principles of youth work are supported by reflective practice and peer education, establishing and maintaining relationships with young people and community groups. Principles include the following:

• knowledge of how young people develop during adolescence and appropriate support;

• the trusted relationships and voluntary engagement of young people;

• understanding how to establish boundaries, challenge behaviour and de-escalate conflict;

• the importance of safeguarding in providing a safe environment for young people.

Youth services provide valuable provision and are often a lifeline for the young people who use them, providing a safe space for young people to explore a range of issues while engaging purposefully in activities to support their development, well-being and aspirations. The Council of Europe (nd) sums this up as providing a tool for personal development, social integration and active citizenship of young people. Figure 5.2 below is adapted from their model for youth work.

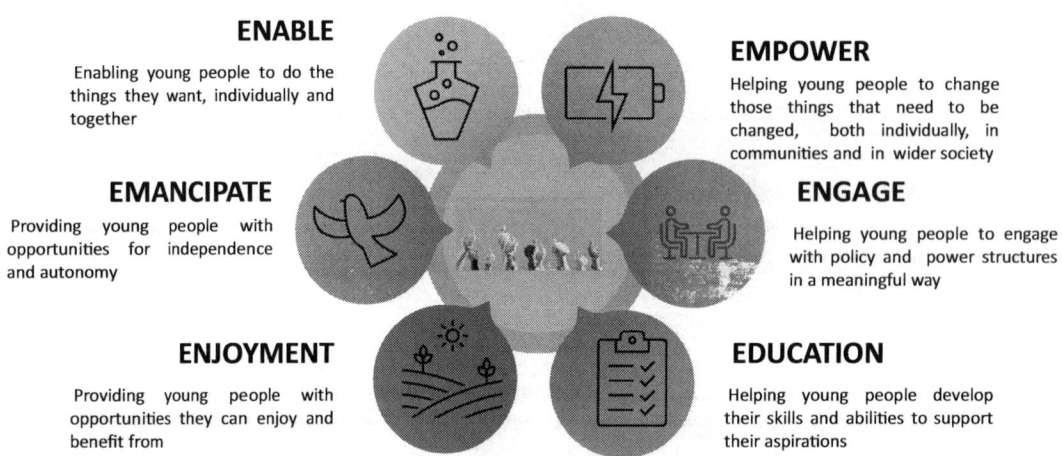

ENABLE
Enabling young people to do the things they want, individually and together

EMPOWER
Helping young people to change those things that need to be changed, both individually, in communities and in wider society

EMANCIPATE
Providing young people with opportunities for independence and autonomy

ENGAGE
Helping young people to engage with policy and power structures in a meaningful way

ENJOYMENT
Providing young people with opportunities they can enjoy and benefit from

EDUCATION
Helping young people develop their skills and abilities to support their aspirations

Figure 5.2 *Supporting young people in strength-based ways*

Clearly, such principles and activities have a focus on strengths at their very heart. However, as well as youth workers, young people encounter a wide range of other professionals, including teachers, health professionals and work coaches. In all these areas, using strength-based approaches can be highly effective.

Youth services provide safe spaces where young people can explore their interests, be with friends, learn, develop and grow in a supportive environment. Given the immense potential of youth work, it is worrying to note that public spending on youth work has been decreasing for over a decade (YMCA, 2022).

Positive discourses of young people

Too often in our society young people quite literally get a bad press. A youth research project (Hertsmere Young Researchers, 2011) found compelling evidence of unbalanced media reporting of young people, focusing on the sensational rather than the factual, and portraying young people in a negative way. According to the report, this impacted significantly upon how young people were perceived in society. They gave examples of how knife crime is portrayed as a teenage issue (whereas in fact more than two thirds of knife crime did not involve teenagers). These perceptions of young people's violence then became a self-fulfilling prophesy for young people who in turn may feel unsafe and decide to carry a weapon for self-protection. While negative images of young people were abundant and exaggerated, more positive portrayals of young people were rarely reported. Those working with young people can help create a positive discourse of young people. Figure 5.3 has a few ideas.

Figure 5.3 *Creating a positive discourse of young people*

Young people's participation

Youth participation refers to the active participation of young people in all aspects of decision making that affect their lives. The United Nations Convention of the Rights of the Child (1989) enshrines the rights of young people to participate. Article 12.1 states:

> Parties shall assure to the child who is capable of forming his or her own views the right to express those views freely in all matters affecting the child, the views of the child being given due weight in accordance with the age and maturity of the child.
>
> (OHCHR, 2023)

In practice, some examples of youth participation may include the following (Figure 5.4).

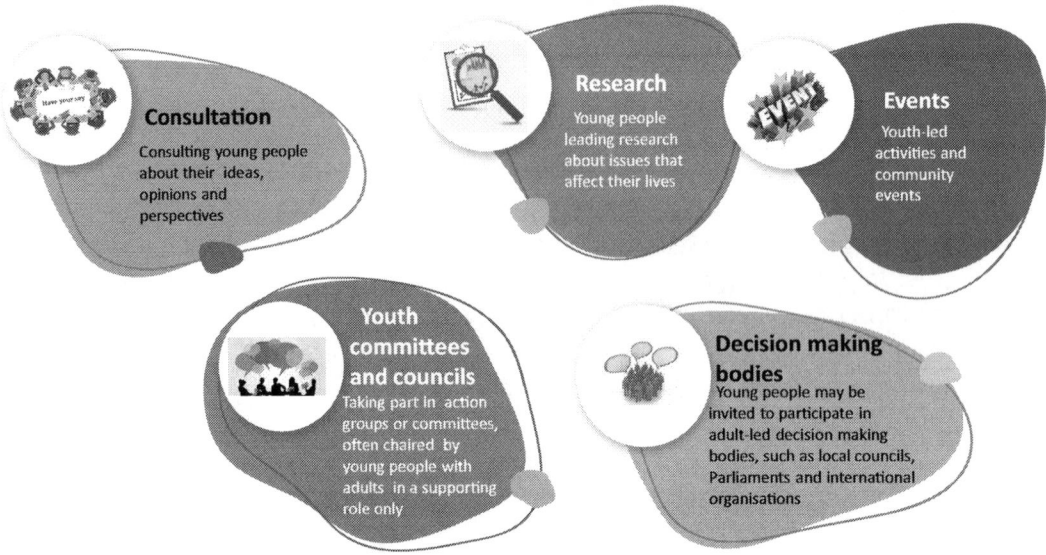

Consultation
Consulting young people about their ideas, opinions and perspectives

Research
Young people leading research about issues that affect their lives

Events
Youth-led activities and community events

Youth committees and councils
Taking part in action groups or committees, often chaired by young people with adults in a supporting role only

Decision making bodies
Young people may be invited to participate in adult-led decision making bodies, such as local councils, Parliaments and international organisations

Figure 5.4 *Examples of participation*

Hart (1992) recognises that not all activities that might be termed participation are equal. He conceptualises a ladder of participation where the first three rungs are not participation at all, but rather manipulation, using young people as decoration or being tokenistic. The upper rungs of the ladder provide progressively more opportunities for young people's meaningful and active involvement, culminating in the eighth rung which is youth-initiated decisions shared with adults.

In the next case study, Samuel Taylor, a musical theatre student at the Guildford School of Acting and a passionate advocate for young people's participation in public life, shares his experiences. This case study is presented as a reflective conversation.

CASE STUDY 👐

Alison   *So, it's lovely to chat with you, Samuel. Could you start by telling me a little about yourself?*

Samuel   *I grew up in the South Wales Valleys, in a very close family. I had a hard time at school because I was a bit different from the norm – high achieving and into the arts. I've had so many opportunities. My interests are youth engagement and politics on one hand. And then there is the arts. I'm training to be an actor now, which is very exciting!*

Alison	*Tell me a bit about the youth engagement you have been involved with.*
Samuel	*I did four and a little bit years as a member of the local youth parliament delegate and I also served a term as deputy youth mayor, a term as youth mayor. I was also the inaugural chair of the Young Wales Project Board at Children in Wales, which was a Welsh government initiative; a group of young people who were a mix of youth trustees and a consultation board of young people from across Wales and diverse backgrounds. Some were youth parliament representatives; others were young carers. There were people who had come from adverse childhood experience backgrounds and young people who were in working life. In Wales, the definition of a young person goes up to age 25. Between 19 and 25 is that funny in-between place, which often gets sort of forgotten about. You're expected to be an adult, but at the same time there's no transition from children and young people's services to adult services. It is all a bit arbitrary. I really realised that when we did a little bit of work on sort of children and young adults' mental health services.*
Alison	*Yes, that's an interesting point.*
Samuel	*I had an example recently. I ended up in hospital and I was put on a ward with people who were all at least 80. Obviously, I'm never going to be put on paediatrics, but at the same time, I don't always feel like enough of an adult to be there. It's those odd sorts of gaps, but in policy there is often this strange cut off – children and young people stop here and young adults start there, but realistically that's just a tick of the clock. Just a birthday, and people mature at different rates.*
Alison	*So tell me more about your role on the board.*
Samuel	*We were quite highly regarded by many decision makers. I regularly met with the education minister and the communities minister. We were consulted regarding young people's views on Brexit. We were taken seriously. It wasn't just a tick in the box. I mean, for those of us in representational roles, we saw it as a job.*
Alison	*That's interesting what you said about a tick in a box. Did you ever feel that you were experiencing tokenism?*
Samuel	*Sometimes we would meet people who really wanted to know what we thought, and they obviously cared. They would listen and then actually tailor what was happening going forward around what we had said. Other times, you would meet people who were like, 'Okay. We've seen what the kids think. We can tick the box off, and off we go, it doesn't matter'. The tokenism showed, and we could tell. But there were examples of people coming in with that approach and then walking out surprised by what we had to contribute.*
Alison	*So you were winning hearts and minds?*

→

Samuel	Yes. Some people have a very negative view of young people. The minority label sticks to the majority. You will always get a minority who are not motivated and not making a positive contribution and basically letting young people down, but that is not the majority. We need to prove that stereotype wrong.
Alison	What are some of the ways you have done that?
Samuel	I think I'm very, very fortunate that I was presented with so many opportunities. I took the attitude of never saying no. Like even now, next week, I'm involved in a production. There's no money in it, but I can put it on my sort of acting CV. Others might say 'You don't get paid and it's a week off the holidays. No, don't go'. But the opportunities that I have been given I am tremendously grateful for. I was being able to speak at the Commons more than once, and then also to go over to Geneva and speak at the UN. I'm also very acutely aware of the fact that they're opportunities that wouldn't exist for other people because they've been put in a box.
Alison	Put in a box?
Samuel	Yes, stereotyped and given a label. Once you get your label, it is hard to move beyond it. In Year 7, once you have your label, that's how people will see you. But people change. Stereotypes and categories can be damaging and follow you right through the system. So, I got those chances and opportunities because I was always seen as a 'good lad' and was very much into the arts as opposed to the sporting worlds of many of my peers. Others might find it harder to get their voices heard.
Alison	So I'm quite interested in how you have used your opportunities to advocate for others.
Samuel	So for me, it is all about listening and trying to understand others' perspectives. Not necessarily agree, but really understand where they are coming from. I think that informs everything. I think in a representational role, you cannot assume that you know what that person is going to say next. Don't assume. People have very understandably different opinions about anything. My job is to represent those views. If we disagree, let's explore why. And let's just accept that we probably will disagree, and it probably won't be a resolve conversation. But at the end of it we both have two perspectives. Instead of one. Being open-minded is a learned behaviour and it helps overcome a lot of entrenched positions, to build tolerance and understanding. Open dialogue. Let's talk about it.
Alison	That's interesting. You represented an area with a lot of social needs, didn't you?
Samuel	Yes. If you look at the statistics, there is a lot of bad news. But recently I brought a London friend to stay, and she was amazed how far it is from the deprivation stereotype. I mean, the landscape is incredible. Deprivation doesn't define you.

It will impact you, but it isn't your destiny. If people looked at people as people not as numbers, not as sort of dots or statistics, that's where your strength approach comes from. Because then you see the person and ask, what does this person need? What can I do for this person? Not think, 'this person needs this'.

Alison   Who has helped you along the way?

Samuel   It's so important to have people who believe in you. For me that's my family and some of the great people I've met along the way, youth engagement workers, politicians. I think with young people, the best thing you can give them is a safe space and support.

Alison   How has your performance career also helped you in the representational work?

Samuel   You learn so much about yourself and how you process, and it gives you the space to breathe and then be able to stand up and go. It also teaches you hard work and dedication. So much of working for change is just chipping away at the block and taking the small wins.

Alison   So, what's next for you, Samuel?

Samuel   At the minute I wake up every morning and I'm living the life that I've dreamed of living since I was six years old! But long term, yes performance, teaching, then maybe return to the politics and I have a romanticised notion of coming back to my hometown and screaming about the arts from the rooftop.

Alison   Any advice for other young people and for professionals working with young people?

Samuel   It's more important to listen than to talk, especially if you're the adult. If you are a young person who is sure of themselves, you're going to be OK. And most importantly if someone gives you an opportunity, never say no. Never.

Alison   What a great place to end. Thank you, Samuel.

Reflective questions ⑦

»   Why is it important for young people to have a say in decisions that affect their life? Can you think of examples where you have involved young people in decision making?

»   Samuel highlights how young people can be subject to negative stereotypes and how some young people may be labelled and then denied opportunities

→

because of that label. Do you agree? Can you think of examples from your own practice?

» Samuel explains how sometimes young people's views can be sought *tokenistically*. Do you agree? How can you guard against this in your own practice?

» For Samuel, active listening is at the heart of true participation and representation. How do you prioritise active listening? Writer Stephen Covey suggests, '*Most people do not listen with the intent to understand; they listen with the intent to reply*'. Do you agree? How can we guard against this?

Asset-based approaches to working with young people

The term '*asset-based approach*' to youth work refers to ways of working with young people in a way that not only addresses the issues they face but also concentrates on identifying and building on their strengths. Strength can be found in many places; it could involve their talents and abilities, relationships, interests or personality traits. Moreover, strengths can be found in their families, friendship groups, organisations that support them and the wider community. As Thornton (2019) points out, the individual person is at the heart of asset-based working and the support is tailored to help them identify and achieve their own goals. To systematise an assets-based approach to supporting young people, the Search Institute (see Further resources) identified 40 positive strengths that young people need to be successful. Half of these assets are internal and focus on social and emotional strengths, values and commitments. The other half are external and focus on relationships and opportunities in their families, schools and wider communities.

It is important to recognise that part of an asset-based approach will involve identifying risks and then amassing assets to address and potentially mitigate these risks. So, for example, it is natural for teenagers to seek new experiences as these light up the thrill-seeking areas of the brain and give pleasure. An asset approach would look to provide such opportunities for thrill seeking but within a safe environment. Other areas of risk may involve social media, peer groups and substances.

Supporting healthy habits for life

Many of the risks associated with young people relate to their health and well-being. Building on the neuroscience explored earlier, this can be a great time for embedding healthy lifestyles and in doing so setting young people up for healthy and successful lives. However, the Prince's Trust NatWest Youth Index (2023) found that the overall well-being of 16–25 year-olds reached its lowest point in its 14 year history. Young people in the survey reported very high levels of anxiety, including worries about financial security and the future. In such a context, supporting confidence and health education can play an important role. However, there is national evidence to suggest that young people do not receive appropriate health information, support or advice. Youth work practitioners may be ideally placed to raise awareness and deliver health-related information and resources to young people. The Council for Wales Voluntary Youth Services presented a series of recommendations for practitioners engaging in this work (CWVYS, 2012; see Figure 5.5).

Figure 5.5 *Working with young people around health issues (adapted from CWVYS, 2012)*

In the following case study, Julia, an experienced youth worker and now a university lecturer in youth and community work at Cardiff Metropolitan University, shares her insights on strength-based working.

CASE STUDY ☺

The context of youth and community work

Youth work's roots can be traced back to the latter half of the nineteenth century, with the provision of 'Ragged Schools'. A space for some of the poorest children and young people to gain an education in an informal, relaxed and safe environment (Doyle and Smith, 1999). Early youth workers described their work as emancipatory, challenging systems of

→

oppression *(Bright, 2015) and despite countless societal and political changes over the last 170 years, youth and community work practitioners continue to offer an approach that values voluntary engagement, is responsive to young people's needs and cares for their welfare. The service works with young people between the ages of 11 and 25 and, while policies and funding vary across the United Kingdom, the profession is underpinned by a set of National Occupational Standards (NOS) (CLD, 2019), which identify the key functions, minimum practice expectations and values-based approach that is not only core to effective practice, but differentiates the profession from other forms of work with young people.*

The deficit arena

A deficit perception of young people is nothing new. 'Politicians and policy makers in Britain and Northern Ireland currently tend to talk about young people in three linked ways – as thugs, users and victims' *(Jeffs and Smith, 1999, p 8). Policies are developed and funding, often short term, provided to 'solve' these issues. As a result, much of my youth work career has been spent in target-based programmes, practising with and managing youth workers in schools, working with young people identified as at risk of becoming 'NEET' (Not in Education, Employment or Training). Within Youth Justice Services, I worked with young people transitioning out of custody (Young Offenders' Institutes) or identified as 'high risk' of entering it.*

In both settings, young people are generally perceived as the problem and subsequent referrals focus on behaviour. I have been asked to work with young people who are described as being 'disruptive', 'disrespectful', *who* 'cannot abide by rules', 'refuse to learn', *are a* 'threat to the public', 'fight', 'drink', 'do' *and* 'sell drugs' *and* 'cannot conform' *to society's rules.*

Youth work itself is a strength-based approach

Despite working in targeted environments which you could argue 'pathologise' young people, I have always aimed to work 'holistically' (CLD, 2019). What this means in practice terms is using an iceberg approach (Schopler, 1991) – if the focus of the referral for a young person is 'challenging behaviour' (what can be seen), my engagement is rooted in attempting to understand their needs and strengths (what is going on underneath). This is achieved through developing a voluntary relationship with the young people, despite the statutory environments in which I often practised. It is made explicit from the outset that working with me is the young person's choice, and while there are professional boundaries to the relationship, what we work on together is led entirely by them as 'Youth Work starts at whatever point young people are in their lives and recognises their potential' *(CWVYS, 2022, p 4). This approach purposefully aims to tip the power balance in young people's favour, enabling them to experience a sense of control.*

When working within schools, I strove to offer consistent one to one and small group support, where, through arts and crafts, physical activity or simply a place to come, engage in dialogue and often just 'be', young people developed social skills, emotional intelligence and experienced feeling heard. De St Croix (2016, p 4) summarises this approach beautifully, explaining that 'youth workers work with young people to create and claim spaces for conversation, fun, challenge, relationships and collective learning'. While in the short term this often enabled them to manage school routines more positively, it also acted as a microcosm for wider society. Being able to navigate these systems means they can begin to challenge structures they feel are unfair, in alignment with the Freirean concept of praxis (1970).

Utilising Rogers' (1957) core conditions was vital in my youth justice role. I empathised with young people, who often told me they felt judged – not only via the court system, but within their own communities. For those leaving custody every element of their lives had been rigidly controlled, so the transition back into society could seem daunting. While I recognised these young people had criminalised histories, I endeavoured to see past the behaviour which was only part of their story and focus on building relationships, based on congruence (kindness, compassion) and unconditional positive regard. I visited one young person on a community order 14 times before they acknowledged me. Eventually they told me they felt they could trust me as I was 'stubborn and hadn't given up'. Resilience, patience and adaptability are three of the many skills effective practitioners require, along with an innate belief that young people have all they need within them (Belton, 2010, pp 29–40).

I believe a youth worker's role is to support young people to become conscious of their power through the creation of a safe space and building bridges (Williamson, 2015). One of the ways this can be achieved is using models of experiential learning, as explored in Smith's Creators not Consumers (1980). Creating opportunities for young people to 'do for themselves' has always been pivotal to my practice. While more time-consuming and therefore often at odds with targets linked to funding, providing young people with space and time to consider what is important to them and who they want to be, and to plan for themselves, plants the seeds for growth in self-belief and confidence. It has been a privilege to work with young people who have learnt how to tell the time, open and manage a bank account, cook for themselves, choose to leave unhealthy relationships and even produce a video campaigning for national youth club provision – the focus must always be about the journey, not the destination.

Pestalozzi's Head, Heart, and Hands theory (cited in Heafford, 1967, p 47) provides a holistic framework for my practice and lends itself to a strength-based approach. I use the knowledge in my 'head', which includes the theories explored in this case study, awareness of specialist agencies that can support when requested or required and awareness of my 'self' in the relationship. My role is not to be a gatekeeper or provider of knowledge but to create an environment where young people can think thoughtfully and critically for themselves (Eichstellar and Holthoff, 2011, p 41). I utilise my hands to actively support young people – this could be through activities, workshops and games that are my youth work 'toolbox'. My heart: the love, passion, enthusiasm, and commitment to the profession that I truly believe in and the trust, faith, and confidence I have in young people themselves.

Reflective questions ⓘ

» According to the case study, what are the key features of youth and community work practice?

» Identify and explore the strength-based approaches utilised by the youth and community work practitioner in this case study.

» What do you think may be the challenges of using strength-based approaches in multi-agency services, which have fixed targets, agendas and cultures?

» Consider societal perceptions of young people and how these influence how agencies work with or for them.

» Think about the current societal issues highlighted in this case study (crime, surveillance, education). Do you think young people caused them or inherited them?

Chapter summary ⓘ

In this chapter, strength-based approaches have been explored in relation to working with young people. We have recognised that the period of 11–25 is an important phase in the life-course, but also a time when young people are developing and changing rapidly. Hence, a one-size-fits-all approach is not going to be effective, and practitioners need to respect a growing autonomy of young people and tailor their responses to the individual. While this period is awash with opportunities, it is a time fraught with risk for many young people, particularly in relation to identity, mental health and well-being. Having practitioners who can understand, value and support individuals in a strength-based way can help young people to navigate the challenges they may face. Samuel's case study explored the importance of young people having a voice in all matters that affect their lives. Julia helped us to consider the great potential of strength-based youth work to make a positive difference in people's lives.

Further reading ✎

- The Search Institute has developed a framework for thinking about and supporting young people's assets, both internal and external. There are also many resources for using the framework with young people. These resources can be found online at: www.search-institute.org/our-research/development-assets/developmental-assets-framework (accessed 4 August 2023).

- Blakemore, S-J (2012) *The Mysterious Workings of the Adolescent Brain*. TED talks. [online] Available at: www.ted.com/talks/sarah_jayne_blakemore_the_mysterious_workings_of_the_adolescent_brain (accessed 4 August 2023).

  In this TED talk, neuroscientist Sarah-Jayne Blakemore compares the prefrontal cortex in adolescents to that of adults, to show us how typically '*teenage*' behaviour is caused by the growing and developing brain.

• The Young Adult Development Project is a very comprehensive resource, helping us to understand the changes that happen in adolescence and early adulthood. It can be found online at https://hr.mit.edu/static/worklife/youngadult/ (accessed 4 August 2023).

References

Belton, B (2010) *Radical Youth Work*. Dorset: Russell House Publishing.

Blakemore, S-J (2012) The Mysterious Workings of the Adolescent Brain. TED talks. [online] Available at: www.ted.com/talks/sarah_jayne_blakemore_the_mysterious_workings_of_the_adolescent_brain (accessed 19 June 2023).

Bright, G (2015) *Youth Work: Histories, Policies and Contexts*. London: Red Globe Books, Bloomsbury.

Bynner, J (2005) Rethinking the Youth Phase of the Life-course: The Case for Emerging Adulthood? *Journal of Youth Studies*, 8(4): 367–84.

Council for Wales Voluntary Youth Services (CWVYS) (2012) Health and Well Being in Youth Work Method and Resource Handbook. [online] Available at: www.cwvys.org.uk/wp-content/uploads/2014/06/HB-Health-and-Wellbeing.pdf (accessed 19 June 2023).

Council for Wales Voluntary Youth Services (2022) *Youth Work in Wales: Principles and Purposes*. Wales: Youth Work in Wales Review Group. [online] Available at: https://www.cwvys.org.uk/youth-work-in-wales-principles-and-purposes-2/ (accessed 19 June 2023).

CLD Standards Council Scotland (2019) National Occupational Standards in Youth Work. [online] Available at: https://cldstandardscouncil.org.uk/resources/standards-and-benchmarks/national-occupational-standards/youth-work-nos/ (accessed 19 June 2023).

Council of Europe (nd) Youth Work Essentials. [online] Available at: www.coe.int/en/web/youth-portfolio/youth-work-essentials (accessed 19 June 2023).

De St Croix, T (2016) *Grassroots Youth Work*. Bristol: Policy Press.

Doyle, M and Smith, M (1999) What is Youth Work? Exploring the History, Theory, and Practice of Work with Young People. [online] Available at: https://infed.org/mobi/what-is-youth-work-exploring-the-history-theory-and-practice-of-work-with-young-people/ (accessed 19 June 2023).

Eichstellar, G and Holthoff, S (2011) Conceptual Foundations of Social Pedagogy: A Transnational Perspective from Germany. In Cameron, C and Moss, P (eds) *Social Pedagogy and Working with Children and Young People Where Care and Education Meet* (pp 33–52). London: Jessica Kingsley Publishers.

Freire, P (1970) *Pedagogy of the Oppressed*. London: Penguin Books.

Fuhrmann, D, Knoll, L J and Blakemore, S J (2015) Adolescence as a Sensitive Period of Brain Development. *Trends in Cognitive Science*, 19(10): 558–66.

Giedd, J N (2004) Structural Magnetic Resonance Imaging of the Adolescent Brain. *New York Academy of Sciences*, 1021: 77–85.

Hart, R A (1992) *Children's Participation: From Tokenism to Citizenship*. Florence, Italy: United Nations Children's Fund International Child Development Centre.

Heafford, M (1967) *Pestalozzi*. Bungay: The Chaucer Press.

Hertsmere Young Researchers (2011) Unbalanced Negative Media Portrayal of Youth. [online] Available at: www.hertsmere.gov.uk/Documents/08-Parks–Leisure/Children–Young-People/Final-Report—Unbalanced-negative-media-portrayal-of-youth.pdf (accessed 19 June 2023).

Jeffs, T and Smith, M (1999) The Problem of 'youth' for Youth Work. *Youth and Policy*, 62: 45–66.

National Youth Agency (2023) What is Youth Work? [online] Available at: www.nya.org.uk/career-in-youth-work/what-is-youth-work (accessed 19 June 2023).

Office of the High Commissioner for Human Rights (OHCHR) (2023) Convention on the Rights of the Child. [online] Available at: www.ohchr.org/en/instruments-mechanisms/instruments/convention-rights-child (accessed 19 June 2023).

Prince's Trust (2023) The Prince's Trust NatWest Youth Index 2023. [online] Available at: www.princes-trust.org.uk/about-us/research-policies-reports/research (accessed 19 June 2023).

Rogers, C (1957) The Necessary and Sufficient Conditions of Therapeutic Personality Change. *Journal of Consulting Psychology*, 21(2): 95–103.

Schopler, E (1991) Behavioural and Research Influences on Educational and Clinical Programs. In Giddan, N and Giddan, J (eds) *Autistic Adults at Bittersweet Farms* (pp 140–50). New York: Routledge.

Simpson, A R (2018) The Young Adult Development Project. [online] Available at: https://hr.mit.edu/static/worklife/youngadult/index.html (accessed 19 June 2023).

Smith, M (1980) Creators Not Consumers. [online] Available at: https://infed.org/mobi/mark-smith-creators-not-consumers-rediscovering-social-education/ (accessed 19 June 2023).

Thornton, A (2019) *Asset-based Work with Young People: Findings from the Youth Fund Evaluation*. Renaisi. [online] Available at: https://renaisi.com/2020/01/29/findings-from-the-evaluation-of-paul-hamlyn-foundations- youth-fund/ (accessed 24 July 2023).

Williamson (2015), Final Declaration of the 2nd European Youth Work Convention: Making a World of Difference. [online] Available at: https://pjp-eu.coe.int/documents/42128013/47262187/The+2nd+European+Youth+Work+Declaration_FINAL.pdf/cc602b1d-6efc-46d9-80ec-5ca57c35eb85 (accessed 19 June 2023).

World Health Organization (nd) Adolescent Health. [online] Available at: www.who.int/health-topics/adolescent-health#tab=tab (accessed 19 June 2023).

YMCA (2022) Devalued: A Decade of Cuts to Youth Services: A Report Examining Local Authority Expenditure on Youth Services and England and Wales. [online] Available at: www.ymca.org.uk/wp-content/uploads/2022/02/ymca-devalued-2022.pdf (accessed 19 June 2023).

6 Strength-based practice for children and young people with SEND

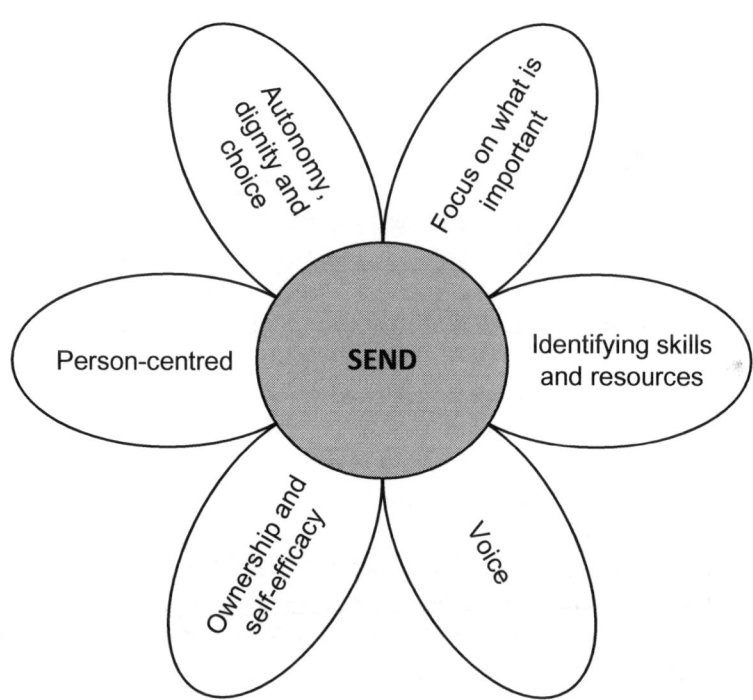

Chapter objectives ◎

This chapter:

- analyses the importance of a positive and open-minded attitude to special educational needs and disability (SEND);

- stresses the need for individualised, child-centred planning;

- celebrates neurodiversity and multiple intelligences;

- applies a strength-based approach to working with children with complex health needs.

Introduction

This chapter begins with discussion on parents of children with SEND and the importance of a positive experience of identification and open-minded learning about a child's needs. Observation is important in identifying the individual child's needs, strengths and individuality and supports the construction of plans in partnership with the child and family. This chapter discusses support and the importance of a child-centred approach which focuses on the child's capabilities, rather than assumptions. Writing strength-based statements is discussed, as is the balance between care and independence. Multiple intelligences are outlined, along with a celebration of neurodiversity strengths, resulting in the empowerment of children and young people with SEND. Two case studies illustrate aspects of strength-based practice. The first is an account by Liv, whose daughter has some specific needs; Liv is a great example of positivity and hope for her child. The second case study is by Gilda, whose positive attitude is invaluable in her role with children who have complex disabilities and health needs.

A positive attitude

The story of Emily Perl Kingsley's personal experience (MCC, 2021) is a difficult one to read. She gave birth to a son with Down syndrome in the 1970s and was advised to send the baby to an institution and to tell her friends and family that he had died in childbirth, a common recommendation at the time but one that Kingsley thankfully dismissed immediately. Emily Kingsley (1987) wrote a wonderful poem called '*Welcome to Holland*' about her experiences, which has been a comfort to many parents of children with disabilities. In the poem she talks about planning a trip to Italy and looking forward to all of the wonderful things that Italy has to offer. This is a metaphor for the excitement of preparing for a new baby. In the poem, the plane lands in Holland instead. Instead of having what you had looked forward to, you then have to cope with having to buy new guidebooks, learn a new language and come to terms with being in Holland. The poem ends '*if you spend your life mourning the fact that you didn't get to Italy, you may never be free to enjoy the very special, the very lovely things about Holland*'. The message that as a parent of a child with SEND your life will be different but not '*less than*' is one that has changed many people's views.

The term '*positive mental attitude*' first appeared in a book by Napoleon Hill in 1937. The book was one of the first self-help books to be written and it was called *Think and Grow Rich*, the premise being that anyone can be anything they want to be, as long as they have a positive attitude. This particular book is focused on success in business and making money, but the idea that a positive attitude attracts positive changes is one that is used in self-help books and by therapists today. In 1995, a horse jumping accident changed the life of Christopher Reeve forever. He went from a fit and healthy, well-loved actor famously portraying Superman on screen, to someone paralysed from the neck down needing assistance to breathe. His positive attitude meant that he remained hopeful, and he worked to raise awareness and improve the lives of people living with disability until his death in 2004. Reeve's philosophy was based on his strength and determination to make a difference.

> *A Hero is an ordinary individual who finds the strength to persevere and endure in spite of overwhelming obstacles. Once you choose hope, anything's possible.*
>
> (Reeve, 1999)

Hope is of the utmost importance; in a '*hope-inspiring relationship*' (Prowle and Hodgkins, 2020, p 139), practitioners will build relationships with children and families which are based on seeing the positives and having high expectations about possibilities.

Reflective questions ⑦

Look at the descriptions of child A and child B below in Figure 6.1. Child A has been written in a strength-based way, and child B in a negative way, viewing the child's characteristics as problems.

» Answer honestly, how might you feel if you were told that child B would be coming to your nursery/school/play setting? How might others feel?

» Reframing labels is important in strength-based practice. With older children, we can help them to reframe their own views of themselves, to enhance self-esteem. Can you write strength-based descriptions to replace the following '*labels*' that children may have about themselves?

- – Hyperactive
- – Bossy
- – Anti-social
- – Difficult
- – Oversensitive
- – Stubborn
- – Clingy
- – Demanding

Child A and child B both describe the same child, but the descriptions come from very different points of view.

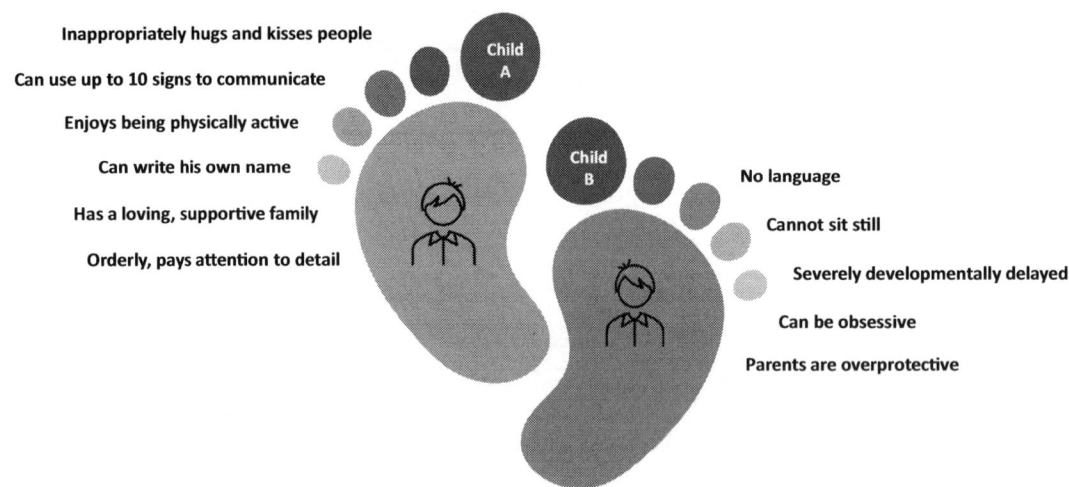

Figure 6.1 *Child A and child B*

Labelling

The reflective activity above looks at negative labels. Labelling is a contentious issue in the realm of SEND, with strong views for and against providing labels for children with a specific need. On the one hand, a label can be useful in accessing support and funding for the child. A label can be useful to professionals working with the child in helping to devise individual education programmes (IEP or EHCP). It is important to consider potential downsides: the possibility of professionals having lower expectations of children and conceivable issues with peer friendships and bullying. However, a study carried out in 2020 (Gibbs et al) set out to investigate how labels of ADHD and dyslexia impacted on teachers' perceptions of, and teaching of, children in their classes. The results showed that a label did impact on teachers' assessment of what children's needs were likely to be, but labels did not affect teachers' perceptions of self-efficacy. The positive results of the study show that teachers generally believed in children's ability to succeed.

CASE STUDY 🔄

What do you think?

A local support group for the families of children who are on the autistic spectrum has been doing some important work in supporting parents and siblings. Being able to share experiences, concerns and advice with others who understand is a great help to families. However, one of the group's new initiatives has caused upset and debate. The group have had T-shirts printed for their children. The idea came from the fact that when a child with autism exhibits challenging behaviour (sometimes referred to as a '*meltdown*') in a public place, eg in the middle of a supermarket, members of the public can be very judgemental of a perceived lack of good parenting. The parents wanted the public to know the reason behind the behaviour in the hope that they would be more understanding.

Figure 6.2 *Labelling*

Some people, however, felt that '*labelling*' the child was wrong, and they did not like the idea of a child being known by their disability label.

Reflective questions ⑦

» What is your initial feeling about this?

» Try to explain the opposing views.

» How does this correspond to a strength-based approach?

The labelling of a child with SEN is very much a part of the medical model of disability, special needs and disabilities being seen as problems to be dealt with. Historically, professional clarification of disability resulted in a published '*statutory classification of handicap*' (O'Shaughnessy, 2008) with appallingly negative labels, such as '*idiot*', '*imbecile*', '*feeble-minded*' and '*mentally defective*' (Cole, 1989). Thankfully, labels today are more positive, and they define the need rather than the child. For example, '*an autistic child*' is now more likely to be referred to '*a child who has autistic spectrum disorder*'. The child should come first, followed by the need, so that the child is no longer defined by the need. It is important to add, however, that the child themselves should be the person deciding on a label (or not).

Nevertheless, some diagnoses today still have very negative language; consider ADHD for example, which stands for attention deficit and hyperactivity disorder. Two of the words in the title are '*deficit*' and '*disorder*', very negative words. Plows (2014) suggests that these labels are very damaging to children and proposes that we ask children how they would like to be treated. Plows (2014) advocates encouraging children to identify their own learning needs, in partnership with parents and professionals.

CASE STUDY ☞

Liv and Alex

When our daughter Lola* was born, as with many parents, we were overjoyed but overwhelmed. After our initial panic about being good enough parents (for us it was a concern about her feeding and being jaundiced when she was a couple of months old) we had started to be able to take a more laid back and calm approach to parenting. I think that after the initial panic we were able to think more clearly and avoid overthinking and excessive and unnecessary stress.

When Lola was a month old and a 'strawberry birthmark' started to appear we monitored it, discussed it with the health visitor and went to see the GP. The GP informed us that haemangiomas are common and are likely to 'go on their own as Lola gets older'. We did however go back as Lola's birthmark was getting bigger and it appeared to be swollen (it became quite significant and dramatic to look at). We went back to the GP and had a different on call doctor from all the other times and she referred us to the hospital. She said we needed to go straight away. We got to the hospital within 30 minutes and then found out that Lola had bronchiolitis, but they were also concerned about the haemangioma. They carried out various examinations and ordered an MRI scan. They explained to us that Lola had a type of birthmark which was also internal and that where the birthmark had swollen behind her ear, it had also extended internally and was pressing onto her windpipe, obstructing her airway. Lola could breathe but the doctor was concerned that without treatment she may not have been able to.

At one point when the lead consultant was off for the weekend, another had explained that the initial scan had picked up an abnormality on the brain. When I asked if this could be an internal birthmark (and due to how big the one was behind her ear – the size of a golf ball), I asked could she die, to which he couldn't answer me and said they were waiting to hear from a specialist in America. My husband and I were left in bits that evening, but the nurses were wonderful and comforted us with a listening ear and words of reassurance. Due to the numerous assessments, we found out that Lola also has an abnormal optic nerve in her right eye, an abnormality on her brain, a small VSD (ventricular septal defect [hole on her heart]) and partial PHACE (posterior fossa anomalies, hemangioma, arterial anomalies, cardiac anomalies and eye anomalies).

Lola had treatment (propranolol, an amazing treatment which had only been used in this way to treat haemangiomas for a few years) to reduce her birthmarks externally and internally. She was referred to cardiology, to ophthalmology, to ENT (ear, nose and throat), for a further MRI (magnetic resonance imaging), for physiotherapy and for an ultrasound of her right eye.

Lack of sleep and trauma of thinking that we may lose our daughter affected us both in different ways. We took turns to be 'the strong one' and the one 'falling apart'. When falling apart we were filled with 'what if's' and would look at this little baby and want to make things perfect for her. Visually she looked like she was in pain, but we were lucky she was not. Her birthmark was swollen, very dark red/purple and covered a large portion of her face. At first, we were told there was an abnormality in her brain, but we did not know what this was; we were told that the hole in the heart was small and was likely to heal by itself. We were told she was likely to have little to no vision in her right eye.

When we were strong, we would tell each other she is not in pain. The birthmark is to do with her blood vessels being close to the skin's surface. We would remind ourselves – she is breathing, and if she has any difficulties, we are in the right place for it to be resolved. In relation to the rest – her eye and brain – we told ourselves she will not know any different, she will just know that she is Lola and loved. We believed we needed to focus on how lucky we are to have Lola here with us and remember how much joy she brings us.

The doctors, however, would remind us that she has got these diagnoses and they may impact her in various ways. At the beginning I saw this as negative and unhelpful, however I now see this as making us aware so we could fully support Lola to access the support as, when and if she needed it. We had and have had lots of specialist support for Lola via the NHS, and we approach each referral as a gift. A gift to gain understanding of our wonderful daughter and a way of reassuring us as her parents. Each referral highlights her strengths and areas which could be supported (and therefore leads to helpful resources) and makes us feel cared for and valued. This keeps us grounded and personally I can say it gives me access to a greater capacity to parent – whatever it means 'to parent'.

One thing that Alex and I have grappled with is the use of labels and sharing information about Lola's diagnoses. On the one hand, we do not want there to be any negative impacts in relation to the expectations of others and some sort of self-fulfilling prophecy. We would not want others to limit Lola by judging her potential through her medical notes, rather than empowering her based on what capabilities she presents. However, on the other hand we do not want to do her a disservice as her parents by ignoring a need and preventing the people in her life from being able to support her to the best of their ability.

We continue to address this dilemma, and it really is all to do with the trust and relationships we have with the professionals in Lola's life. The nursery that Lola attends now know about her diagnoses, but first got to know her and us. Their expectations were based on Lola as an individual not a label/condition. Empathy received from the nursery practitioners and shared understanding between us has led recently to Lola's key worker to suggest that she

→

is referred to speech and language therapy. We appreciate that as Lola's parents we have one perspective and viewpoint, but by gaining other people's perspectives who spend time with Lola, we are more likely to get a clear understanding of what she needs. That makes us feel so much more confident and stronger as Lola's parents. Lola amazes us every day in so many ways; she has her own wonderful personality and most importantly is happy and enjoying life. Who knows what her future has in store but based on what she is showing us, she will take every challenge life presents her with a smile on her face. Lola is meeting milestones and excelling beyond everyone's expectations.

* Lola is a pseudonym and has been chosen by the child, as it is her favourite unicorn name.

Reflective questions ⑦

» Liv and Alex took turns in being '*the strong one*' and '*the one falling apart*'; reflect on the importance of this relationship dynamic. What advice might you give a single parent in a similar position?

» Liv and Alex say that they approach each referral as '*a gift*' – how could we as professionals encourage more parents to approach interventions with this positive attitude?

» What are the benefits of getting to know a child and family before being informed of a medical diagnosis?

» How is Liv and Alex's positive attitude likely to impact Lola?

Inclusion

Inclusion is the state of being included or being made a part of something, but the way that works in practice means different things to different people. In education, the Warnock Report (1978) and the Salamanca Statement (UNESCO, 1994) have driven the inclusion movement in schools so that the learning needs of all children should now all be supported (Crossley and Hewitt, 2021). There has been some controversy lately as a lack of government funding for education has impacted on the support children receive. In a recent survey by the National Education Union, 81 per cent of schools reported not having sufficient staff to provide strategies and support for children with SEND, and 73 per cent said that there had been '*a drop in the number of teaching assistants, as a direct consequence of funding pressures*' (NEU, 2023). A lack of support staff has a devastating effect on these children.

However, a recent green paper shows that there is to be an overhaul of the system in schools which should enable schools to meet children's needs more effectively and consistently, the current system being somewhat of a postcode lottery (Zadawi, 2022). The green paper will announce several changes: earlier intervention, more accountability, new national standards of support in education, health and care, more choice for parents and the publishing of inclusion plans for the sake of transparency.

Segregation, integration or inclusion?

In 1918, local education authorities were required to set up 'special schools' for children with special educational needs and disabilities, and these became even more prevalent after the 1944 Education Act. This segregation of children with SEND was designed to help produce the best possible specialised care and support for children with SEND, with small classes, high levels of staff, specialist equipment and specialist staff. The Warnock Report (1978), the subsequent Education Act (1981) and the later Special Educational Needs and Disability Act 2001 advocated a duty to integrate as many children as possible into mainstream schools. The principle behind this was that the purpose of education was the same for all and so all children must have the same opportunities (Lindsay, Wedell and Dockrell, 2020, p 2). At first, provision was mostly about integration, with inclusion units attached to mainstream schools and a variable amount of integration and inclusion. Some schools allowed children to be together for parts of the curriculum and separated them for other aspects of the day.

Since the Disability Discrimination Act of 2004, there has been an increase in children and young people with a range of difficulties being fully included in mainstream settings. This is a wonderful opportunity for children and adults alike to increase their understanding of diversity and to practise inclusivity and positivity. True inclusion means that everyone is included, regardless of their individual needs, and it is the responsibility of the organisation to make reasonable adjustments so that everyone can be included. Figure 6.3 depicts exclusion, segregation, integration and inclusion.

Segregation

Separate programmes are created to separate individuals from the group

Integration

Individuals are welcomed but not given opportunities to fully participate with everyone else

Inclusion

All individuals are meaningfully supported and valued

Figure 6.3 *Exclusion, segregation, integration and inclusion*

UNESCO (2005) produced a list of guidelines for inclusion, as follows:

- inclusion is a process;
- inclusion is concerned with the identification and removal of barriers;
- inclusion is about the presence, participation and achievement of all students;
- inclusion involves a particular emphasis of those groups of learners who may be at risk of marginalisation, exclusion or underachievement.

Inclusion in education and care settings has its challenges. Staff need comprehensive knowledge and skills to be able to manage a wide range of special needs, so training and development is necessary. There are also challenges with having a large group of children to manage, if there is a wide range of abilities. Providing individualised support to a classful of children is very demanding, as this quote from a teacher demonstrates:

> We have lots of barriers to include children with special needs in the classrooms. Teachers are not trained; it is very important to give them training first on various types of disabilities ... only then is inclusion possible.
>
> (Bansall, 2020, p 192)

However, the benefits of inclusion are very significant too. In an inclusive setting, there will be a focus on meeting the individual needs of each child, and that will benefit all children in the group. Children in such groups will learn at an early age about the fact that difference is a part of life and that everyone has their own character, strengths and needs. This helps to build friendships among the children and also relationships between parents, families and the community. Another benefit is the high expectations of children; those with additional needs are inspired and motivated to learn.

Another approach, one that is very much strength-based and which goes even further than inclusion, is 'inclusive pedagogy', which Sewell (2020, p 53) discusses here:

> This stance argues that specific, specialised educational strategies and intervention for SEND are not required. The approach takes the stance that all needs can be met via good quality, general classroom teaching.

With an inclusive pedagogy approach, there is no view that the teacher has a class of children who all learn in the same way and one or two children with special needs who need something different. The approach sees learning as something that everyone is capable of and that treating a child with a 'special need' differently to the majority with specialist resources or support just for them damages self-esteem and can become a self-fulfilling prophecy, leading the child to believe that they are 'less than'.

Reflective questions ⑦

There are many inclusion audit tools available online. Four examples are given here, but you may find another online that better suits your organisation. Have a go at the audit for your workplace and identify the strengths and the areas to work on in your setting.

> »   Inclusion audit tool for schools www.supportservicesforeducation.co.uk/Page/18898
>
> »   Inclusion audit tool for early years settings www.barnsley.gov.uk/media/21205/ey-sen-support-inclusion-toolkit.pdf
>
> »   Inclusion audit tool for health and care www.inclusion-health.org/inclusion-audit/
>
> »   Inclusion audit tool for youth work https://network.youthmusic.org.uk/how-do-i-know-how-i%E2%80%99m-doing-equality-diversity-and-inclusion-tool

Individualised, child-centred planning

Early intervention

The Early Intervention Foundation's (2017) definition is:

> *Early intervention is about taking action as soon as possible to tackle problems for children and families before they become more difficult to reverse ... about working with children and families to help them. It is a collaborative approach to providing effective support.*

The early years in particular (pre-birth to starting school) is a critical time of development; by the age of three, a child's brain is 80 per cent formed (Allen, 2011). Therefore, early identification of additional needs and development of skills and competencies is essential at this early stage. Early assessment is important in identifying children's strengths as well as their additional needs (Mengoni and Oates, 2014), in order to intervene is a positive way. Continuous observation and monitoring is important in order to understand the individual child and identify any support needs. The importance of involving parents and families at every stage cannot be underestimated, as they know the child best and are able to advocate for the child's voice.

Observation, assessment and planning

Observation and assessment feed into the devising of statements, which are necessary as aims to work towards. Strength-based statements should include:

*   what a child can already do;
*   what a child can do when provided with educational support;
*   what a child will one day be able to do.

At the forefront of the strength-based approach is the underlying principle of enabling the child, accepting that there is a need for additional support but seeing this as a need for the setting, rather than the child. In the Australian government's guidance on assessing children with SEND is the phrase, '*the problem is the problem – the child is not the problem*' (DEECD, 2012, p 6). If we return to the child A and child B exercise earlier, we can see that the deficit stance is that child B has no language, so the child has a problem. On the other hand, in a strength-based approach, the statement for child A reads '*can use up to 10 signs*' (Figure 6.1). Therefore, if adults working with the child are not able to communicate with them, this is a problem with the communication provision within the setting, not a problem with the child. This is the same principle as the medical and social models of disability. The medical model is one based on the disabled person being/having the problem, whereas the social model sees any problems as being with a society that is unable to meet the person's needs (Pickard, 2021).

Although it is important to identify children's needs in order to access support, it is equally important to identify their strengths, creating a holistic view of the child. Focusing on the strengths that the child has is important, but it is also important to look at strengths within the family, within the setting and in the local community.

Reflective questions ⑦

According to Payne (2022), professionals are often asked to describe a child's '*worst day*' to identify services and support needed to support the child within a setting. However, this is a very negative '*deficit*' approach. The following activity is designed to identify a child's interests and strengths to understand what the child needs in order to make it a positive experience for them.

Think about a child that you know well.

»   First, imagine what would make it '*the best day ever*' for that child (Figure 6.4).

»   Reflect on what this would tell you about planning for the child's needs.

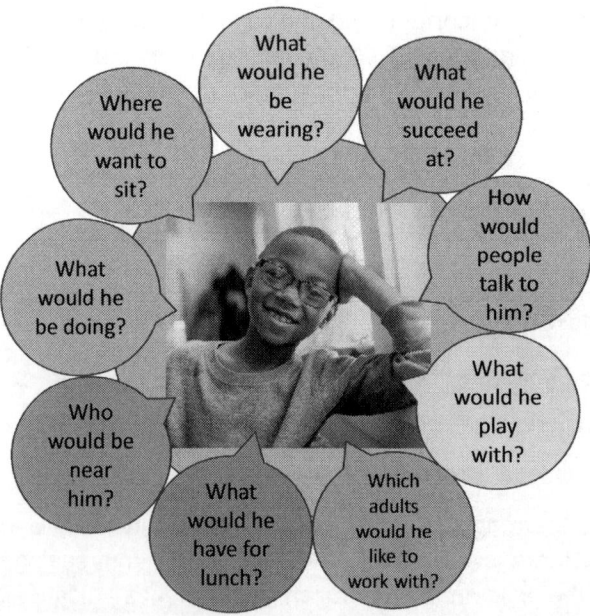

Figure 6.4 '*The best day ever*' (credit to Mike Reed)

The child's voice

It is crucial to learn to communicate with children, whether this is verbal or in another way (signing, visual prompts and symbols, choice boards, etc). Observations which are recorded will be invaluable as they will enable practitioners to gather information about children's interests and preferences.

Neurodiversity

The term 'neurodiversity' signifies a celebration of diversity in neurological differences, in much the same way as we celebrate differences in race, religion, gender, etc. Fung (2021, p 3) defines it as 'a concept that regards individuals with differences in brain function and behavioral traits as part of normal variation in the human population'. This relatively new concept, first coined by Singer in 1998 (Fung, 2021), calls for equality for people with neurological differences. McGee (2012, p 12) explains,

> Like biodiversity, which is seen as critical to the health of ecosystems, advocates of neurodiversity assert that neurological variation is not only natural but is central to the success of the human species.

Kapp et al (2013, p 59) term neurodiversity a 'deficit as a difference model'. The term usually refers to autism but is also ascribed to ADHD and dyslexia. As Leadbitter et al (2021, p 2) describe, 'variations in neurological development and functioning across humans are a natural and valuable part of human variation' rather than a problem to be managed. There is no 'right way' to think, learn and behave; professionals need to get to know individual children and to meet their particular needs.

CASE STUDY ⊕

Natalia: meeting a young person's particular needs

Natalia is a 13 year-old girl with autism in a secondary school. One of the things she is very sensitive to is sound and she can often be seen with her hands over her ears. To meet Natalia's particular needs, her teacher could:

» identify a quiet place for her to go when she needs to;

» allow her to wear noise-cancelling headphones whenever possible;

» give her prior warning about unexpected loud noises like bells and fire drills.

Patience, kindness and empathy are important, as are listening to Natalia and asking her about her own needs, as she is the expert in her own life.

Gardner's multiple intelligences

A useful theory which encourages the investigation of strengths is Gardner's (2000) theory of multiple intelligences. The theory has two important elements. One is that intelligence is not fixed; it develops, so there is always the opportunity for progress and development. The other is that cognitive intelligence, which is highly prized in Western society, particularly in schools and workplaces, is only one type of intelligence, but there are other types of intelligence (Figure 6.5).

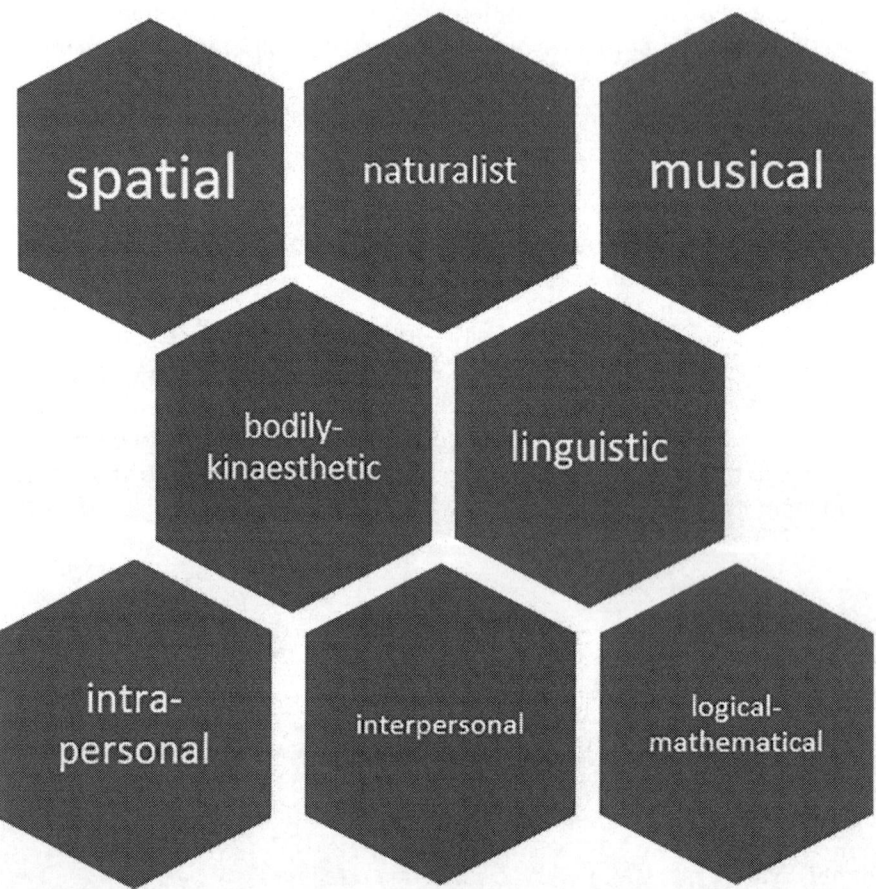

Figure 6.5 *Multiple intelligences (adapted from Gardner, 2000)*

Gardner suggested that only linguistic intelligence and logical-mathematical intelligences are valued in our schools, but with regard to the other intelligences, teachers should use a variety of methods to suit everyone. This, then, fits with the modern theory of inclusive pedagogy, as it appreciates the individual needs of all children, not just those with a diagnosed special educational need or disability. Author and education advisor Sir Ken Robinson (2007) tells a poignant story of a young girl diagnosed with ADHD which illustrates this perfectly (see Chapter 3).

Strength-based approaches with complex needs

Children and young people with 'complex needs' due to disability or illness require a lot of individual help and support on a daily basis. This can be challenging for families and carers, but a strength-based approach can be inspiring and there is much hope and happiness to be found. In the following case study, Pip reflects on her feelings when she worked with a child with complex needs for the first time.

CASE STUDY

Pip: supporting a child with complex needs

I had been working in a mainstream school setting as a classroom-based teaching assistant for two years when I was asked to take on a one-to-one role supporting a severely disabled boy who would be joining the school. I was initially very unsure about taking on the role. I questioned my ability, my skills, my knowledge, and I didn't think I had the personal strength to provide the level of care needed. I became extremely anxious and considered resigning from the role.

I took my concerns to my line manager, and we talked it through. She reassured me that I would be thoroughly trained, which helped, but the discussion reminded me that actually the most important thing was that the child was made welcome and felt valued and that his family felt this too. This is something that guides me when working with any child, so why should he be any different? Furthermore, I was reminded I was not alone in the situation and had the support and experience of my colleagues to draw on.

I undertook the training, which provided the physical skills I would need, but the big turning point came when meeting him and his mum for the first time. It was evident that he came from a loving home and chatting with mum revealed that she was just as anxious about handing him into our care as I had been about taking on the role.

The relationship I formed with mum proved to be the strongest asset of the situation. She was a fountain of knowledge for any queries we had about his care, health, likes and dislikes, because she knew him best. To strengthen this relationship, we included mum as much as possible any time an outside agency or practitioner visited us in school. As mum could see what we would be doing and working towards first hand, she became confident in our abilities and therefore less anxious.

We focused on the boy's pre-existing strengths as a basis for working towards his individual targets, including his peers whenever possible, for example, with messy play and singing. Involving mum in the process allowed her to see that we were putting his best interests first and that he was beginning to thrive. By the end of the school year, he was a valued member of the school, the other children loved playing and chatting with him, and he had become relaxed and happy on a daily basis, smiling and giggling.

Reflective questions ⑦

»   Consider the strengths in this story; what can you learn for your own practice?

»   The relationship between Pip and the child's mother was central to the success of this child's transition to school. What constitutes a good relationship with a parent or family?

Chapter summary ⑧

In this chapter, we have analysed the importance of a positive attitude. Emily Perl Kingsley's poem '*Welcome to Holland*' highlights the importance of looking at a situation in a different way. The two case studies in this chapter, by Liv and Pip, both give examples of a positive approach built on supportive relationships and a genuine desire to see the positives. The debate around labelling has been analysed and its links to segregation.

Inclusion for all is the ultimate aim of the strength-based approach. Everyone has strengths and everyone should be valued, included and listened to. Getting to know children and families and planning for individuals, based on children's needs, choices and talents is ideal, with no one group seen as superior to another. In a nation where tolerance is growing and more and more children are being included in mainstream education, a real difference can be made to people's self-image and self-esteem.

Further reading 📑

* NHS (2021) *Video: Profound Intellectual and Multiple Disabilities.* [online] Available at: www.nhs.uk/conditions/social-care-and-support-guide/caring-for-children-and-young-people/how-to-care-for-children-with-complex-needs/ (accessed 19 June 2023).

   This video, on an NHS website, gives advice about complex needs and includes an interview with the mother of a young person, Victoria, who is now living independently with support from carers. Her mother talks very positively about life with a child who has complex needs.

* Sewell, A and Smith, J (2020) *Introduction to Special Educational Needs, Disability and Inclusion.* London: Sage.

   A comprehensive guide to working with children who have SEND. This book covers numerous special needs in a variety of settings and offers positive inclusive advice which sees the child as the heart of care and education.

References 📚

Allen, G (2011) *Early Intervention: The Next Steps: HM Government.* [online] Available at: https://assets.publishing.service.gov.uk/government/uploads/system/uploads/attachment_data/file/284086/early-intervention-next-steps2.pdf (accessed 19 June 2023).

Bansall, S (2020) Preparing School to Meet the Challenge of Inclusive Education for Children with Disabilities: A Collaborative Action Research Network. *International Journal of Education and Management Studies*, 10(2): 191–4.

Cole, T (1989) *Apart or a Part? Integration and the Growth of British Special Education.* Milton Keynes: Open University Press.

Crossley, N and Hewitt, D (2021) *Inclusion: A Principled Guide for School Leaders*. London: Routledge.

Department of Education and Early Childhood Development (DEECD) (2012) *Strength-based Approach: A Guide to Writing Transition Learning and Development Statements.* [online] Available at: https://wrap2fasd.org/2022/12/16/strength-based-approach-a-guide-to-writing-transition-learning-and-development-statements/ (accessed 30 June 2023).

Early Intervention Foundation (2017) *What is Early Intervention?* [online] Available at: www.eif.org.uk/why-it-matters/what-is-early-intervention (accessed 30 June 2023).

Fung, L (ed) (2021) *From Phenomenology to Neurobiology and Enhancing Technologies.* Washington, DC: American Psychiatric Association Publishing.

Gardner, H (2000) *Intelligence Reframed: Multiple Intelligences for the 21st Century.* New York: Basic Books.

Gibbs, S, Beckmann, J F, Elliott, J, Metsäpelto, R, Vehkakoski, T and Aro, M (2020) What's in a Name: The Effect of Category Labels on Teachers' Beliefs. *European Journal of Special Needs Education*, 35(1): 115–27.

Hill, N (1937) *Think and Grow Rich.* New York: Simon and Schuster.

Kapp, S K, Gillespie-Lynch, K, Sherman, L E, and Hutman, T (2013) Deficit, Difference, or Both? Autism and Neurodiversity. *Developmental Psychology*, 49(1): 59–71.

Kingsley, E (1987) *Welcome to Holland.* [online] Available at: www.dsasc.ca/uploads/8/5/3/9/8539131/welcome_to_holland.pdf (accessed 19 June 2023).

Leadbitter, K, Buckle, K L, Ellis, C and Dekker, M (2021) Autistic Self-Advocacy and the Neurodiversity Movement: Implications for Autism Early Intervention Research and Practice. *Frontiers in Psychology*, 12: 1–8.

Lindsay, G, Wedell, K and Dockrell, J (2020) Warnock 40 Years On: The Development of Special Educational Needs since the Warnock Report and Implications for the Future. *Frontiers in Education*, 4(164): 1–20.

Making Chromosomes Count (MCC) (2021), *Emily Perl Kingsley, the Woman Behind Sesame Street and 'Welcome to Holland' Poem.* [online] Available at: https://makingchromosomescount.co.uk/2021/09/28/emily-perl-kingsley-the-woman-behind-sesame-street-and-welcome-to-holland-poem/ (accessed 19 June 2023).

McGee, M (2012) Neurodiversity. *Contexts: American Sociological Association*, 11(3): 12–13.

Mengoni, S E and Oates, J (2014) A Tool to Record and Support the Early Development of Children Including Those with Special Educational Needs or Disabilities. *Support for Learning*, 29(4): 339–58.

National Education Union (2023) *Latest Data from Government on Special Educational Needs in England.* [online] Available at: https://neu.org.uk/latest/press-releases/latest-data-government-special-educational-needs-england (accessed 28 July 2023).

O'Shaughnessy, M (2008) Labelling Children with Special Educational Needs: To Label or Not to Label? *REACH Journal of Special Needs Education in Ireland*, 21(2): 67–76.

Payne, K (2022) Observations – Using a Strengths-based Approach. *Teach Early Years*. [online] Available at: www.teachearlyyears.com/learning-and-development/view/observations-using-a-strengths-based-approach (accessed 19 June 2023).

Pickard, B (2021) A Framework for Mediating Medical and Social Models of Disability in Instrumental Teaching for Children with Down Syndrome. *Research Studies in Music Education*, 43(2): 110–28.

Plows, V (2014) Labelling Kids: The Good, the Bad and the ADHD. *The Conversation*. [online] Available at: https://theconversation.com/labelling-kids-the-good-the-bad-and-the-adhd-31778 (accessed 19 June 2023).

Prowle, A and Hodgkins, A (2020) *Making a Difference with Children and Families: Re-imagining the Role of the Practitioner*. London: Red Globe Books, Bloomsbury.

Reeve, C (1999) *Still Me*. London: Arrow Books.

Robinson, K (2007) *Do Schools Kill Creativity?* TED talk. [online] Available at: www.ted.com/talks/sir_ken_robinson_do_schools_kill_creativity (accessed 19 June 2023).

Sewell, A (2020) Chapter 4: SEND Support and Intervention: Overcoming Barriers. In Sewell, A and Smith, J (eds) *Introduction to Special Educational Needs, Disability and Inclusion* (pp 49–62). London: Sage.

UNESCO (2005) *Guidelines for Inclusion*. Paris: UNESCO.

UNESCO (1994) *The Salamanca Statement and Framework for Action on Special Needs Education, World Conference on Special Needs Education: Access and Quality, Salamanca, Spain, 1994.* [online] Available at: https://unesdoc.unesco.org/ark:/48223/pf0000098427 (accessed 28 July 2023).

Warnock, H M (1978) *Special Educational Needs: Report of the Committee of Enquiry into the Education of Handicapped Children and Young People*. [online] Available at: www.educationengland.org.uk/documents/warn... ...arnock1978.html (accessed 30 June 2023).

Zadawi, N (2022) Ambitious Reform for Children and Young People with SEND. Press release. [online] Available at: www.gov.uk/government/news/ambitious-reform-for-children-and-young-people-with-send (accessed 19 June 2023).

7 Strength-based practice with parents and carers

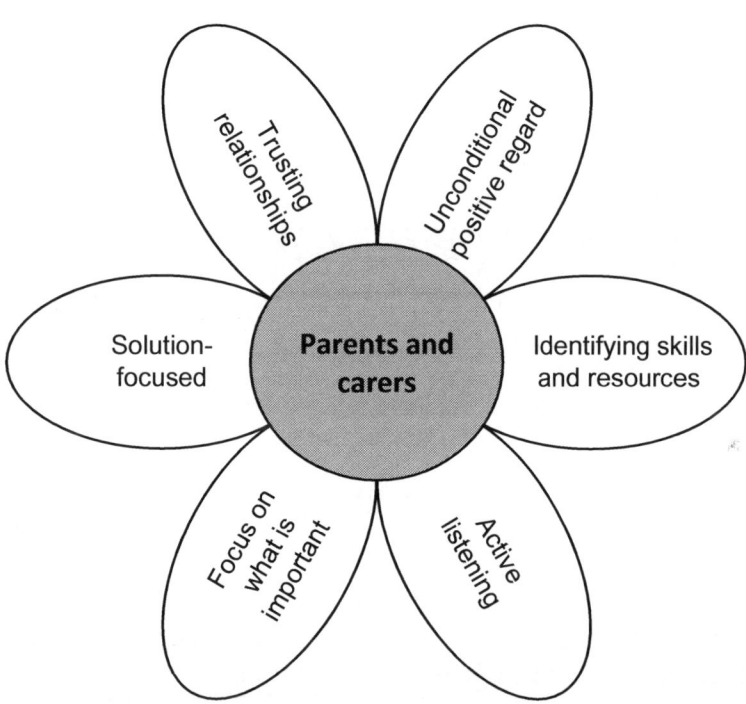

Chapter objectives ◎

This chapter:

- discusses the importance of parenting for creating secure attachments, enabling happy childhoods and setting up children for positive trajectories;

- analyses a range of approaches to positive parenting;

- evaluates ways of supporting parents within their role.

Introduction

When undertaking the research for this chapter, I stumbled upon a job description *'for a parent'* constructed by Karen Stephens (a retired academic, practitioner and herself a parent and grandparent). The fictitious job description laid out the numerous essential and desirable skills for the role, the extensive knowledge and abundant personal qualities to be embodied by the applicant, before specifying the huge responsibilities and accountabilities demanded by the role. The hours were 24/7, vacations were non-existent and the contract lasted a lifetime. When discussing pay and conditions, Karen wrote, *'expanded opportunities for contentment and self-fulfilment offered in lieu of monetary compensation'*. She ended her tongue-in-cheek document with a statement that although parenting was often undervalued, it remains *'the most critical job around; and the most demanding, too!'* This job description can be found in the link under Further resources.

The parenting that children experience during their childhood can have a strong and long-lasting effect on their well-being in the short term and their longer-term outcomes across a range of indicators including relationships, self-regulation, communication, academic achievement and physical and mental health (Sanders and Turner, 2018). The quality of the parent–child relationship and the cultural and community context in which that relationship operates can influence the parenting a child receives and have effects that ripple beyond childhood into adult life and even beyond into intergenerational cycles. Hence, supporting parents in the complex and important roles they undertake with their children is of utmost importance.

Blaming the parents

We have already noted that parenting plays a complex and crucial role in determining children's outcomes and therefore it is important that parents receive support with this role. For many parents this support will come from within their own social networks and from other sources that they can access independently. Other parents may need additional support to help them address specific challenges they may be facing.

However, too often, the need for parenting support can be couched in very negative terms as part of a societal *'blame culture'* which seeks to place the responsibility for a child's difficulties, or indeed wider social ills, firmly with the parents. This happens at an individual level, for example the widespread societal disapproval a parent may experience when their child has a meltdown in the supermarket. However, it can also be seen in the widespread public outcry following the 2011 UK urban riots, where *'bad parenting'* was held up as an overarching cause of the disorder resulting in the UK government's Troubled Family Programme, launched in 2012, which aimed to transform the lives of 120,000 families with multiple problems across England by May 2015. The programme's premise was that the best way to work with families with multiple problems involved identifying the underlying and interconnected problems that the family faced and dealing with them holistically in order to initiate change within that family. In doing so, it was argued, the programme would save the public purse approximately £9 billion a year which it currently spent dealing with the problems the families faced (eg substance misuse, youth justice issues, mental health difficulties), because their needs had not been addressed through earlier intervention (Department for Communities and Local Government, 2016). While the emphasis on early intervention and holistic support offered a welcome new focus on supporting families, the whole programme started from a deficit model, identifying multiple problems and deficits in families, and indirectly placing the responsibility for these failings with parents.

This chapter seeks to challenge this discourse, by presenting a model of strength-based parenting which seeks to acknowledge and celebrate strengths in families and consider how such strengths can be fostered, expanded and used to strengthen families and enable parents to feel empowered within their roles. Such an approach, does not, as some have argued, ignore risks, but rather tries to understand (and, where appropriate, manage) those risks within a holistic context of relationships, family culture and family functioning.

CASE STUDY ☺

Helen: supporting parents to help their children

Helen Coleman, a speech and language therapist, explores how she works with parents in a strength-based way in order to help them to support their child's speech and communication. You hear more from Helen in Chapter 8.

Sometimes the work I do with parents and school staff can be just as important as the work I do directly with the child. Here too, I always try to focus on strengths. Often parents can be quite emotional about the fact that their child is having difficulty with an area of their development. They can often also feel like they have done something to cause the problem or feel like their parenting skills are at fault. However, often parents instinctively know what helps and no one has more motivation than they do to get it right for their child! I often spend time talking to them about situations which are tricky and what they are doing now, so we can pull out what is working now and how we can extend that. For example, parents can often identify that their child with comprehension difficulties responds well when they show them what to do rather than tell them, or when they give one instruction at a time. We talk about how useful that strategy is, why it helps and how they can extend it into situations which the child is finding harder. Not only is it building on the parent and child's strengths, but it's something they have already seen working and so they are more likely to take on my recommendation of trying to do it more.

Reflective questions ⑦

» Helen mentions that often parents blame themselves for their children's difficulties. Why do you think this is the case? In what ways does Helen's strength-based approach attempt to challenge and change this?

» Helen notes that focusing on what is working right now can be a helpful strategy for families dealing with adversity or challenges. It is also helpful for practitioners. Can you reflect upon a challenging situation that you are facing (in life or work)? What is currently working for you in addressing this issue? How can you build upon that moving forward?

Parenting styles

Since the 1960s there has been an interest in how different parenting styles impact on children. Parenting styles incorporate the emotional environment in which a parent and child relationship develops as well as the strategies and approaches that parents use to manage situations and behaviours. In 1967s, Diane Baumrind conducted a seminal study focusing on parent and child interactions, using naturalistic observations which she then went on to analyse, interpret and categorise, resulting in three distinct parenting styles: Authoritarian, Authoritative and Permissive. Her work was later expanded by Maccoby and Martin (1983) who identified a fourth parenting style, which they defined as Uninvolved or Neglectful parenting. Parenting style theory suggests that all parents will gravitate naturally towards one of these four styles. These styles will be characterised by different emotional responses, communication styles and support and behaviour strategies. Moreover, they can be understood in terms of levels of emotional warmth and levels of control (as shown in Figure 7.1).

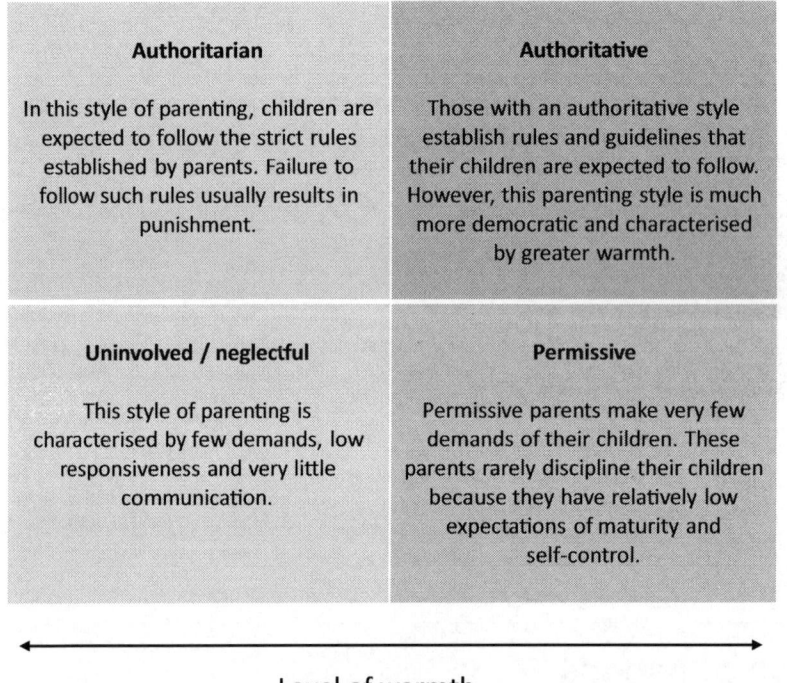

Figure 7.1 *Parenting styles*

According to Baumrind and later researchers, not all parenting styles are equal in terms of their benefits or otherwise to children. Ideally, one needs to aim for high levels of both emotional warmth and control. Consider each of the styles in more detail.

*   **Authoritarian** parents show high levels of control. They place high demands on the child and have high expectations of their child in terms of achievement,

behaviour and obedience. They are the parent, and they expect their rules to be followed unquestioningly because of their position. This form of parenting can be quite rigid and unyielding, punishments can be quite harsh and often there is little responsiveness to the child's perspective and little emotional warmth. According to Power (2013), children brought up with this style are often competent and self-regulated but may report less happiness and lower self-esteem than others.

- **Permissive** parenting could be considered the exact opposite of authoritarian parents. Here there are high levels of emotional warmth and parents are often very indulgent. However, levels of control are low. Parents are very responsive to their child but tend to place low demands upon them. Discipline is lax, often inconsistent, and parents tend to have low expectations of their child. Children are allowed to make their own decisions, regardless of age and maturity, and parents often assume the role of friend. According to Power (2013) children parented under this style tend to lack self-regulation and struggle with authority. This often results in underachievement at school.

- **Uninvolved/Neglectful** parenting is characterised by low warmth and low levels of control. Parents may meet the child's basic needs such as for food, shelter and clothing but are otherwise detached or uninvolved in their children's lives. As a result, children's emotional needs may go unmet. There is often little communication between the child and the parent, and there may be few rules or guidelines to support the child. In extreme cases, the parents may be neglectful even of the child's basic needs. Powers (2013) identified that of all the parenting styles, this style had the most adverse effects for children, and that children parented in this way may lack self-esteem and experience significant difficulties in later life, struggling to achieve positive outcomes.

To an extent, parenting style theory suggests that all the above styles are unsatisfactory and lead to sub-optimal outcomes for children. The fourth parenting style, authoritative parenting, is seen as the ideal approach, combining high levels of emotional warmth with high parental control, and ultimately resulting in happy children who achieve positive outcomes in both the short and long term.

- **Authoritative** parents, Baumrind argues, are involved and responsive to their child's needs, they set high standards and support their child to achieve them. They are more democratic than authoritarian counterparts and place an emphasis on coaching and nurturing rather than punitive measures. They have realistic expectations and put measures in place to support the child to achieve independence and self-regulation.

You can certainly learn something from the parenting styles theory and understanding parenting approaches in relation to warmth and control is particularly helpful. In this society control is often seen pejoratively with connotations of power, domination and restriction. Control does not equate to controlling. Within this parenting context, what we are striving for is for is for parents to set appropriate standards and expectations, to listen to children and to be responsive to their child's needs, while at the same time regulating their own emotions and responses.

One of the dangers of accepting parenting style theory uncritically is that, if we are not careful, it can result in determinism, whereby we assume that people are unable to change their default parenting style and therefore the negative outcomes resulting from a particular style are inevitable for the child. It is important to note, however, that it is possible for parents to consciously and reflectively challenge their default style in order to support better outcomes for children. Moreover, the cause-and-effect links between parenting styles and future outcomes are unproved, and parenting is likely to be just one factor among many that influence later outcomes. Also, in, many families, children will have more than one caregiver and hence may be affected by different styles and expectations. There may also be cultural dimensions to how children are parented.

Towards a strength-based parenting style

Bi et al (2018) suggest that by being cognisant of the advantages and potential pitfalls of different parenting styles, parents can strive towards a more authoritative stance. In doing so, they can often maximise the benefits of the authoritative parenting style and can enjoy a happier and calmer family life. Below are some of the factors that may help parents to develop an authoritative parenting approach.

Figure 7.2 Authoritative parenting

Tsabary (2015) considers the importance of what she terms '*conscious parenting*', looking inwards at self rather than focusing on the child and their behaviour. This is seen as a mindful approach, which fosters parental self-awareness as well as an enhanced understanding of the child as a separate and individual being. This mindfulness can support better outcomes in the moment and help develop a positive relationship over time. Within this model, the parent is required to be emotionally present and attuned to their child, to relinquish control and to learn from their child and to allow children to grow through challenges instead of always solving the problem. D'Apice and von Stumm (2020) suggest that this form of parenting requires parents to engage with and authentically communicate with their child. In turn the conversations that a conscious parent has with a child will have benefits for the parent–child relationship as well as possibly resulting in better child cognition, self-regulation and a stronger sense of self.

It is important to recognise that there is no such thing as the perfect parent, and that all parents will have bad days and make mistakes. Recognising this, the next section considers what it means to be a '*good enough parent*'.

Reflective questions ⑦

Consider the following scenarios.

Sadir (aged seven) is playing on his games console and trying hard to reach the next level. He ignores his mum when he is called to come out to the kitchen for supper. His dad brings him his food on a plate and Sadir misses a cue and the game ends. He kicks the plate out of his dad's hand and shouts angrily.

Bella (aged 12) has several older friends that she enjoys spending time with. Recently she has started staying out late on school nights and coming home smelling of alcohol and cigarettes. Last week a £10 note went missing from her stepdad's wallet. Bella said she knows nothing about it. Her mum is sure it was Bella that took the money as there does not seem to be any other plausible explanation.

Parents Kate and Dee are at the supermarket with their son, Rory (aged three). Rory spots a toy dinosaur that he wants. The toy is expensive, so Dee puts it back on the shelf. Rory gets incredibly upset and starts crying. Despite Dee's attempts to soothe and distract Rory, the situation escalates and soon he is lying on the floor screaming and kicking. Kate is mortified and feels that everyone is watching and judging their parenting. She picks up the dinosaur and heads off to the till.

→

> » In each of these situations, how might someone with the following three parenting styles react:
>
>   – authoritarian parenting style?
>
>   – permissive parenting style?
>
>   – uninvolved parenting style?
>
> » What might an authoritative parenting approach look like in each of these scenarios?
>
> » Beside parenting styles, what other factors might impact on how the situations above unfold?

Good enough parenting

The concept of '*good enough parenting*' was first used by Winnicott (1965). Winnicott recognised that it is both unhelpful and unrealistic to demand perfection of parents. He extolled the virtues of the vast majority of parents, who, despite imperfections and occasional lapses in responsiveness, are in all practical respects '*good enough*' to meet their children's needs. Winnicott talks about most parents being able to exercise sound instincts and provide stable and healthy environments for their children. Such parents he described as both ordinary and devoted, and he wanted to defend them against a perceived threat of intrusion of the state (through professional expertise) into the private family lives of such parents. Such parenting he argued, is not perfect, but it is good enough to ensure positive outcomes for the child. The emphasis he argued, needed to be on the nurturing environment, and meeting the child's needs responsively most of the time was sufficient to create happy, well-attached children. This nurturing environment is best characterised by emotional connection, affection and presence, and is supported by further studies including the famous still face experiment undertaken by Edward Tronick in 1970 (Weinberg and Tronick, 1996).

This concept of good enough does not negate the reality that some parenting is simply '*not good enough*' and hence there is a need for safeguarding structures to recognise where parenting is abusive or neglectful to the detriment of the child's well-being, and where appropriate, to provide alternative parenting. However, the concept of being good enough to secure positive outcomes for your child can be a helpful one, allowing parents to avoid the pitfalls of comparison, and focus on responsiveness and getting it right for the child in the present moment. The difficulty lies in defining what '*good enough*' parenting is. There have been several attempts to explore what good enough parenting might look like. These are explored below.

Research undertaken by Kellet and Apps in 2009 defined '*good enough*' parenting as consisting of four main elements:

1. meeting children's health and developmental needs;

2. putting children's needs first;

3.   providing routine and consistent care;

4.   acknowledging problems and engaging with support services.

However, some have suggested that this sets the bar low. It is also acknowledged (Hoghughi and Speight, 1998, p 94) that there are both cultural and temporal issues that influence our understanding of good enough parenting. Hence, they argue that good enough parenting is '*a process that adequately meets the child's needs, according to prevailing cultural standards which can change from generation to generation*'. Others have noted that parenting is often affected by wider structural issues in society. Hence as well as focusing on supporting parents, poverty and inequality also need to be addressed in order to help families break out from cycles of deprivation (Field, 2010). This is not to suggest that parents living in poverty are not '*good enough*', but Field recognises that the numerous additional challenges these parents face day in and day out may make it even more difficult to provide the physical and emotional security, attuned responsiveness and consistent approaches that lead to positive outcomes. Under this view, parenting support needs to be accompanied by measures to reduce poverty.

Joussemet, Landry and Koestner (2008) consider that good enough parents are driven by recognition of the child's autonomy. Hence parents need to support the child's own self-determination and self-regulation in order to support their development and well-being. The central tenet of this approach is the parents' trust in their child to develop as an autonomous human being.

Reflective questions ⑦

» Define what good enough parenting looks like in a series of bullet points.

» To what extent is good enough parenting a helpful concept?

» Going back to the parenting scenarios above (Sadir, Bella and Rory), what would constitute a good enough parenting response in these cases?

Towards a strength-based approach to good enough parenting

Given all that has been considered in the chapter so far, one of the best things we can do to support parents is to help them realise that no parent is perfect and that what they need to strive for is making effective parenting choices in the moment, while providing their children with emotional environments in which they can flourish and meet their potential. Maslow (1943) helpfully created a five-level model of human needs which he presented as a hierarchy. This paradigm has been reimagined below with a parenting focus.

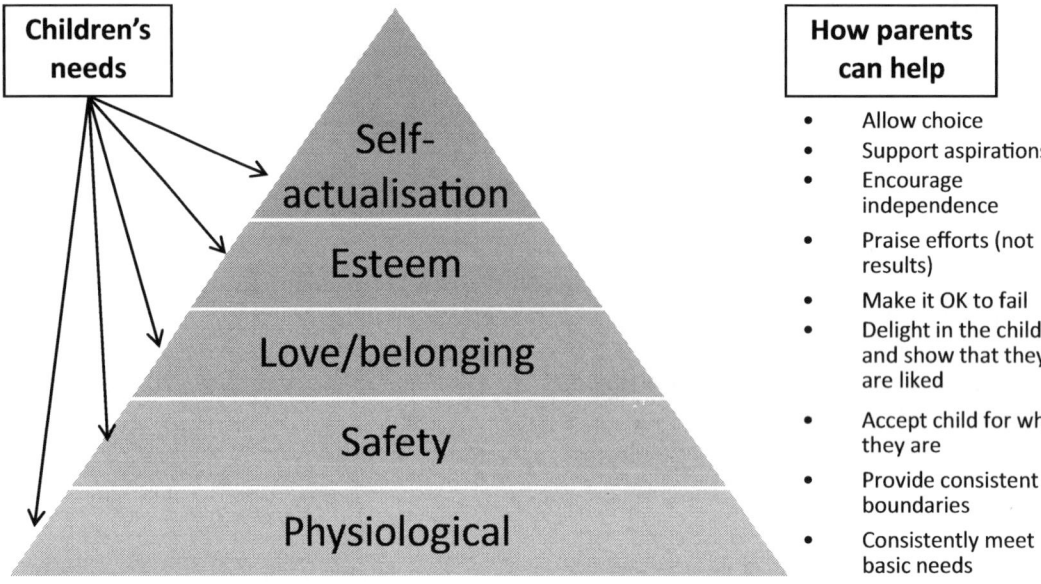

Figure 7.3 *Supporting parents to meet children's needs*

In supporting parents to consistently meet children's needs, the focus needs to be upon creating and sustaining positive relationships between parents and child, encouraging parents to spend positive time with their child, to listen to their child and to create consistent boundaries that are sufficiently flexible to adapt to children's changing needs. It could be argued, therefore, that good enough parenting is characterised most strongly by attuned responsiveness on the part of the parent, coupled with the parent having unconditional positive regard for the child (Rogers, 1951).

Attuned parenting involves listening to, understanding and responding to children's cues (the way that they communicate their needs through their words, actions or body language). According to Kobak et al (2017) 'attunement' is also linked to emotional literacy and a demeanour of warmth. Unconditional positive regard, in this context, means an attitude of unwavering acceptance and love for the child that is not dependent on behaviour. This does not mean accepting everything the child does but accepting them as an autonomous human being who is doing the best they can in their current circumstances or situation. Originally developed by Rogers to inform the therapist–client relationship, through building empathy and trust the concept of unconditional positive regard has a broader resonance for relationships in general and, in this instance, for parent–child relationships.

How mobile phones can affect attunement

Kildare and Middlemiss (2017) studied how parental use of technology was impacting on parenting. They concluded that the increased dependence on mobile communication devices and the pressure to respond instantaneously resulted in interruptions to parent child interactions and less parental attunement. This finding was supported by Lemish, Elias and

Floegel (2020) who found that parental mobile phone use while visiting playgrounds with their children, resulted in parents being less attentive to both emotional and safety concerns, while also missing out on opportunities for shared experiences and loving communication. This in turn, argued Steiner-Adair (2014), results in children feeling undervalued, unimportant and ignored.

This is not to decry the importance of mobile technology, which can be helpful to parents in keeping in touch with older children and young people, as well as being used to access information to support parenting. It does suggest, however, that the technology needs to be used sparingly in the presence of children and that parents need to be supported to develop strategies for managing and containing their phone use.

Creating a village to raise the child

'It takes a village to raise a child' is a well-known proverb. It reminds us that we are interconnected and part of a community. This is especially important for parents who may be feeling isolated. A strength-based approach to parenting will involve finding assets within the wider systems supporting the family (Bronfenbrenner, 1979) and finding ways to maximise these assets for the family. Such resources may include extended family members, other parents, neighbours, community projects and organisations, and other professionals working with the family. The important thing is to help parents to feel well supported and less isolated. In the case study below, we hear from Luiza, an experienced social worker who currently heads up a fostering and adoption team for a consortium of local authorities. In this case study, she reflects upon her work to support Emma, a first-time adoptive parent.

CASE STUDY ⊖

Evie is five years old. She was adopted at 18 months old by Emma who is a single adoptive parent. Emma went through a rigorous assessment process and preparation training before being able to adopt Evie. Up until Evie's third birthday Emma and Evie had a lot of support from professionals helping Evie to settle in, and for both to get used to being a family together. Emma works as a special needs teaching assistant in the local school, and she has a lot of knowledge about children's needs and development.

Emma is requesting adoption support as she struggles with Evie's behaviour, and she feels she is not able to manage Evie's care. In the last year Evie started to have angry outbursts, hitting Emma, refusing to follow the routine and rules in the house, taking a long time to settle to sleep and a long time to get ready in the mornings. Taking Evie to school often ends up in a meltdown in front of the school gates. Often Emma is late to work in the morning and Evie is late going into school. Emma is worried she will lose her job and she wonders if she is a good parent to Evie.

Traditionally, a child and family assessment are based on the assessment framework triangle considering all aspects of the child's developmental needs, parents' ability to care, the

→

environmental factors and, more importantly, safeguarding concerns. Over the years I have learnt that while this framework is essential in understanding the needs of the child from all perspectives, it should not prevent practitioners from thinking outside the framework. Considering the parenting capacity from a strength-based perspective is about the parent's needs as much as the child's: what does the parent need to enable them to provide not perfect but good enough care to the child?

So how does this apply to our case scenario?

To start with it helps to connect with the parent in their vulnerability, to acknowledge how difficult things seem for them right now using phrases which start with 'I wonder/imagine/ notice'. An empathic response generates connection where the other person feels listened to and empowered to share their story and their truth. It also promotes the view that the person is not the problem. As a professional it is important to develop an attitude of professional curiosity and positive regard, allowing those we support to explore and reflect on where they are at and what they would like to see changing.

Rather than offering a solution of what needed to change for Emma and Evie, I enabled Emma to explore what was happening for them right now and what she felt were the triggers for Evie's change in behaviour. Emma was able to reflect on how the start of school has been difficult for Evie and a huge milestone in her life. She recognised Evie would struggle more with change because of her experiencing early trauma through adoption. By offering Emma a safe space to explore things without judgement or blame it helped her develop empathy for Evie's reality and struggles, reminding her of all of Evie's previous experiences and how these may impact on her present needs.

One of the models we use in our work with parents is that of PACE, which stands for Playfulness, Acceptance, Curiosity and Empathy. This comes from dyadic developmental psychotherapy-informed approach advocated for use with children who have experienced early developmental trauma. In our conversations with parents about children's needs and when the situation seems very complex, as in Emma's case, we advise parents 'if in doubt go to A&E – acceptance and empathy'. The same model applies when engaging parents who find themselves overwhelmed by the demands of parenting and we model for them as practitioners the experience of acceptance and empathy. Only when this connection is made can we explore with curiosity what is going well, what are the strengths, inviting the parents to take an active role in identifying what feels to them the right solution. Rather than feel ashamed she was the parent whose child was misbehaving, Emma felt empowered to see Evie's school as a partner in their journey. Emma was able to identify as a strength what she already knew through her job and embraced the role of an advocate for her daughter's needs, continuing to promote and raise empathy in others for her daughter's early life experiences and needs. Looking closely at the routines in the home to allow regular moments of connection between Emma and Evie using PACE, working with school to ensure Evie's needs were understood and that she was having the right support when not with mum, improved things significantly.

Thirteenth-century poet and scholar Jalaluddin Rumi wrote: 'you think, because one and one make two, that you understand two. But to truly comprehend the nature of two, you must first understand *"and"*.'

The strength-based approach enables practitioners to not forget about the 'and' not only as the relationship between individuals, but the significance of the quality of this relationship. Applying this within the systems we are part of as practitioners, to the way we work with professionals and families, and to our critical self-reflection as practitioners can only enable growth where one and one makes more than two.

Reflective questions ⑦

» What did Luiza put in place to support Emma, and what difference did it make?

» Why is it a helpful approach to focus on strengths when supporting parents in their parenting role?

» How can practitioners model the strength-based approach in their working relationship with a parent?

» Can you think about a work situation where you may choose to act differently now you know more about the strength-based approach?

The importance of parental self-care

As we have noted in the job description at the beginning of the chapter, parenting is a difficult but hugely rewarding job. It is little wonder that parents can become frazzled and overwhelmed from time to time, especially in situations where they may be dealing with additional pressures. In such cases, they can often ignore their own well-being needs. Parents' self-care is of utmost importance to enable them to deal with inevitable stresses of life and to make the most of their time with the children. At a basic level, this will involve taking care of their own physical needs, being kind to themselves, staying connected to others, asking for help when it is needed and finding time for things they enjoy. As practitioners, we can model this self-care in the way we take care of ourselves and encourage parents to regularly audit their own well-being and find ways to prioritise self-care.

Chapter summary 📖

In this chapter, strength-based approaches have been explored in relation to working with parents. Once again, the importance of strong relationships has been noted, in this case between parent and child. We have considered the challenges and rewards of parenting, and dispelled the myth of parental perfection, advocating an understanding of '*good enough*' parenting while also stressing the importance of parental attunement and unconditional positive regard for their child. Luiza's case study demonstrates how parents can be supported to take a strength-based perspective and in doing so to become more confident in their parenting. Finally, we thought about the importance of parents' own self-care in enabling them to look after their own well-being needs, alongside caring for their children. The aim of all of this is to create strong families, who support one another and enjoy one another's company, and where ultimately the children achieve positive outcomes.

Further resources

- The parent job description mentioned at the beginning of the chapter can be found at: www. easternflorida.edu/community-resources/child-development-centers/parent-resource-library/ documents/daunting-but-rewarding-job.pdf (accessed 19 June 2023).

- TED talk: www.ted.com/talks/yuko_munakata_why_most_parenting_advice_is_wrong (accessed 19 June 2023).

- In this challenging talk, Yuko Munakata, a professor in the Department of Psychology at the University of California, challenges conventional wisdom about advice given to parents and also about the role parents play in shaping their children's life chances.

References

Baumrind, D (1967) Childcare Practices Anteceding Three Patterns of Preschool Behaviour. *Genetic Psychology Monographs*, 75(1): 43–88.

Bi, X, Yang, Y, Li, H, Wang, M, Zhang, W and Deater-Deckard, K (2018) Parenting Styles and Parent-adolescent Relationships: The Mediating Roles of Behavioural Autonomy and Parental Authority. *Frontiers in Psychology*, 9(2): 187.

Bronfenbrenner, U (1979) *The Ecology of Human Development: Experiments by Nature and Design*. Cambridge: Harvard University Press.

D'Apice, K and Von Stumm, S (2020) The Role of Spoken Language and Literacy Exposure for Cognitive and Language Outcomes in Children. *Scientific Studies of Reading*, 24(2): 108–22.

Department for Communities and Local Government (DCLG) (2017) *Troubled Families Programme: Evaluation Overview Policy Report*. [online] Available at: https://assets.publishing.service. gov.uk/government/uploads/system/uploads/attachment_data/file/665504/Troubled_ Families_-_Evaluation_Overview.pdf (accessed 30 June 2023).

Field, F (2010) The Foundation Years: Preventing Poor Children Becoming Poor Adults. Report of the Independent Review on Poverty and Life Chances, National Archives. [online] Available at: https://webarchive.nationalarchives.gov.uk/ukgwa/20110120090128/http://povertyreview. independent.gov.uk/media/20254/poverty-report.pdf (accessed 19 June 2023).

Hoghughi, M and Speight, A N P (1998) Good Enough Parenting for All Children – a Strategy for a Healthier Society. *Archives of Disease in Childhood*, 78: 293–6.

Joussemet, M, Landry, R and Koestner, R (2008) A Self-determination Theory Perspective on Parenting. *Canadian Psychology/Psychologie Canadienne*, 49(3): 194–200.

Kildare, C A and Middlemiss, W (2017) Impact of Parents' Mobile Device Use on Parent-child Interaction: A Literature Review. *Computers in Human Behaviour*, 75: 579–93.

Kobak, R, Abbott, C, Zisk, A and Bounoua, N (2017) Adapting to the Changing Needs of Adolescents: Parenting Practices and Challenges to Sensitive Attunement. *Current Opinion in Psychology*, 15: 137–42.

Lemish, D, Elias, N and Floegel, D (2020) 'Look at me!' Parental Use of Mobile Phones at the Playground. *Mobile Media & Communication*, 8(2): 170–87.

Maccoby, E E and Martin, J A (1983) Socialization in the Context of the Family: Parent-child Interaction. In Mussen, P H (series ed) and Hetherington, E M (vol ed) *Handbook of Child Psychology: Vol. 4. Socialization, Personality, and Social Development* (pp 1–101). New York: Wiley.

Maslow, A H (1943) A Theory of Human Motivation. *Psychological Review*, 50(4): 370–96.

Power, T G (2013) Parenting Dimensions and Styles: A Brief History and Recommendations for Future Research. *Child Obesity*, 9(Suppl 1): 14–21.

Rogers, C R (1951) *Client Centred Therapy*. Boston, MA: Houghton Mifflin.

Sanders, M R and Turner, K M T (2018) The Importance of Parenting in Influencing the Lives of Children. In Sanders, M and Morawska, A (eds) *Handbook of Parenting and Child Development Across the Lifespan* (pp 3–26). Cham: Springer.

Steiner-Adair, C and Barker, T (2014) *The Big Disconnect: Protecting Childhood and Family Relationships in the Digital Age*. New York: Harper Collins.

Tsabary, S (2015) *The Conscious Parent*. London: Yellow Kite Books, Hodder & Stoughton.

Weinberg, M K and Tronick, E Z (1996) Infant Affective Reactions to the Resumption of Maternal Interaction after the Still-face. *Child Development*, 67: 905–14.

Winnicott, D W (1965) *The Maturational Process and the Facilitative Environment*. New York: International Universities Press.

8 Strength-based practice with people who have suffered adverse life experiences

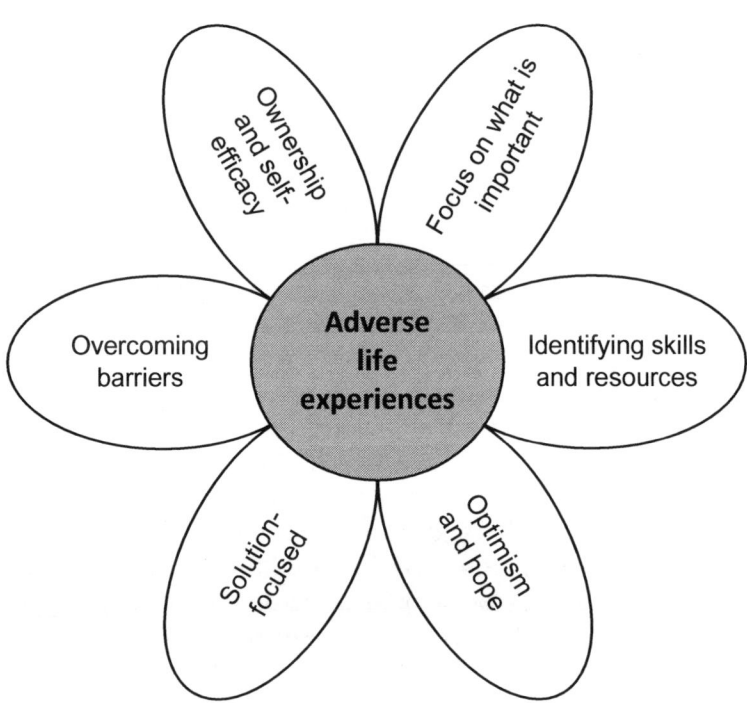

Chapter objectives ◎

This chapter:

- discusses the various ways in which adverse life experiences impact upon children's lives and well-being;

- explores how strength-based approaches can be used to support children and families experiencing adversity to manage their situations and find hope, even in difficult circumstances;

- evaluates approaches practitioners can use to promote a strength-based perspective.

Introduction

Most children and adults will face adversity at some point in their lives, and for many families living with multiple adversities can be one of the defining features of their experiences. In these circumstances, a strength-based approach can enable individuals to look beyond their immediate circumstances, harness their own inherent strengths as well as assets in their wider networks and communities, and look to the future with optimism and hope. This chapter focuses on strength-based approaches with those facing adversity. Such approaches may be relevant for practitioners working with children and young people across the entire age range and in a wide range of health, education, social care, leisure and community settings. While strength-based approaches may already be prevalent in some settings, for others this will represent a different way of working. The chapter looks in detail at what we understand by adversity, how it impacts upon those experiencing it and the contribution that a strength-based approach can have in supporting those children and families affected by adversity. A case study from palliative care shows how, even in extremely sad circumstances, a focus on strengths can be a helpful approach.

What is adversity?

In all our lives, there are elements of difficulty, challenge and loss as well as times of transition and change. These are part of the universal human experience and help us to develop resilience in facing challenges. However, as Brown and Prowle (2022) point out, children may also encounter losses that do not happen to everyone, sometimes referred to as 'circumstantial losses'. Such losses may encompass a range of situations, such as loss of a parent through death, family breakdown, being forced to flee your home, experiencing domestic abuse or parental substance misuse, or witnessing devastating events. Some ⸻ se experiences may be sudden and life-changing (eg the sudden death of a close family member or being caught up in a natural disaster). Others may occur over an extended period (as in the case of abuse, family breakdown or parental imprisonment). However, what is evident is that childhood adversity can have significant impact on children's well-being and outcomes both immediately and in the longer term. Such experiences may be described as trauma, defined by the mental health charity Mind (nd) as 'going through very stressful, frightening or distressing events'. However, it is important to note that trauma is the emotional response to the distressing event and not the event itself. Our experiences of trauma are highly individualised; some people may have an immediate reaction, but for others the traumatic response may occur months or even years later. This individual response to trauma is shaped by a multiplicity of factors including our own personalities, environments, relationships and life experiences. In children, this response will also be affected by the age and development of the child, the severity of the event, the child's proximity to the event and the reactions of caregivers. What is evident is that without intervention childhood trauma can affect the brain and nervous system. In Figure 8.1 below are some of the signs that a child might be experiencing trauma, an emotional and physiological response to extremely upsetting events.

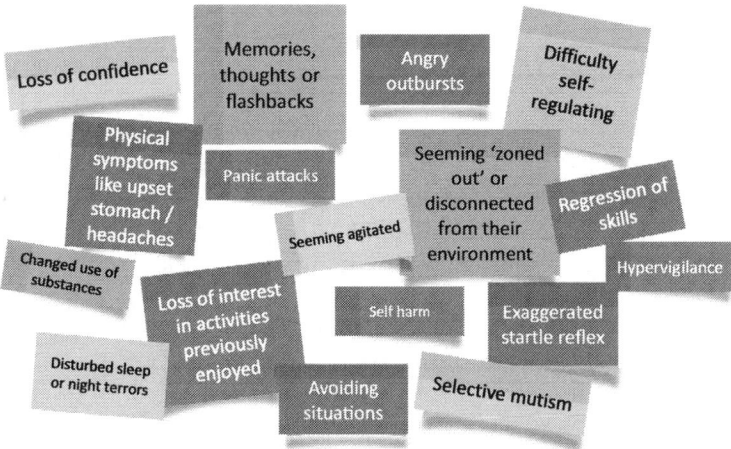

Figure 8.1 *Possible signs of trauma*

Clearly, all the signs above may have several different causes, but it is important for practitioners to be aware of the possibility of trauma, especially in cases where the child is known to have experienced distressing events or circumstances.

There are several ways in which practitioners can support a child or young person experiencing trauma. Perhaps the first and most important step is to be trauma informed or trauma aware, in other words to upskill yourself to understand more about trauma, how it manifests itself and how it impacts on children. This awareness can, in turn, help you to create an environment that is conducive to supporting a child experiencing trauma. In Figure 8.2 below are some further examples of how the practitioner can support a child experiencing trauma.

Figure 8.2 *Supporting a child with trauma*

Reflective questions ⑦

Loukia, aged nine, came to the UK in 2021 having experienced violent conflict in her village in South Sudan, including seeing her grandparents' house destroyed by fire. Loukia is doing well at school, has learned to speak fluent English and has many friends. However, following a loud, unidentified noise in the playground, Loukia takes shelter beneath a table and cannot be coaxed out. She is inconsolable and is rocking to and fro and kicking out at anyone who comes near her. The other children in her group are visibly shocked and upset.

» How is Loukia's trauma manifesting itself in this situation?

» As a practitioner, how could you support Loukia both immediately and in the longer term?

» How would you support the rest of the group?

Multiple adversity

There is no single definition of multiple adversity (Lea, 2011), although most definitions refer to a range of complex and interconnected issues and challenges that impact upon the individual or family. For children experiencing multiple adversity, these issues are likely to have far-reaching effects for the child in both the short term and the long term. Rankin and Regan (2004) identified the essence of multiple adversity as implying both '*breadth of need*' (more than one need with multiple needs interconnected) and '*depth of need*' (profound, severe, serious or intense needs). However, a possible third dimension relates to longevity of need (Prowle and Musgrave, 2018), relating to how long the adversity lasts. Some theorists attribute the causality to societal changes (such as demographic mobility, changes to structure of families, decline of religion, decline of authority). Others highlight that while there are a multiplicity of factors impacting on the family, the strongest impact is linked to economic factors (poverty). However, what is evident is that growing up in adversity is likely to have negative impacts for children. Many studies identify poor outcomes for children related to health (physical and emotional), education and, later, employment. What is more, these negative effects can continue to impact right into adulthood and beyond, and there have even been links drawn between childhood adversity and how long a person can expect to live. Figure 8.3 below highlights the different types of adversity that may combine to create multiple adversities which are hard for individuals to break out of or change.

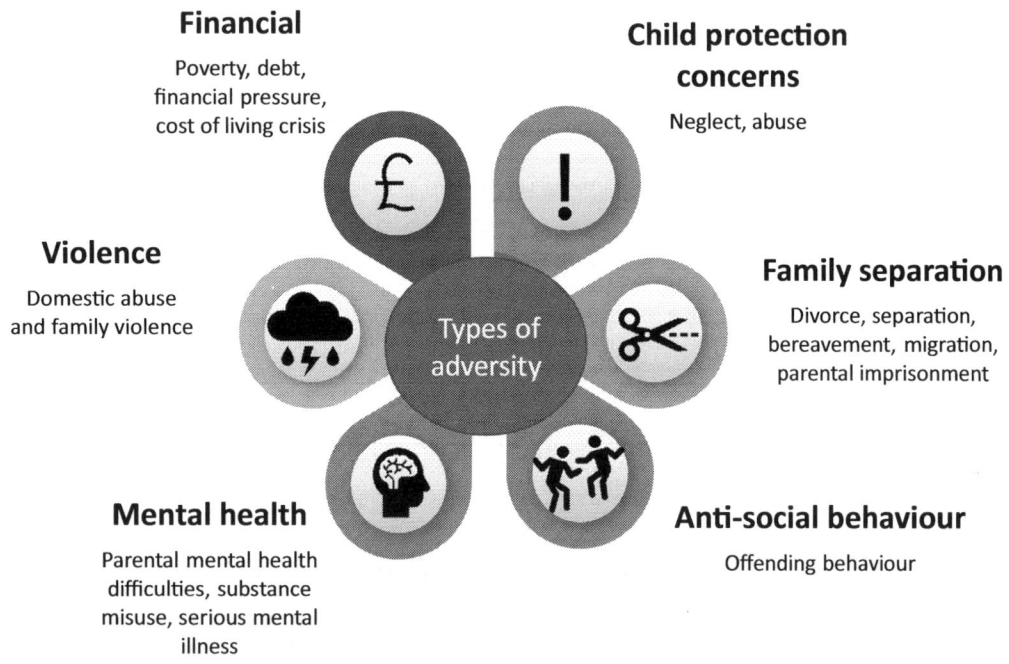

Figure 8.3 *Types of adversity*

When there are multiple issues facing a family, it is important for services to provide an integrated response that works holistically with the family's circumstances rather than address the needs in a piecemeal way that may lack coordination and result in duplication or needs being missed. Some services have found that having a keyworker or lead professional to coordinate the work and act as the main point of contact for the family can be particularly useful. It is also critical to ensure that the voice of each family member is heard and respected throughout the support given, and that the family is engaged with the support plan and feels ownership over it. It goes without saying that a strength-based approach can make all the difference to the quality of the support in these circumstances, where parents may be feeling overwhelmed and inadequate.

Child poverty

There is growing evidence from research that when a family is experiencing any adversity, poverty can act as an amplifier to that adversity, making their situation more difficult and intransigent. There are many ways of defining poverty, with many writers arguing that poverty is not simply economic but includes access to opportunities and resources. However, the most common method for calculating child poverty in the UK is to consider the relation of a family income to the UK median household income. Households with less than 60 per cent of the median income are considered to be living in relative poverty; in 2021 this equated to 3.9 million children in the UK living in poverty. However, the figures had decreased on the previous year as a result of coronavirus government support in the form of additional Universal Credit payments, and the numbers are projected to rise further. This is exacerbated by the current cost-of-living crisis, which is affecting families' abilities to provide for their children and resulting in choices between fuel or food, for example.

Charlotte Selvey works in a nursery where she often encounters families experiencing multiple adversities and hardships. In this short case study, she shows how, as a setting, they seek to support families without stigmatising those who may be struggling.

Reflective questions ⑦

» Charlotte recognises that adversity comes in many forms. How has the setting found ways to support families?

» It is crucial that such support is presented sensitively to families, with a focus on their own dignity, autonomy and choice. How do you think the nursery achieves this?

» Charlotte mentions the importance of non-judgemental support. How could you apply this in your own practice?

CASE STUDY 👝

Charlotte Selvey

Supporting children and families is at the forefront of what we do every day, making sure that every child in our care feels safe, welcome and included in all activities. As the nursery is in what is considered a low-income area, many families are experiencing multiple vulnerabilities, such as having SEN children and coping with the cost-of-living crisis. We take a holistic approach to working with the families and we try to overcome any barriers.

Hot meals are provided at a low cost and are sometimes free, as the nursery is run by a charity. We distribute food bank vouchers, but we also access Vitamin Angels (a charitable organisation who provide protein-rich foods, fresh fruit and vegetables to disadvantaged families) every week. Because of this initiative, the children have healthy meals and snacks, and the most disadvantaged families can access nutritional foods without additional financial pressure. As a result, children enjoy trying new foods and engage well in transitioning from processed foods to healthy snacks.

We have a clothes bank where families can swap old children's clothes for items more suited to their needs. We always have a good supply of coats and wellies for the winter months. Essential everyday items such as nappies and baby wipes are supplied at no extra cost to the families. Our aim is to work in partnership with families, so practitioners will always find an empty room where parents/carers needing a friendly ear can talk without fear of judgement.

Adverse Childhood Experiences

ACEs is an acronym for Adverse Childhood Experiences. In 1995, a large-scale American study (Felitti et al, 1998) explored the relationship between childhood exposure to ACEs and later risk factors in adulthood. The results were startling. Firstly, ACEs were found to be extremely common with half of the respondents reporting at least one adverse childhood experience in their past and 12.55 per cent of respondents reporting exposure to at least four ACEs. The study found that the more ACEs a person encountered in childhood, the greater their risk of developing social, emotional or physical issues. They concluded that exposure to toxic stress via ACEs in childhood caused physiological changes in the brain and body and that these in turn led to health behaviours in adulthood that were linked to negative outcomes. The findings of this study have been replicated in other countries including England (Bellis et al, 2014), thus strengthening the link between exposure to ACEs and later poor outcomes. The ACEs studies are not without critics. Firstly, many have criticised the 10 ACEs identified in the original study as not being inclusive of all adverse childhood experiences. The original ACEs are identified in Table 8.1 below.

Table 8.1 *Types of ACEs*

Abuse	Physical
	Emotional
	Sexual
Neglect	Physical
	Emotional
Household dysfunction	Mental illness
	Substance misuse
	Domestic abuse
	Divorce
	Incarcerated relative

Some have argued that there are some important omissions from this list. For example, bereavement through death of a parent or sibling does not feature at all in the list. Moreover, the list reflects mainly adversities that are common in Western nations, and does not include adversities such as natural disasters, war and conflict, or indeed hunger and absolute poverty. Moreover, exposures to ACEs should not be seen in a deterministic way as it is not predictive at an individual level (Kelly-Irving and Delpierre, 2019). Furthermore, although understanding ACEs provides practitioners with a useful conceptual framework, it is simply a starting point for attuned, trauma-informed work to engage the individual within their own support needs. This goes beyond quantifying adversities into '*overcoming adversity, whilst also potentially subtly changing, or even dramatically transforming, (aspects of) that adversity. Beating the odds whilst also changing the odds*' (Hart et al, 2014, p 7).

Strengths in adversity

Even when families are dealing with significant difficulties and challenges, there will always be strengths. However difficult things have got for a family, something has helped them to survive it thus far. The role of the practitioner is to help the child or family to identify their own strengths and then build on these further. Some examples of such strengths are found in Figure 8.4 below, although this is by no means an exhaustive list.

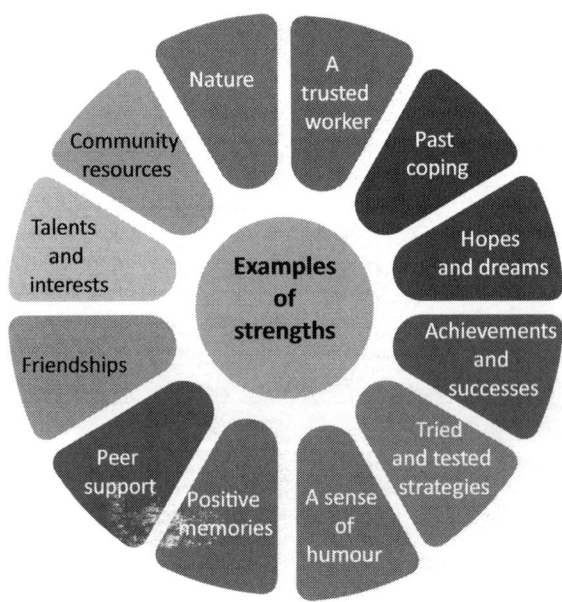

Figure 8.4 *Strengths in adversity*

All these strengths represent elements that can help the individual to feel supported, to build their self-esteem and to develop positive coping mechanisms. While in some cases work can be undertaken to reduce or remove the adversity, for example actions to combat poverty, in some cases, the adversity itself cannot be changed. An example of this might be a chronic illness. In this case, it is more about reframing the adversity, accepting what cannot be changed and supporting the individual to live a fuller life despite it. By shifting the way we think about adversity, we can find ways to live healthier and happier lives. Similarly, peer support can be helpful in showing how individuals coping with similar adversities have managed to thrive. Watching others succeed can lead to vicarious self-efficacy (Bandura, 1997).

Internal strengths and external assets

Helping an individual to embrace their own uniqueness and identify their own internal strengths is a useful way to support a child to become resilient in the face of adversity. Such internal strengths may include aspects of their personality, their sense of humour, their coping strategies and their emotional intelligence. Figure 8.5 shows some prompts for helping children identify their strengths.

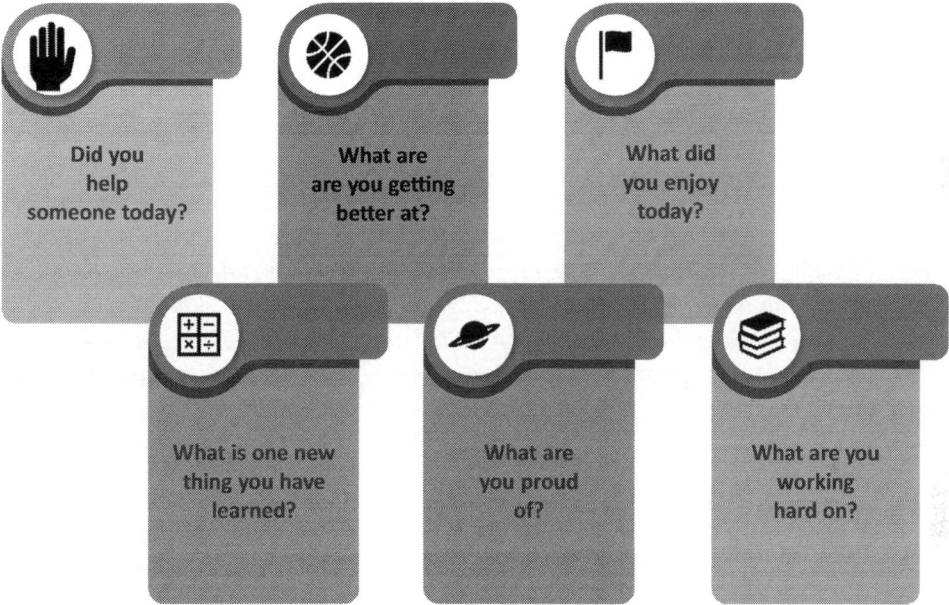

Figure 8.5 Helping children identify their strengths

However, there will also be strengths and assets in families, communities and the wider environment. These may include trusted individuals, friends, interests and hobbies or access to safe outdoor and indoor spaces. Getting to know the child will be the first step in beginning to map these strengths and assets which can all contribute to a child's resilience. It really is all about positive relationships.

In the case study below, Helen Coleman, the speech therapist mentioned in Chapter 7, talks about her work with children who are experiencing speech and language issues. In many cases, children may have been made to feel like they were failing, so Helen's approach is to focus strongly on strengths, celebrating small successes and praising every effort. In doing this, the children in her care can make great strides forward with their speech but also experience wider benefits of well-being.

CASE STUDY ⊖

Helen Coleman

When I assess a child's speech and language skills, the aim is to identify whether there is a difficulty or not. However, that's not the only thing I'm looking for. It's equally important to identify what the child is good at. For example, one little boy wasn't really vocalising much at all at the age of two and a half. However, he had great attention and listening skills and his physical co-ordination and visual memory were very good for his age. When I put his therapy plan together, I looked at how to use these strengths to support his expressive language development. I thought that signing would work well for him as he was able to copy signs well and the visual support would help him to remember the words.

Similarly, when assessing a 10 year-old, I discovered that she found putting long sentences together challenging and had word-finding and vocabulary difficulties. However, she had fantastic general knowledge on certain topics which interested her, and her comprehension skills were mostly age appropriate. So, I began her therapy by working on describing items and giving lots of information about them. Initially I chose items related to some of her favourite topics. Not only did this make it easier for her to describe them, but it also kept her engaged and positive about my sessions. This, in turn, meant that she wanted to come back and work with me, and being engaged and enthusiastic always facilitates learning.

Not only does focusing on strengths help the child to make faster progress, but it also supports their self-esteem. Often when I see children with unclear speech, they are very aware of the sounds that they find difficult to say and when I ask them to repeat a sound, they might say 'I can't say that one' and be reluctant to try. If I keep asking them to do it repeatedly, they are likely to become demoralised and reluctant to join in. Instead, I focus on asking them to say sounds I know that they can say for a while, so that they can experience success. Once they trust me and are engaged, I can usually persuade them to attempt the tricky sound, reassuring them that it's fine if they can't say it, I just want them to have a go. I make sure to praise their attempt even if it's not right; this child has learned to have the courage to try something difficult – what a great strength to take forward into future sessions and life in general!

Reflective questions ⑦

» Helen talks about balancing an appreciation of strengths with clear understanding of the child's developmental needs. Can you think of examples from your own practice where you have experienced a similar balancing act?

» Helen talks about encouraging children to '*have a go*' without fear of failure or judgement. Here she is encouraging a growth mindset (see pages 58–9). Why is this so important in enabling children to meet their potential?

» In your own context, how do you support children to develop a growth mindset?

Hope

Collins (2015) regards hope as an essential quality for practice, especially when working with those who are facing adversity. Hope helps to maintain practitioners' belief in the possibility of good outcomes and transformation, even when working with individuals in extremely challenging circumstances. Having hope can motivate a person to keep moving forward even when things are difficult. It can mean the difference between giving up and finding a way through a situation.

So, what do we mean by hope? It is important to recognise that there are different understandings of hope, ranging from psychological and cognitive constructions that focus on individual goals and aspirations, to humanistic constructions (Freire, 1994), which view hope within a context of injustice and inequality. In an article in *The Conversation* (2020), right in the middle of the Covid-19 pandemic, Professor Everett Worthington wrote,

> *Hope is not Pollyannaish optimism – the assumption that a positive outcome is inevitable. Instead, hope is a motivation to persevere toward a goal or end state, even if we're sceptical that a positive outcome is likely.*

In this context, hope can be an inspiration and motivation to keep going. Sælør et al (2015) highlight that self-esteem and self-belief are crucial for having hope. When these two things are in place, a person can recognise opportunities and can intentionally exercise optimism.

Strength-based practice, values and beliefs, and individual aspirations play an important role in allowing the practitioner to model a hopeful perspective. It is important to recognise, however, that hope cannot be rushed or manufactured. Instead, it involves a balance between acknowledging the real hurts, difficulties and challenges a person is facing, while simultaneously modelling hope for a positive future (Lemma, 2010).

Practitioners' ability to sustain hope can be adversely affected by stress and burnout in their own lives. Hence practitioners working with those in adversity need to also prioritise self-care.

Practitioner resilience and self-care

McCashen (2007) recognises the dangers of seeing practitioners as experts who may take over the responsibility for fixing problems, thereby denying individuals the opportunity to participate, identify their own problem-solving abilities and exercise dignity, autonomy and choice in the face of their adversity. Where practitioners can really help is through helping to remove barriers, challenge power structures, believe in the individual and in doing so support the individual's own abilities and solutions to emerge (Navarro, 2006). Practitioners can do this through using their own professional networks and knowledge base and signposting the individual to organisations and people that can help.

So much of this chapter has been about becoming an attuned, trauma-aware and compassionate practitioner. However, working in this way is emotionally demanding work and continued exposure to high levels of stress can, if left unchecked, result in burnout. Figure 8.6 below shows just some of the ways in which this may manifest itself.

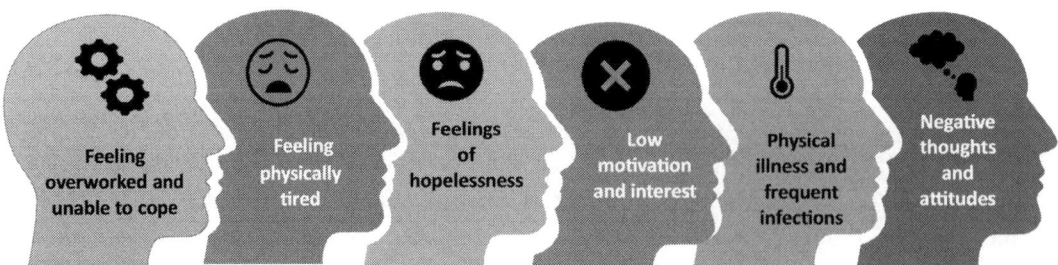

Figure 8.6 *Signs of burnout*

Burnout can be debilitating and hence it is important to have proactive strategies in place to avoid things getting to this stage. We need to recognise that working with individuals who are experiencing adversity demands a high degree of practitioner resilience. It is important to recognise in this context that resilience is not simply a fixed attribute, rather it is like a muscle that we need to exercise and look after. Our resilience fluctuates and is affected by many factors, both internal and external. Being prepared for and having strategies in place to manage stress, making time for our own interests and well-being and being able to access high-quality supervision are all ways of supporting our own resilience, and avoiding burnout. Chapter 12 explores the importance of practitioner self-care.

However, despite the evident demands of the role practitioners undertake it is important to recognise that such work is enormously rewarding and intrinsically satisfying. In the case study below, Gilda Davis, a university lecturer and paediatric nurse specialising in palliative care, gives us an insight into her work with families facing profound adversity in the form of a seriously ill child. Gilda's case study draws together many of the themes from this chapter, not least the enormous privilege of working to support families in adversity, learning from them and creating moments of beauty and meaningful connection.

CASE STUDY ☺

Gilda Davis

Most of my clinical career as a children's nurse has been spent working in children's hospices. Children who access hospices for both respite and palliative care have a range of diagnoses, with some accessing support only at the end of life and others regularly visiting the hospice for respite stays for many years (and everything in between).

The Together for Short Lives diagnostic categories clearly demonstrate this range.

Table 8.2 Adapted from Together for Short Lives (Chambers, 2018)

Category 1	Life-threatening conditions for which treatment may be available but may not succeed
Category 2	Conditions where premature death is inevitable, and treatment is aimed at prolonging life
Category 3	Progressive conditions where there are no treatment options
Category 4	Irreversible but non-progressive illnesses causing severe disability

In my years of working with children with life-limiting and life-threatening conditions, and their families, I never cease to be in awe of the resilience of both the child and their family, in their ability to keep going when life isn't going well. By this I do not mean to imply that the families of children with complex needs are all like Mary Poppins or the Waltons, they are not, they are us, with good days, not so good days and awful days; and a child/parent who needs extra support. It is these children who have taught me the most, and it is to them I am most indebted. They have taught me to appreciate each day. I am not talking about abdicating responsibility – we need to remember our commitments, the appointments, the things that structure and order our lives – but we also mustn't forget the small things, the pleasure in a smile, the sense of wonder when we smell, see, hear or touch something new to us.

I would like to share with you two incidents. Neither of them is particularly remarkable and either could easily have been missed.

Jay* was a nine year-old boy with cerebral palsy and an unnamed neuro-degenerative disorder. He had very minimal muscle control, verbal communication was limited to cries when he was distressed and smiles when he was happy. He required total care. Part of his disorder was severe spasmodic episodes that caused him distress and occurred several times daily.

Jay had come into the hospice for respite. On one day he was particularly distressed, and I had taken him into the multi-sensory room as he seemed to find the environment soothing. The play specialist set up one of the lights so that when his arm was lowered onto the switch pad (I was supporting his arm under his elbow), he could turn the light on. The switch was sensitive enough to respond to the light pressure caused by the weight of his hand. This was a new activity for Jay and having even a limited control over any of his movements was an unfamiliar sensation for him. The look of wonder and amazement on his face is a memory I carry with me. What to us may seem like such a small movement was, to Jay, a moment in which he climbed a mountain.

Mo* was a 15 year-old boy with duchene muscular dystrophy (DMD). The disease progression meant that he had some upper body movement but required support for all aspects of care. Mo received overnight ventilation and was finding that he was increasingly needing non-invasive ventilation for periods of time during the day too. He was aware of his condition and his prognosis.

→

Mo viewed himself as a singer who happened to have DMD. He loved to sing, but this was becoming more difficult for him to do. However, 'difficult' wasn't a word that Mo used, and we structured his daytime ventilation sessions around activities like singing. By this time, we could hear the difference in his voice, it had lost its strength and he was unable to hold notes that he had previously managed. In anticipation of the approaching day when Mo's singing voice would no longer be audible, the music therapist helped him 'cut' his own CD – Mo selected the songs he wanted to record himself singing, music copyrights were checked, backing music was arranged and the CD was recorded.

When we talk about quality of life (QoL) we often mean this in the macro sense, considering the individual in the context of society, in relation to the expectations of the individual and the expectations of the community around them. We tend not to think QoL in the micro, in the importance of the little. The actions of Jay managing a switch and Mo recording a CD may not have had an impact on the function of a community, but for those of us privileged to work with these children and with the many others like them, we are reminded of the importance of appreciating the small things.

So, go outside, smell the air, feel the rain on your face, appreciate the small positives and enjoy today.

* Names have been changed.

Reflective questions ⑦

»   Having read the case study, what are your immediate thoughts and reflections?

»   In what ways does Gilda build on the strengths of the children she is working with? And what benefits do the children gain from her approach?

»   Gilda talks of resilience as not being '*like Mary Poppins or the Waltons*'. What has she learned about resilience from the families she supports? What is your understanding of resilience?

»   Gilda recognises the importance of the little moments, in the here and now. How can this focus on the present support well-being for children, parents and practitioners?

Chapter summary ⑭

In this chapter, strength-based approaches have been explored in relation to working with children and families facing adversity. The importance of relationships has again been emphasised, recognising the need for practitioners to be attuned and responsive and to invest time in getting to know the child as an individual. Recognising the potential for childhood adversity to lead to negative long-term outcomes, we have nonetheless stressed that this is not written in stone and that sensitive intervention and support can make all the difference to individuals. Charlotte reminded us that there is lots that we can do to help alleviate the impacts of adversity. Meanwhile, Helen has shown us how we can work with children to spot their strengths and use these as superpowers to help them overcome difficulties and challenges. We have also considered how important it is to have hope, even in difficult circumstances, and as Gilda's case study showed, even in situations which are extremely challenging and desperately sad, we can come alongside families to help them experience moments of hope and happiness.

Further reading ✎

- Worthington, E (2020) How Hope Can Keep You Healthier and Happier. *The Conversation.* [online] Available at: https://theconversation.com/how-hope-can-keep-you-healthier-and-happier-132507 (accessed 4 August 2023).

  An interesting article on hope by Professor Everett Worthington.

- Webb, M, Bunting, L, Shannon, R, Kernaghan, D, Cunningham, C and Geraghty, T (2014) *Living with Adversity: A Qualitative Study of Families with Multiple and Complex Needs.* Barnardo's Northern Ireland. [online] Available at: www.ncb.org.uk/sites/default/files/uploads/files/08%2520briefing_paper_living_with_adversity_nov_2014.pdf (accessed 4 August 2023).

  A Barnardo's report reviewing the literature around supporting children with multiple adversity. This is an excellent resource, which encompasses the findings of many different research projects about multiple adversity. It does not need to be read in its entirety but is useful for dipping into.

- BoingBoing Website (nd) www.boingboing.org.uk (accessed 4 August 2023).

  This helpful website includes a myriad of resources to support practitioners in promoting children's resilience. There are thought-provoking articles, useful activities and up to date research. The website also includes a helpful resilience framework: Resilience Framework (Children and Young People) 2012 – adapted from Hart and Blincow with Thomas, 2007.

References ≋

Bandura, A (1997) *Self-efficacy: The Exercise of Control.* New York: Worth.

Bellis, M A, Hughes, K, Leckenby, N, Perkins, C and Lowey, H (2014) National Household Survey of Adverse Childhood Experiences and Their Relationship with Resilience to Health-Harming Behaviours in England. *BMC Medicine*, 12: 72.

Brown, E and Prowle, A (2022) Understanding and Responding to Adverse Childhood Experiences (ACEs) in Practice. In Richards, H and Malomo, M (eds) *Developing Your Professional Identity: A Guide for Working with Children and Families* (pp 97–112). St Albans: Critical Publishing.

Chambers, L (2018) *A Guide to Children's Palliative Care*, 4th ed. Bristol: Together for Short Lives.

Collins, S (2015) Hope and Helping in Social Work. *Practice: Social Work in Action*, 27(3): 197–213.

Felitti, V J, Anda, R F, Nordenberg, D, Williamson, D F, Spitz, A M, Edwards, V and Marks, J S (1998) Relationship of Childhood Abuse and Household Dysfunction to Many of the Leading Causes of Death in Adults: The Adverse Childhood Experiences (ACE) Study. *American Journal of Preventive Medicine*, 14(4): 245–58.

Freire, P (1994) Pedagogy of the Oppressed, 3rd ed. New York: Continuum Publishing Company.

Hart, A, and Blincow, D, with Thomas, H (2007) *Resilient Therapy: Working with Children and Families*. London: Brunner Routledge.

Hart, A, Gagnon, E, Aumann, K and Heaver, B (2014) *Uniting Resilience Research and Practice Development with Activism to Challenge Social Adversity*. Brighton: University of Brighton.

Kelly-Irving, M and Delpierre, C (2019) A Critique of the Adverse Childhood Experiences Framework in Epidemiology and Public Health Uses and Misuses. *Social Policy and Society*, 18(3): 445–56.

Lea, A (2011) *Families with Complex Needs: A Review of Current Literature*. Leicester: Leicestershire County Council.

Lemma, A (2010) The Power of Relationship: A Study of Key Working as an Intervention with Traumatised Young People. *Journal of Social Work Practice,* 24(4): 409–27.

McCashen, W (2007) *The Strengths Approach*. Bendigo: St Lukes Innovative Resources.

Navarro, Z (2006) In Search of a Cultural Interpretation of Power: The Contribution of Pierre Bourdieu. *Institute of Development Studies Bulletin*, 37(6): 11–22.

Prowle, A and Musgrave, J (2018) Utilising Strengths in Families and Communities to Support Children's Learning and Wellbeing. In Cheeseman, S and Walker, R (eds) *Pedagogies for Leading Practice: Thinking About Pedagogy in Early Childhood Education* (pp 125–41). London: Routledge.

Rankin, J and Regan, S (2004) Meeting Complex Needs in Social Care. *Housing, Care and Support*, 7(3): 4–8.

Sælør, K, Ness, O, Borg, M and Biong, S (2015) You Never Know What's Around the Next Corner: Exploring Practitioners' Hope Inspiring Practices. *Advances in Dual Diagnosis*, 8(3): 141–52.

Worthington, E (2020) How Hope Can Keep You Healthier and Happier. *The Conversation*. [online] Available at: https://theconversation.com/how-hope-can-keep-you-healthier-and-happier-132507 (accessed 19 June 2023).

9 Strength-based practice in safeguarding and child protection

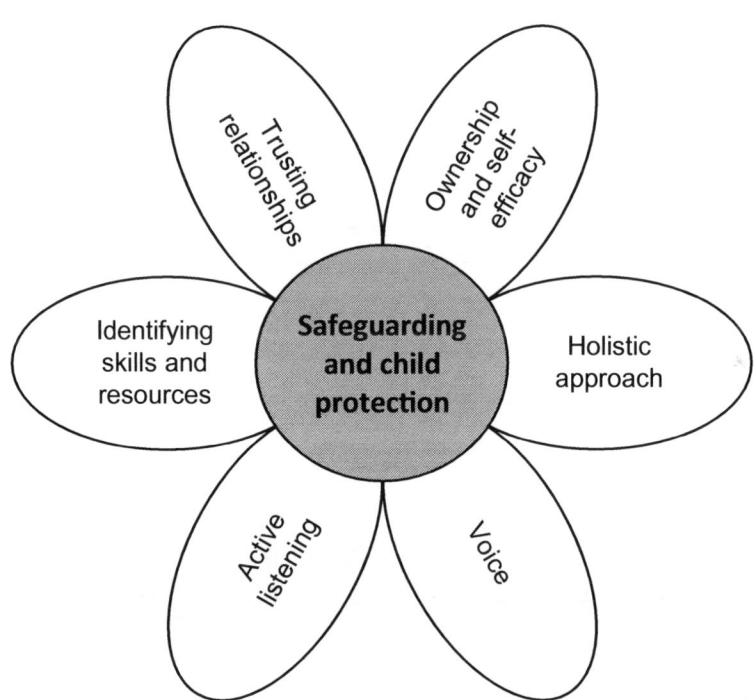

Chapter objectives ◎

This chapter:

- explores children's understanding of safety;
- discusses positive approaches to risk and challenge;
- outlines strength-based child protection approaches;
- illustrates ways of hearing the child's voice in child protection.

Introduction

This chapter encompasses a strength-based approach to both safeguarding and child protection, which are undertaken in two distinct parts, although there are noticeable overlaps. The chapter starts with a discussion on safeguarding with an emphasis on prevention and on building children's understanding of their safety, including risk and challenge in physical play. Two linked case studies from a day nursery that embraces risk-taking give a thought-provoking insight into their ethos. The role of the designated safeguarding lead is discussed, as the role is central to building a strength-based culture within the setting.

In terms of child protection, considering strengths in relation to this seems oxymoronic. However, increasingly, social workers are recognising the efficacy of this approach, especially in their work with foster carers, birth parents and children. This part of the chapter explores '*solution-focused*' and '*signs of safety*' approaches and includes a case study of a practitioner working with families where the children are deemed to be on the cusp of being taken into care. Intensive support, relationship building and a focus on strengths helps to turn the situation around, resulting in better than anticipated outcomes. Clearly, this will not be the case for all families, but there are often key strengths that can be identified and built upon to improve situations and relationships. Strength-based, child-focused safeguarding should place the child at the heart of all decisions, so ways of obtaining the child's voice are explored.

Safeguarding

Children's understanding of safety

A strength-based approach with children and families focuses on the positives and strengths of the child. The EYFS states that '*every child is a unique child, who is constantly learning and can be resilient, capable, confident and self-assured*' (DfE, 2021a, p 6). A strength-based approach to children's safeguarding means acknowledging these capabilities and working with children to keep themselves safe. Whether at home, at school, at sports and leisure clubs or out and about playing, this is an important skill which enables children to be independent. Demonstrating and talking to young children about ways of keeping safe, being consistent about safety rules and supervising children who are learning to manage risk are all important in empowering children (Figure 9.1).

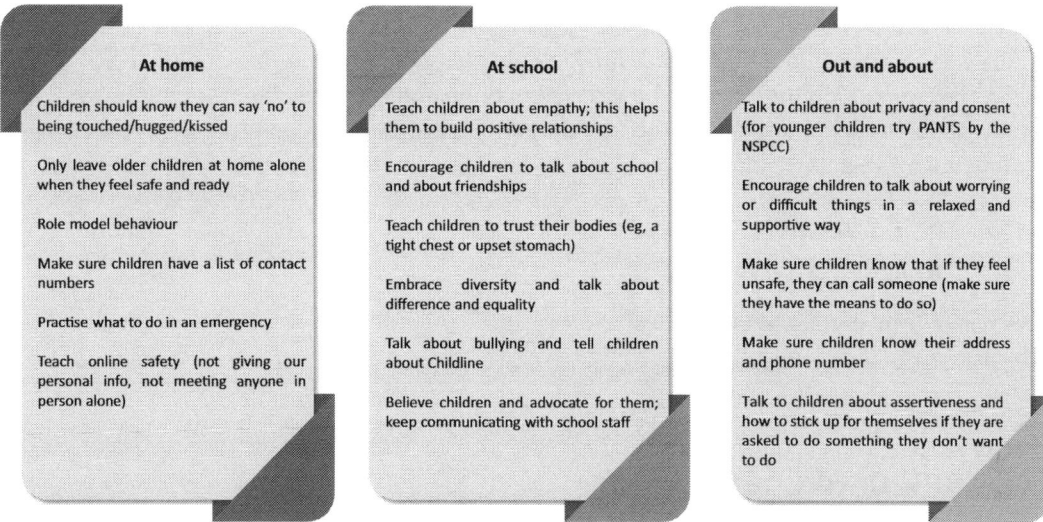

Figure 9.1 *Helping children to keep themselves safe*

Reflective questions ⑦

How might you respond to the following scenarios?

You are visiting relatives who have a four year-old daughter. Several people are there to celebrate a birthday. The child's parents say to her, '*go and give everyone a kiss, go on …*' and push her towards everyone in turn. The child looks very uncomfortable.

» What might you be thinking?

» What would you do/say?

» Why is it important?

You are looking after a friend's children for the evening. The nine year-old boy is playing on his iPad with his headphones on and you can hear him talking to people and laughing. He is hiding the screen from you and says he wants to play on the iPad in his bedroom on his own.

» What might you be thinking?

» What would you do/say?

» Why is it important?

→

You are at a girl guides' weekend away, helping to supervise a group of girls aged 10–14. You notice that one of the girls is becoming increasingly quieter and always seems to be alone. While it is fine for someone to prefer being on their own, it is very unusual for this particular girl.

» What might you be thinking?

» What would you do/say?

» Why is it important?

Risk and challenge

The balance of risk and challenge versus protection is a theme that is incorporated in other chapters within this book (see Chapters 3 and 4), but it is important to address it here when discussing safeguarding. Providing opportunities for risk and challenge in children's play is to '*encounter or create uncertainty, unpredictability, and potential hazards*' (Play Wales, 2023), which allows children to explore and learn about what their bodies can do. Safety is important, but removing all risk is unnecessary. Justice Munby once famously said, '*what good is it making someone safer if it merely makes them miserable?*' (Open Justice, 2022). Children and young people want and need to test their abilities, challenge themselves and problem-solve; this is an important element in the development of physical, social and emotional development. Young children are capable and confident learners (Berg, 2021); adults who trust this belief allow children to explore.

> *Young children are able to question, theorise, experiment, reason and solve problems during their play, yet inappropriate teacher mediation and fear for safety can limit children's curiosity to explore their learning spaces, develop well and be safe.*
>
> (Agbenyega, 2011, p 171)

From a safeguarding perspective, the balance between risk/challenge and hazards is crucial. Risk should be assessed, and safeguards put in place; no child should be put in danger of significant harm. This may mean that, if you are allowing children to engage in risky play, safeguards need to be put in place, see Figure 9.2.

Allow the child to decide when they are ready, and allow them to lead

Provide activities which gradually become more challenging

Teach skills (eg finding foot and hand holds when climbing trees)

Ask children if they feel safe

Don't react with panic; accidents happen when children panic

Figure 9.2 *Providing risky play*

The following linked case studies describe a setting which embraces risk and challenge.

CASE STUDY ⊕

Poppie Ephgrave: a unique approach to physical development

At Hitchin House Day Nursery, we place emphasis on physical development right from the start, enabling development of skills and encouraging confidence from our youngest babies right up to our strong and empowered pre-schoolers. Embedding physical development in everything they do is crucial and ensures that we retain the children's happiness and independence at the heart of our philosophy. Within our pedagogical approach we allow children to explore and develop their skills at their own pace and interest while always considering the unique child.

Practitioner input (or not!)

When staff first join our setting and hear about our unique approach to play involving risk taking, they often nod their heads in excitement and agreement. However, when observing the play taking place it is hard for them to refrain from hovering, holding out a hand or telling children they will 'catch them if they fall' while being unaware that their actions are in fact removing the sought-after elements of 'dangerous' play. The key element to our approach is for the practitioners to take a step back and allow the children to explore with independence. The role of the practitioner is to allow children to create their own risk assessments, to observe and to offer guidance through asking the children questions such as 'do you feel safe?' We begin this approach right from the start in our baby rooms, allowing children to climb and move rather than being removed from their play or taken down from play at height.

→

This allows children to become aware of the effects of their movements and to understand the world around them. This generates security and independence for the children and developing these transferable skills is something we need to encourage. We do not erase key learning opportunities by removing all elements of 'danger'.

The child

A crucial factor in enabling risky play is for us to trust the children's skills, calculations and independence. They are much more qualified than we give them credit for! Our practitioners have in-depth knowledge of the children in their care, which we achieve through secure partnerships with parents and having a loving pedagogy that supports children in secure attachments, developing relationships and feeling safe. At Hitchin House, we believe these are the foundations to supporting children in exploring play involving risk; when children feel safe and secure, this is when they learn.

The environment

Another key element to enabling children to take physical risk is by providing them with opportunities to do so. Our environment is designed around the child, ensuring that there are many opportunities for the children to express themselves physically and stretch their skills. This is essential to the development of the child; when we know what our bodies are capable of, we feel empowered and safe.

Within our environment, we use lots of indoor climbing equipment such as wobble boards for our babies and rainbow bridges. We use shelving and windowsills to place resources at height, which encourages standing and reaching from a young age. In our rooms for older children, we continue providing these opportunities through our climbing walls and Pikler frames. Within our garden space we do not focus on bringing the inside outside but instead appreciate that this is a different space and with this comes the opportunity to develop new skills. We do not have set climbing equipment but rather lots of crates, tyres and beams so the children can create endless structures. It is very common to see that our children have created a slide that is four tyres high, or a complex obstacle course. The team at the nursery ensure that the resources are open ended, so the children have flexibility in their play. This is also important as our practitioners can grow the environments to suit the groups of children they are working with at that time, further encouraging reflective practice.

We enable children to develop security in their fine motor skills, too, by providing the children with opportunities to pour their own drinks and use tools such as hammers in our workshop and knives to prepare their snack.

Our environment is designed so that the children and staff feel 'at home', which creates security and familiarity for the children in our care and a relaxing environment for the staff team. This is fundamental as it helps the children to feel comfortable developing their risk-based skills, so they are ready to take on new challenges. Fundamentally, having a focus on holistic development within our pedagogy and environment is what allows us to enable the children in our care to take ownership of their play.

CASE STUDY ⊖

Zoe Wright: is it risky play or is it just playing?

When staff start working in an environment that fully embraces child-led learning, there are invariably two things that we need to unpick from their practice: letting children fail and giving children space to work it out for themselves. We want them to 'step back and watch the magic'.

One of the most important things is for staff to recognise that each child has their own unique understanding of what is risky for them, so we teach staff to be present and available if needed, but not to intervene unless invited by the child. Alongside this, they need to learn cues that are not always obvious, so a deep knowledge of the child and their learning and play style is very much part of that process. We recognise that risky play is not always about gross physical learning – it can equally be putting a hand into the cold messy play tray or talking out loud to the doll.

Our team's practice development agenda is presented in two ways: modelling – with advice and support from colleagues while actively working with children; and direct active teaching opportunities. Our ethos around play and risk taking is introduced to staff from their first visit and followed up with induction and ongoing training. We invest heavily in staff development and provide internal and external training opportunities: 'lunch and learn' sessions, face to face, online, self-sought, directed training and supervision. These practice development opportunities may not specifically be about risky play, but our aim is to support staff to understand the deep concept of child-led learning:

child-led = child-managed = child being the agent of their own learning

Once the practitioner has embedded this theory and concept into their practice and is able to step back and let the play and adventure unfold before them, they can see the benefits and recognise that facilitating risky play is now, in reality, just playing.

When children trust adults to be part of their self-evaluated risk management plan, they feel more comfortable taking the risk that they are considering. Trust is built through the setting's ethos of a loving pedagogy and robust key worker system, with all staff members taking an active approach to support the child and colleagues, building on each child's feeling of security and safety. The nursery is designed environmentally to feel safe and give cues and links that will remind them of their safest space of all, 'home'. Staff are supported to ensure that all children are given the time they need to build confidence and relationships that will enable them to manage their feelings and adventures. The children know that wherever they go there is a safe adult to help them if they want it. Staff use the language of safety (not fear) when supporting the children in their play – for example, 'do you feel safe?' not 'be careful', 'would you like some help?' not 'let me show you'. Overall, supporting early years staff to enable risky play requires collaboration between staff, child, environment and ethos.

Reflective questions ⑦

In the two linked case studies above, Poppie and Zoe introduce their nursery's *'unique approach'* to risky play.

» Poppie's description of children playing in the outside play area is wonderful: can you identify how this approach would benefit the child in each area of learning (physical, intellectual, emotional and social)?

» Zoe talks about the importance of *'letting children fail'* and Poppie talks about new staff struggling with allowing children to take risks. What are the factors that might make practitioners nervous about fully embracing the ethos at Hitchin House?

» Reflect on changes that you could make in your own practice which would encourage children or young people to manage their own risks.

In Agbenyega's (2011, p 163) research into children's learning spaces, results showed that

Children felt safe in spaces that offered them the best opportunities for play. These are the spaces where they behaved well, laughed freely, reacted positively, and played without too much restriction and intimidation.

Agbenyega recommends play spaces that are free from hazards but that allow children to explore and be creative without adult intrusion. A risk assessment is a process of identifying and removing hazards and controlling risks and is a non-negotiable aspect of Health and Safety at Work Act (1974).

A strength-based approach to risk assessment will examine the balance of strength and risk, rather than simply eliminating all risk.

The designated safeguarding lead

Every organisation working with children must have a named person in charge of safeguarding and child protection within the setting, and this person is the designated safeguarding lead (DSL). This named person is responsible for ensuring that appropriate arrangements are in place for keeping children and young people safe and to promote the safety and welfare of children and young people at all times (NSPCC, 2019). The role of DSL was specified in The Children Act (DfE, 2021b) and some settings also have a deputy DSL (Figure 9.3). The DSL must have good knowledge of safeguarding guidance (eg DfE (2022) *Working Together to Safeguard Children*).

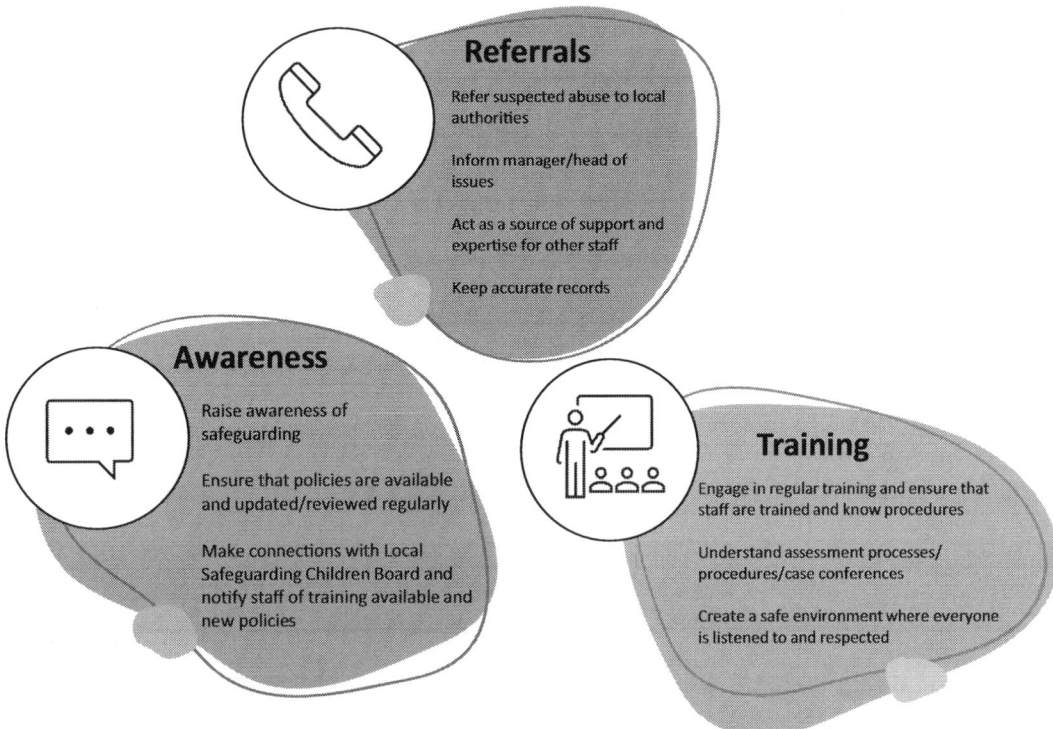

Figure 9.3 *Strength-based responsibilities of the designated safeguarding lead*

Being a DSL is an important responsibility, but it is also an opportunity to educate, to inspire and to make a real difference. Safeguarding is an extremely serious area of practice, and nothing is more important than protecting the children and young people we work with, but the responsibility can be an incredibly rewarding one.

Child protection

A strength-based approach to child protection is one that is rights-based and person-centred and has a clear ethical and values-based position. It embraces the core belief that '*even if people are experiencing problems, they have the strengths, skills, resources and capability to effect positive change in their lives if enabled and supported to do so*' (SCIE, 2018). The case study at the end of the chapter about the Supporting Change project illustrates this very well. Child protection is a complex subject; here, two of the strength-based approaches used today are examined.

Solution-focused practice

Solution-focused practice, as the name suggests, focuses on solutions and on finding positive ways forward, rather than focusing on the problem. The view taken is that children and young people are experts in their own lives and that they can use their own skills, strategies and ideas to move forwards in a positive direction. There are many books and guides with ideas for solution-focused activities. Table 9.1 gives some question examples that are relevant for working with children and young people: miracle questions, exception questions, scaling questions and coping questions.

Table 9.1 *Solution-focused activities*

Miracle questions	Imagine that after a normal day, you are in bed and going to sleep at the usual time. During the night, something happens – a miracle! When you wake up the following day, something exciting has happened. The problem that you had is no longer there. How would you feel? How would you behave? What will you do next?	The miracle questions help people to decide what they want their lives to be like and to explore new possibilities.
Exception questions	Tell me about times when you don't feel_____ Tell me about times you felt the happiest. When was the last time that you felt you had a better day? Was there ever a time when you felt happy? What was it about that day that made it a better day? Can you think of a time when the problem was not there?	Thinking about times when things weren't so bad helps us to realise that things aren't as awful as we think. If a young person says '*I'm always depressed*', for example, identifying occasional times when that wasn't the case can help them to feel more hopeful.
Scaling questions	On a scale of 1–10, where 10 is the happiest and most wonderful feeling you have ever felt, and one is the worst, most terrible agony, how do you feel today? Why is it a four and not a five? What could you do to get to a six? What do you need to be able to move higher?	These are questions that allow a person to rate their mood. They also allow people to evaluate their motivation to change. Scaling questions allow practitioners to add follow-up questions to create positivity and hope.

Table 9.1 (*Cont.*)

Coping questions 	How have you managed so far? What have you done to keep going? What is working? Who is your greatest support and what do they do to help? What stops you from giving up?	These types of questions can help young people to accept and appreciate their resilience. They are experts in their own lives, so helping them to see what works allows them to grow from a place of strength.

The Signs of Safety approach

The Signs of Safety approach originated in Australia in the 1990s. The aim of the approach, when used in a child protection situation, is to focus on the social worker building relationships with children and families in order to identify strengths, periods of safety and good care that can be built upon to stabilise the family situation (Signs of Safety, 2023). The approach is based on the overarching question in Figure 9.4.

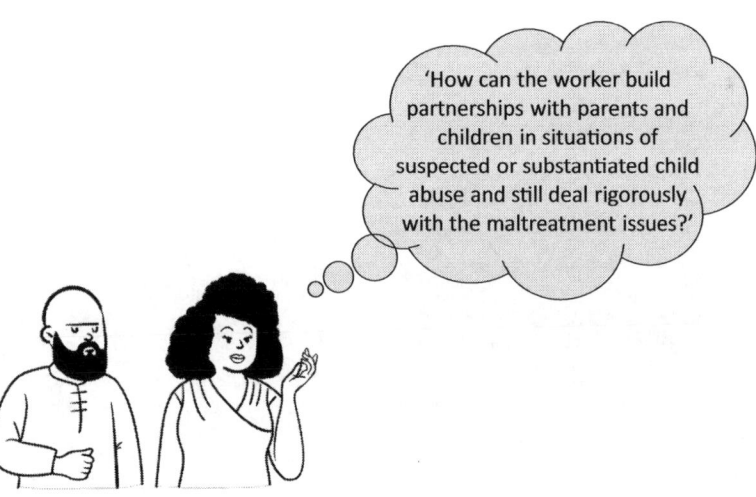

Figure 9.4 *Signs of Safety*

Listening to the voices of children and families is at the forefront of the Signs of Safety approach. The aim is that everyone involved – professionals (social workers, teachers, police, etc), children and families – have the same understanding of the strengths, concerns and goals in the child's life. Assessment of the safety of the child is then based on these three standpoints: concerns, strengths and goals.

Reflective questions ⑦

Think of a fictitious child who may be considered to be at risk, were they a real person (eg Bart Simpson, Kevin McCallister from *Home Alone*, Tracy Beaker, Snow White). It is much easier to do this objectively than it is with a real child who is known to you.

»   Consider the strengths, concerns and goals for this child and identify these on a diagram with three sections as in Figure 9.5.

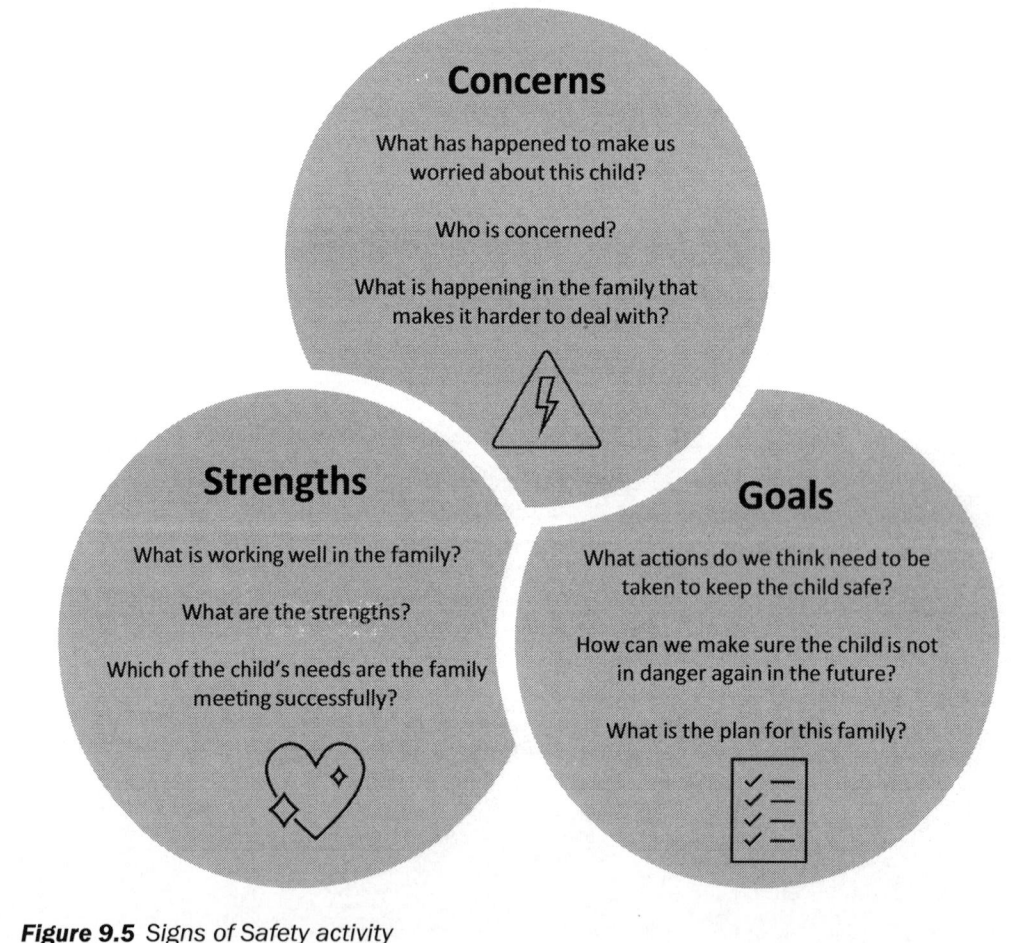

Concerns

What has happened to make us worried about this child?

Who is concerned?

What is happening in the family that makes it harder to deal with?

Strengths

What is working well in the family?

What are the strengths?

Which of the child's needs are the family meeting successfully?

Goals

What actions do we think need to be taken to keep the child safe?

How can we make sure the child is not in danger again in the future?

What is the plan for this family?

Figure 9.5 *Signs of Safety activity*

Both of the approaches detailed above – solution-focused practice and the Signs of Safety approach – have the identification of strengths at their core. The following case study illustrates how a social services child protection team works with families to try and prevent children from going into the care system.

CASE STUDY ⊕

Michelle: supporting change

The Supporting Change team works with children, young people and their families where there is a real risk of them coming into care. They might be going through the court process, or they might have had several periods of registration on the child protection register; it would be at any point where there's an identified need, where there is a real escalating concern. Often, the families that the team works with have already gone through various support services. They may have gone through 'families first', our preventative service, and may have been managed on a child protection plan or a care and support plan, but those things haven't worked. They may be working with other service providers like domestic abuse and drug abuse services, but there hasn't been any real identified change within those services. At that point, referrals are made to the Supporting Change team, essentially with the remit to try and prevent those children from entering care. We know that care is very costly and it's not the best outcome for children in most cases. So, the team will work on a very intensive basis with those families, generally for around 12 weeks, but there is a lot of flexibility. We recognise that people may have, for want of a better term, poor parenting that needs some level of intervention. It's not often going to be resolved within a 12-week intensive programme but, nonetheless, that's what the team try to deliver on most occasions.

And so, the support workers will visit families for as often as needed over that period, which might be a minimum of twice a week, but could, if necessary, be five times a week; very recently one of the workers was going in twice a day for the first two weeks, so it's a very, very intensive service. The aim is to look at what the priority risks are within the family, because the team are specifically allocated to the families that they work with. There's always an allocated social worker working alongside the support workers, because generally they are either children who are looked after who we are trying to perhaps bring out of care, or they are children who are being managed on child protection plan. They will always have an allocated social worker to their case and then the Supporting Change team go in and deliver very intensive parental support to try and effect positive change. There's a short waiting list, which is unfortunate, but that is often the case because of the level of need for the service at the moment. I think it's probably fair to say it is quite a successful service and it comes in at a point where other services haven't worked.

For some of the families, the team recognise that, sometimes, a positive outcome for children and young people might actually be that the children need to be removed from their parents, that they need to be placed with other family or in foster care, because sometimes that is in the best interest of the children. It's always about balancing trying to keep children out of care but looking at what is in the best interest of children long term. Sometimes, the positive outcome might not necessarily be for them to be with their families.

As always, the strength-based approach is fully embedded within the Supporting Change team. I think it's fair to say when the team started back in 2017, we were a bit like the new kids on the block, coming into a local authority which was quite risk averse in their practice. It was very much about looking at what the risks are in the family and removing the children

→

into local authority care, and that was the end of it. I don't think there was much in the way of reviewing those care plans, so long-term foster care meant that children would be there until they were 18 years old. There wasn't any thought about trying to rehabilitate these children back into the family in the future. It was just a case of these are risks, we can't manage them, we'll take it into court, we'll have a care plan of long-term fostering. That would be the end of it until they left care. Then the Supporting Change team started and came in talking about strength-based practice and building on the strengths within families to try and bring about positive change. Initially I think that came as a massive shock to the social workers who were wondering what we were talking about, and we faced massive opposition in respect to that. We were often butting heads, saying 'yes, we know that there are risks, we need to manage those risks, but we will look at the strengths in the family, we'll build on those strengths, and we'll utilise those strengths to mitigate the risk that you're concerned about'. It wasn't an easy process for the first few months, but what the teams quickly saw were the positive outcomes from the Supporting Change team, and they saw that there were opportunities to do something different and not just remove these children straight into local authority care. So as the team started to demonstrate a couple of successes, we were able to bring the social workers and the support workers on board and then at that point we were inundated with requests for the Supporting Change team.

Reflective questions ⑦

»   What do you think makes the Supporting Change service so effective?

»   Reflect on the tensions between strengths and risks in relation to safeguarding. How can risks be managed while remaining strength-based?

»   Which aspects of this approach might you be able to adopt in your own practice?

Child voice in child protection

Any examination of serious case reviews will highlight the importance of listening to children, and this is regularly one of the recommendations for practice following a child abuse case. An Ofsted report (2011), which examined 67 serious case reviews, provided five main lessons to be learned regarding the voice of the child.

1.   The child was not seen frequently enough by the professionals involved, or was not asked about their views and feelings.

2.   *Agencies did not listen to adults who tried to speak on behalf of the child and who had important information to contribute.*

3.   *Parents and carers prevented professionals from seeing and listening to the child.*

4.   *Practitioners focused too much on the needs of the parents, especially on vulnerable parents, and overlooked the implications for the child.*

5.   *Agencies did not interpret their findings well enough to protect the child.*

(Ofsted, 2011, p 4)

Another piece of research, by Allnock and Miller (2013), heard the stories of young people who had been abused and identified some worrying examples of children who had disclosed or tried to disclose abuse but had not been heard. The report emphasised that young people who wanted to tell someone about the abuse they were suffering tried to speak up, but no one picked up on signs or noticed that they were struggling. Other children had told some-one, but their disclosure was ignored. With hindsight, it is easy to wonder how professionals could have been oblivious to what was happening. However, sometimes the thought of a child being abused is too terrible for professionals to bear, so

> *we readily grasp at shreds of evidence, a smile from the child or an apparently plausible explanation for an injury or bruising, to defend us from thinking about other disturbing aspects of information that contradict this, but which we cannot bear to imagine.*
>
> (Butler, 2015, p 20)

This is a way of protecting ourselves from the harsh reality of child abuse. Child protection work is emotionally challenging, but we must have the strength to act on behalf of children in order to protect them. In a case study in our first book (Prowle and Hodgkins, 2020, p 33), social worker Sophie talks about '*bearing the unbearable*'. Sophie talks about building up her emotional resilience over time through experience. Because of this, she believes that stress and burnout are not inevitable in her challenging role.

Race and Frost (2021, p 8) explain why the child's voice is so crucial in child protection work:

> *Listening to the voices of children promotes empowerment and enables their contribution to be valued so that children can be acknowledged as social actors and co-creators of a more effective and child-centred safeguarding system.*

Listening to the voice of the child does not always mean literally listening to the child speaking. Listening to a baby or a non-verbal child can be more of a challenge but is even more important, if we are to give all children a voice. Figure 9.6 provides some ideas of other ways of gaining children's voices.

Exploring the lived experience of children caught up in child protection processes increases understanding of their perspectives and insights.

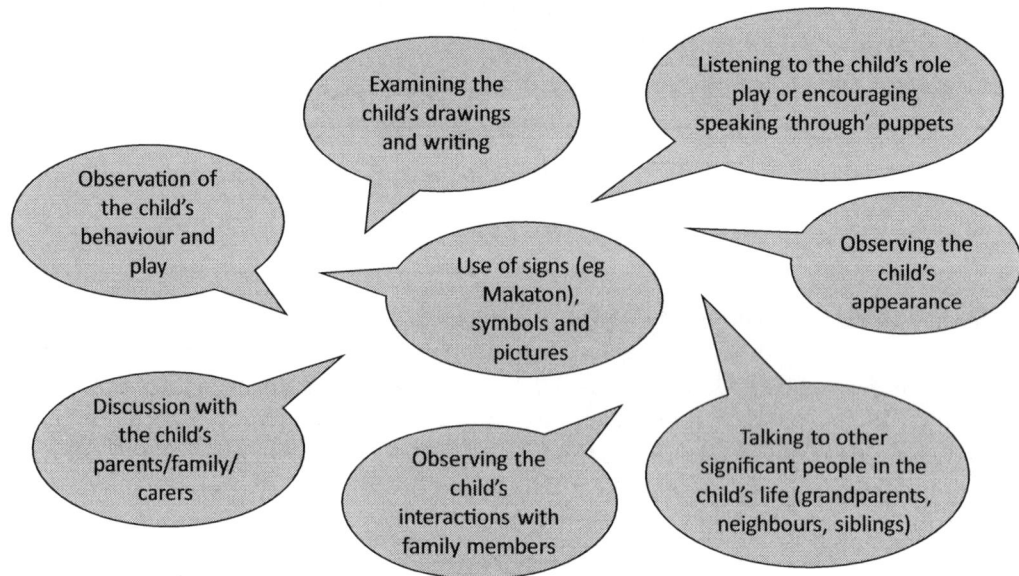

Figure 9.6 *Gaining the voice of the child*

Chapter summary

In this chapter, safeguarding has been explored with a focus on children's understanding of safety. Risk and challenge have been discussed and a case study of a unique approach to physical play at a day nursery illustrates the importance of encouraging children to explore their own capabilities. Risk assessments are just one of the responsibilities of the designated safeguarding lead, a role which is an important and accountable one, but which can also be rewarding if seen as a strength-based position.

In the second half of the chapter, a strength-based approach to child protection has highlighted some examples of strategies which allow for finding positive ways forward for children and young people who are struggling. Solution-focused activities and Signs of Safety are two strategies that can help children and families find a way through difficulties and identify positive areas of change. A case study about the work of a Supporting Change team shows how powerful targeted support can be in preventing children from entering the care system, and in returning children in care to their family home. The chapter concludes with the importance of the child's voice. All too often, children's voices are not heard, and this has led to some terrible child protection failings. Positive ways of enabling the voice of the child to be heard give us the opportunity to step in when necessary and make a real difference in children's lives.

Further reading ⟫

- Prowle, A and Hodgkins, A (2020) Making a Difference with Children and Families. London: Red Globe Books, Bloomsbury.

  Chapter 3: *The resilient and self-efficacious practitioner* includes content that relates to this chapter. It includes the case study from Sophie, which is mentioned earlier, and it discusses ways of developing resilience.

  Chapter 4: *The practitioner as advocate* discusses ways of advocating for children and standing up for their rights.

- Signs of Safety (2023) *What is Signs of Safety?* [online] Available at: www.signsofsafety.net/what-is-sofs/ (accessed 19 June 2023).

  Read more about this useful approach to strength-based practice in child protection.

- NSPCC (2015) *Solution-focused Practice Toolkit.* [online] Available at: https://learning.nspcc.org.uk/research-resources/2015/solution-focused-practice-toolkit (accessed 19 June 2023).

  This toolkit for people working with children outlines the solution-focused approach and also provides ideas and practical activities to use with children.

References ⩣

Agbenyega, J (2011) Researching Children's Understanding of Safety: An Auto-driven Visual Approach. *Contemporary Issues in Early Childhood*, 12(2): 163–74.

Allnock, D and Miller, P (2013) *No One Noticed, No One Heard: A Study of Disclosures of Childhood Abuse.* NSPCC. [online] Available at: https://learning.nspcc.org.uk/meia/1052/no-one-noticed-no-one-heard-report.pdf (accessed 19 June 2023).

Berg, V (2021) *The Reggio Emilia Approach to Early Years Education.* [online] Available at: www.daynurseries.co.uk/advice/the-reggio-emilia-approach-to-early-years-education (accessed 19 June 2023).

Butler, G (2015) *Observing Children and Families – Beyond the Surface.* Northwich: Critical Publishing.

Department for Education (DfE) (2021a) *Early Years Foundation Stage (EYFS) Statutory Framework.* [online] Available at: www.gov.uk/government/publications/early-years-foundation-stage-framework–2 (accessed 19 June 2023).

Department for Education (DfE) (2021b) *The Children Act 1989 Guidance and Regulations. Volume 2: Care Planning, Placement and Case Review.* [online] Available at: https://assets.publishing.service.gov.uk/government/uploads/system/uploads/attachment_data/file/1000549/The_Children_Act_1989_guidance_and_regulations_Volume_2_care_planning__placement_and_case_review.pdf (accessed 19 June 2023).

Health and Safety at Work Act (1974). [online] Available at: www.hse.gov.uk/legislation/hswa.htm (accessed 19 June 2023).

NSPCC (2019) *Role Description for Nominated Chid Protection Lead*. [online] Available at: https://learning.nspcc.org.uk/media/1587/role-description-for-child-protection-lead.pdf (accessed 19 June 2023).

Ofsted (2011) *The Voice of the Child: Learning Lessons from Serious Case Reviews*. [online] Available at: https://assets.publishing.service.gov.uk/government/uploads/system/uploads/attachment_data/file/526981/The_voice_of_the_child.pdf (accessed 21 July 2023).

Open Justice (2022) *"What Good is it Making Someone Safer if it Merely Makes them Miserable?" A Contested Hearing and Delayed Trial of Living at Home'*. [online] Available at: https://openjusticecourtofprotection.org/2022/06/03/what-good-is-it-making-someone-safer-if-it-merely-makes-them-miserable-a-contested-hearing-and-delayed-trial-of-living-at-home/ (accessed 4 August 2023).

Play Wales (2023) *Play and Risk*. [online] Available at: https://play.wales/play/play-and-risk/ (accessed 30 June 2023).

Prowle, A and Hodgkins, A (2020) *Making a Difference with Children and Families*. London: Red Globe Books, Bloomsbury.

Race, T and Frost, N (2021) Hearing the Voice of the Child in Safeguarding Processes: Exploring Different Voices and Competing Narratives. *Child Abuse Review*, 31(6): 1–9.

Signs of Safety (2023) *What is Signs of Safety?* [online] Available at: www.signsofsafety.net/what-is-sofs/ (accessed 19 June 2023).

Social Care Institute for Excellence (SCIE) (2018) *Strengths-based Social Care for Children, Young People and their Families*. [online] Available at: www.scie.org.uk/strengths-based-approaches/young-people (accessed 19 June 2023).

10 Celebrating diversity as a strength

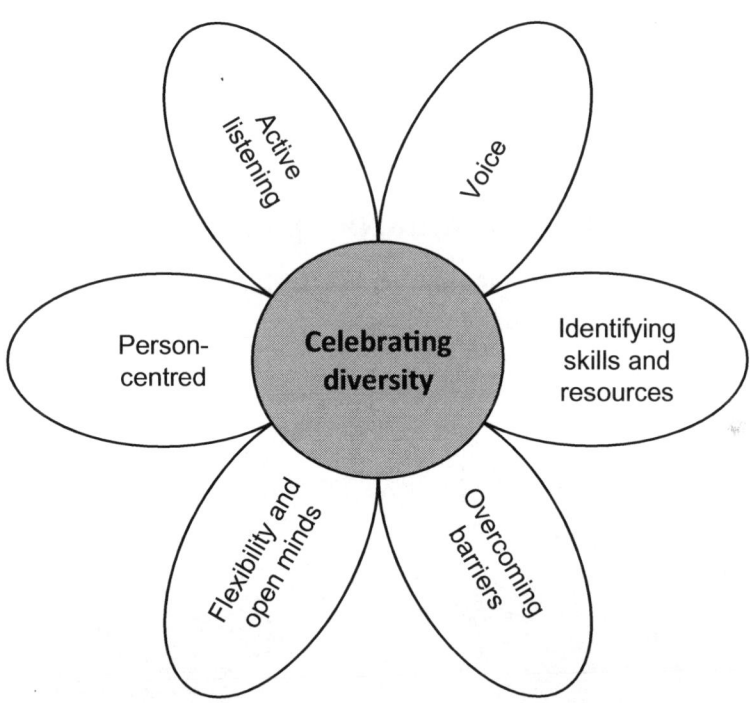

Chapter objectives

This chapter:

- discusses diversity and anti-discriminatory practice;
- stresses the importance of celebrating diversity with children and families;
- identifies ways of celebrating diversity within settings, without tokenism;
- outlines the benefits of diverse teams/staffing.

Introduction

By law, all education, care and health settings must adhere to anti-discriminatory practice guidance and accept diversity. Ofsted (2023) make it clear that schools are expected to create a culture where discrimination is not tolerated. In the health and social care sector, the Care Quality Commission also have regulations against unlawful discrimination (2013, p 10). Our view is that this is not enough, and that the emphasis should be on actively celebrating diversity as a strength. Children and young people benefit from experiencing diversity within their communities and, the more they understand, the more they are likely to treat everyone equally and make a contribution to a diverse society.

This chapter warns against tokenism and stereotyping and instead advocates a positive strength-based approach to difference. People's unique characteristics are seen as positive attributes, yet it is important to learn about what we have in common too.

Diversity and anti-discriminatory practice

Diversity, in simple terms, means difference or variety. There is a multitude of diversity types, some of which are outlined in Figure 10.1 below.

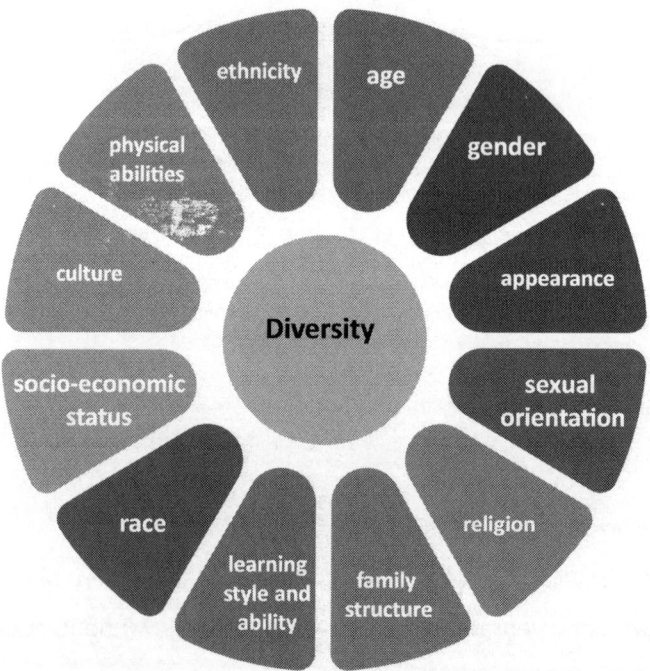

Figure 10.1 Some types of diversity

The approach to diversity taken in this chapter is one that aligns with Thompson's (2021) '*diversity approach*', which encompasses two main themes.

1.   Diversity is a positive and valuable characteristic – it should be valued and affirmed and treated as '*a source of learning, variety, stimulation and interest*' (p 14).

2.   Any form of discrimination is to be challenged – the approach goes much further than just ensuring equality of opportunity and following anti-discrimination legislation.

The first theme above will be discussed later in the chapter. The second theme, discrimination, can be defined as the unfair treatment of a category of person and it threatens the celebration of diversity. The Equality Act (2010) is a single Act which protects people against discrimination on the grounds of race, gender, age, disability, religion, belief or sexual orientation. However, as seen in Figure 10.1, there are many more areas of diversity, some of which are hidden. Stereotypes and prejudice are precursors to discrimination; when we make an assumption about someone, this leads to a belief and that belief establishes actions (see Figure 10.2).

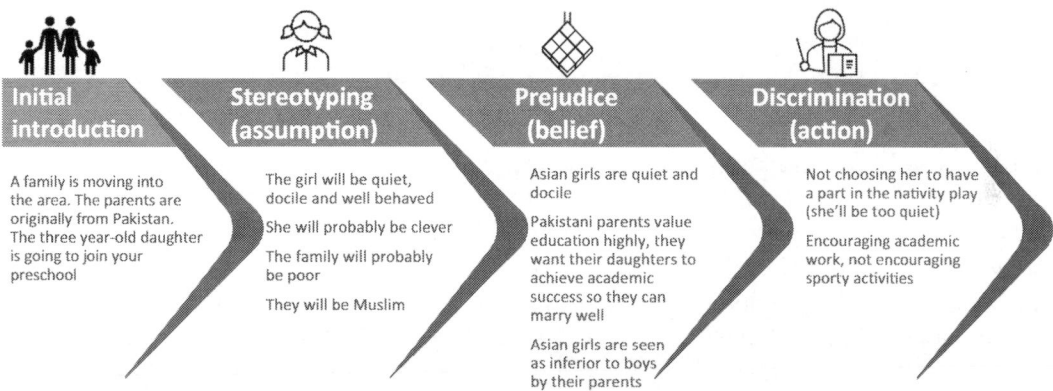

Figure 10.2 *Stereotypes, prejudice and discrimination*

In Figure 10.2 the child's opportunities may be diminished. By making assumptions about the child's culture, we would be denying the child a full range of possibilities. One thing about this child is her racial origin, but there are lots of other things that define the child. She may also grow up to be a gifted musician, a fast runner or a passionate speaker, so she must be offered all opportunities, as all children should. Some characteristics of people can be seen (eg skin colour, physical disability) but others are invisible. When working with others, it is important to get to know the child or family member well in order to identify invisible forms of diversity, so that the person's needs are met effectively; '*adults supporting the child must acknowledge and identify all the needs of the children considering visible and invisible diversity rather than homogenising the child's needs under the visible category*' (Devarakonda, 2020, p 17). Examples of invisible diversity are culture, religious or spiritual beliefs and education level. Here is an example of the latter from practice.

CASE STUDY ☝

Anisha: making assumptions

When I was a young teaching assistant working in a primary school, I was helping out with sports day. Because of a tightening of health and safety regulations by the LEA, we were told that we had to get parents to read and sign a disclosure form before they could run in the parents' race. I dutifully took my forms to the parents who had entered the race and each one read the form and signed. When I got to one of the dads and showed him the form, he looked really angry, and I had no idea why. He glared at me, then walked off and he didn't join in the race. I was completely confused about what could have upset him until someone let me know that the man concerned was unable to read or write. I had inadvertently made him feel stupid and angry and it was easier for him to walk off than to explain. I felt really bad about this, but I haven't made that assumption again since; I have always explained forms verbally.

In cases of blatant discrimination against another person, most people would be appalled and most people would want to do something about it. For example, if someone you worked with on a social work team expressed a strong belief that homosexual couples should not be allowed to adopt children, this would be completely unacceptable. It would be challenged and may well lead to disciplinary action. However, there are many ways of show   reotypical thinking and prejudicial beliefs which go unnoticed and unchallenged.

Reflective questions ⑦

» Table 10.1 provides some examples of challenging discriminatory language. What is the problem with these examples and how should (or would) you challenge them in a positive way? Complete the table with your answers.

Table 10.1 *Challenging discriminatory language*

Example	Why is this unacceptable? What damage could this do?	How might you challenge it?
You overhear a boy saying to another boy '*ha, ha, you throw like a girl!*'		
You hear a teacher saying to the class '*I need two big strong boys to help me carry these books*'		
A local school is collecting money for '*the homeless*'		
You overhear a colleague talking about a '*coloured family*'		
Someone you work with describes a child as being '*wheelchair-bound*'		
The local community centre organises a '*mother and baby group*'		
You overhear a father joking to his young son, '*you can't wear that, it's gay!*'		

Celebrating diversity

A positive attitude towards diversity is about '*recognising and celebrating differences between people and groups and treating those differences with respect*' (Prowle and Hodgkins, 2020, p 145). A diverse society like the UK today offers a huge range of opportunities and each person we work with brings their own unique experiences, strengths and ideas to enrich the lives of others (Kampen, 2020). Diversity should be embraced as a strength, a valuable characteristic (Thompson, 2021), a learning opportunity and a chance to influence people's views of difference in a positive way (Figure 10.3).

Figure 10.3 *Practical ways of embracing diversity*

Culture

A good example of celebrating diversity is described in an article by school librarian, Rosalind Jensen (2020), who organises '*cultural fortnights*' at her middle school. The examples that she describes are intended to educate and to promote respect and understanding of diversity. Jensen's cultural fortnight based on Arabic countries included:

- making links with a school in Gaza, with help from the British Council;

- an information exchange with the Gaza school, focused on the children's first names, favourite foods and favourite authors;

- a display of natural beauty in the area – migrating turtles in Oman, the Baatara gorge waterfall in Lebanon;

- craft activity based on Arabic script;

- teaching children some basic phrases in Arabic;

- reading books about the Islamic empire;

- trying out card games from Daradam;

- learning steps from a rural wedding dance;

- food tasting – sweet desserts.

The range of activities planned by Ms Jensen is wonderful, giving the children a real flavour of all aspects of the culture and what it is like for children who live there. Events such as this can also go some way to redressing the balance of news that children may hear about the area, which often focus on war and extremism. Planning such events is very time-consuming and can be expensive to organise, but they are wonderful learning experiences for the children. Visits to museums and exhibitions are useful ways of introducing children to other cultures, and these are often free of charge to visit. Sometimes, the best resources available are those within your own community. Families can be asked to suggest music from their culture, or films for an international movie night. Children could learn a new game or sport, or some words in another language, and they could listen to traditional stories from other cultures.

LGBTQIA+

A survey commissioned by Stonewall, the lesbian, gay, bisexual and transgender rights charity, in 2014 found that 45 per cent of UK teachers said that pupils in their school had experienced homophobic bullying or name-calling. This is an issue that does not just affect older children; according to Stonewall (2022a, p 8), '*53 per cent of lesbian, gay and bi (LGB) people said they knew they were LGB by the age of 13*', and '*58 per cent of trans young people knew they were trans by the age of 13*'. Stonewall (2022a) have produced guidance for primary schools to prevent and tackle homophobic, biphobic and transphobic bullying in primary schools. The approach has five steps (see Figure 10.4).

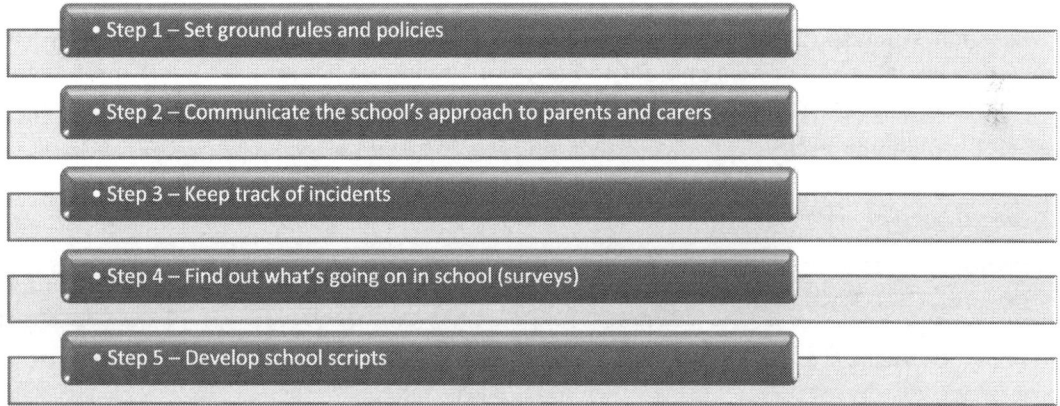

Figure 10.4 *Tackling homophobic bullying in primary schools (adapted from Stonewall, 2022a)*

One of the most important things we can do to change attitudes is to challenge inappropriate language when we hear it from children and families. According to Stonewall (2022b, p 1), '*more than half of secondary school staff and two in five primary school staff admit to not always intervening when they hear homophobic language being used*', due to a lack of confidence or support to do so (consider your responses to the activity in Table 10.1 earlier in the chapter). Homophobic language, just like racist or sexist language, lowers self-esteem and damages people. Children should be able to be themselves and know that who they are is accepted and celebrated. Empowering children and young people by setting up equality groups and children's councils and encouraging children and young people themselves to set up peer mentoring schemes or playground buddies are all positive ways of enabling children to be themselves.

Race and nationality

Today, race is beginning to be understood as a social construct without biological meaning. Society makes assumptions about genetic differences between different races, which then have repercussions and can fuel racism (Gannon, 2016). Any type of racism, treating people differently (often as inferior), is wrong and should be challenged. It is often assumed that young children do not process race, yet research by Sullivan, Wilson and Apfelbaum (2020) found that this is incorrect and advised that we should have conversations with, and educate them about, race at an early age. There is evidence that babies as young as nine months use race to categorise faces (Sullivan, Wilson and Apfelbaum, 2020, p 395), and that by the age of three they associate particular racial groups with positive or negative traits.

In a strength-based approach, race should be seen as a reason for pride. It is important for children to honour their roots, the language, values, beliefs and traditions that have been passed down to them from those they love. Approaches where adults say things like '*skin colour doesn't matter*', or '*we're all the same on the inside*' may not be appropriate. Sullivan, Wilson and Apfelbaum (2020) say that this '*colourblind strategy*' is a missed opportunity for constructive education about race.

White and Wanless (2019) developed a programme in the United States, entitled PRIDE (Positive Racial Identity Development in Early Education), designed to support the healthy development of racial identity in black children. Table 10.2 below outlines some examples for young children, based on their developmental framework.

Table 10.2 *Learning about race (based on a programme by White and Wanless, 2019)*

Children often learn that …	Adults must teach them that …
Being from a particular race is sometimes not safe.	Racial discrimination is wrong and will be challenged by the adults who care for them.
The race of the majority is the best; minority races are not as good.	All aspects of a child's identity are valued, including race, gender, ethnicity and ability.
Talking about and playing out feelings about race is unacceptable.	Adults caring for the child will respond in a developmentally appropriate way and will help children to understand their feelings through play.
Racial/ethnic stereotyping is uncomfortable and may not be discussed or dealt with.	Stereotyping and prejudice are harmful; adults will intervene and promote treating others with respect.

Read the case study below and consider ways that Ahzan's experience could have been very different, if her school had encouraged conversations about racial identity.

CASE STUDY ⊕

Ahzan: positive representation

Ahzan Ghalib is now a lecturer at Birmingham City University. Here, she talks about her own experience as a child and what she learned about positive representation.

As a young child I came to England, and I recall looking around my Year 2 classroom and being unable to see anybody that looked like me. Not the teacher, nor the children or the poster displays. I felt different and over time this affected the way I felt about myself and eventually it impacted my confidence. This lack of confidence contributed greatly to my learning as I didn't want to be seen and therefore I wouldn't put my hand up or ask for help when I needed it. I didn't want to draw attention to myself. I felt as if I was inferior when I was around my classmates, and this was purely because of their skin tone and the fact that I was the only one who looked 'different'. Further to this, my teacher couldn't pronounce my name correctly. I accepted her pronunciation and still now as a 30 year-old woman I introduce myself with the same incorrect pronunciation. Everyone outside of my family circle calls me by this name, a name I wrongly adopted as a six year-old girl.

My confidence in my abilities grew as I got older, and I decided that I wanted to be the teacher who had an impact on that little girl who felt different. I took positive steps to pursue a career that enabled me to be a role model and an advocate for equality and diversity. As a teacher now, I can see the importance of representation and how it allows people from minority groups to obtain a sense of validation. Positive representation encourages expression, that one thing I once lacked. This approach also allows students to see people like themselves reflected in course materials and supports them to identify with and be able to imagine themselves as belonging in that field. Belonging shouldn't be subject to race; the protected characteristics of our future generations need to be valued.

Reflective questions ⑦

» Ahzan's Year 2 teacher could not pronounce her name, and so Ahzan has allowed people to call her by a different name to this day. How could this affect a child's sense of identity? How can you ensure that this does not happen in your workplace?

» Do you think you would notice if a child was reluctant to draw attention to herself like Ahzan did? How might you address this sensitively while ensuring the child's emotional well-being?

» Examine the resources in your own work setting. Do the images and resources truly represent the children in the group? Could it be improved?

» Consider what you might learn from Table 10.2 in relation to a child like Ahzan.

Diversity as a strength

In a strength-based approach to diversity, we need to challenge inappropriate language and behaviour before we can begin to celebrate difference and acceptance. Having an open mind and getting to know people individually is key once again.

CASE STUDY 🔁

From 'celebrating diversity' to 'promoting equity'

Writer and researcher Bettez (2017) is regularly invited to visit high schools and colleges to deliver presentations about diversity and equality issues. In her article, she expresses concern about the ways that schools and colleges teach 'celebrating diversity', which she feels is often 'a passive appreciation of differences' (p 91). Bettez believes that it is more important to educate young people about oppression and privilege.

In her presentations, she shows young people a photograph of Balpreet Kaur, a young Sikh woman with facial hair, and the social media story that used the image without her consent (National Storytelling Network, 2012). Bettez uses the example to endeavour to get young people to consider the feelings of others and to show courage in speaking up against discrimination.

Reflective questions ❓

» What could have resulted in a devastating impact for Balpreet did, in fact, become a very positive event that changed someone's thinking about difference. What is it about Balpreet that enabled her to respond in the way she did?

» Bettez (2017) advocates for young people to show courage in fighting against discrimination and taking action. Reflect on ways that you could do this in your setting.

Tokenism

The Oxford English Dictionary defines tokenism as *'the practice of making only a perfunctory or symbolic effort to do a particular thing, especially by recruiting a small number of people from underrepresented groups in order to give the appearance of sexual or racial equality within a workforce'*. Despite curriculum and legislation requirements to respect all groups, tokenism is still rife in schools and early childhood settings. Too often we see settings with one book about same sex parents, one black doll, one teddy in a wheelchair, tokens that make it look as if we are inclusive, but which, by themselves, are much less meaningful. A child who has two mums will only feel that their family is valued if it is represented all the time, in conversation, in stories and in positive images. The celebration of cultural festivals is another occurrence that is often tokenistic. An example of this might be a group of nursery children celebrating Chinese New Year by eating Chinese food with chopsticks. No other elements of Chinese culture are explored at any other time, the impact being that the festival is celebrated as something exotic and different, rather than investigating the culture in a respectful and meaningful way. This approach is usually well intentioned but, as Mohammed (2021) points out, '*by celebrating linguistic and cultural practices that are different to the dominant group in society, we are highlighting the existing inequity that keeps some families marginalised and disempowered*'. The following case study illustrates a worryingly inappropriate view of Indian culture, and a parent who stepped in to make a real difference.

CASE STUDY

Nisha: Diwali

My family is the only Indian family in the school; my kids are mixed heritage. When my boy was little, his school had a Diwali day and in Reception the activity the teacher chose was to write letters using curry sauce. My boy came home and asked me why I wasn't writing my shopping list in curry sauce!

I'm no expert in Diwali lessons but I went in as I figured I could do better than curry sauce! So, I offered to go in to do a Diwali talk and now I do it every year. In Reception, we read the Diwali story and coloured pictures from it and also did some magic candle and paint pictures. Then in Years 1 and 2, we read the story and reordered it. Then I spoke about what I did at home with the kids (like lighting a candle, creating rangoli with bird seed and leaving a window open for Lakshmi). I also had a chat about what we ate, and I brought some food in.

In Year 3 and the older years, I asked the children what they wanted to find out, because I felt it was important to dispel any myths and get to the heart of what they thought. Many of the parents hadn't been very friendly to my family, so it was a good chance to find out why. The children came up with lots of questions. What is a sari? How do you put it on? What do the men wear? What do you eat? (The answer is we eat everything you do, but sometimes we have Indian food if we are poorly as it is comforting.) What does a temple look like? Why don't you eat beef? Why are the gods blue? Will the brown ever run off your skin? Will it rub onto us? Why are you brown? The teachers were embarrassed but I just let the kids talk so I could make them feel at ease and I brought in physical items where I could.

We ended with the Diwali story using puppets or craft activities because even Year 6 children love crafts. We bonded and it was nice, and the parents were friendlier with me afterwards.

Reflective questions ⑦

» How could the Reception class have got things so wrong with their original plans to inform children about Diwali?

» Reflect on Nisha's story and Mohammed's (2021) view above. Consider your own workplace; is there an element of cultural tokenism in your practice? What are the implications of this for children and families?

» Every June since 2008, people in the UK have celebrated Gypsy, Roma and Traveller History Month. Imagine that you have families from the GRT community living near your workplace. A whole month should be long enough to explore the culture; how would you go about this? Why is it important?

Ensuring that diversity is celebrated without resorting to tokenism can be tricky, in an education system that is constantly making more and more demands on teachers and other staff. Sometimes, actively celebrating diversity can be overlooked in the demands of the role. Nonetheless, showing an interest in individual children and celebrating their uniqueness has a significant impact on their self-esteem and identity. In the following case study, Gemma describes the primary school she works at, which demonstrates good practice in celebrating the diversity of children, families and the staff team.

CASE STUDY ☺

Gemma: welcoming and celebrating diversity

Gemma is an assistant headteacher at Wollescote Primary School in the West Midlands.

Eighty per cent of the children at the school are from ethnic minority families, predominantly Asian families and Eastern European families. Sixty-six per cent of the children are living in homes where English is not the first language. Here, Gemma illustrates her passion for diversity and describes what makes the school an example of excellent practice.

Wollescote is the embodiment of a diverse setting, where difference is seen as a strength and a reason to celebrate. Within our ever-expanding community, we welcome children from a variety of races, cultures and religions. Many of our families say we are their chosen school because we value everyone and treat everyone with respect. At Wollescote, British values are at the heart of our core principles, and we ensure that children, parents and staff respect differing beliefs and celebrate those differences, both in and out of the classroom. This is achieved in many ways.

Firstly, it is important to acknowledge that much of what causes segmentation within society is a lack of understanding; therefore, we encourage children to ask questions about why things are different, we encourage children to admire the cultural differences between them and their peers and, finally, we encourage children and their families to be proud of who they are and to share their experiences with us and others. This may be done within the school day or through other media such as the newsletter, website or the school's Facebook site. We also ensure there are as many opportunities as possible for families to be involved in school life. Parents/carers are encouraged to join us for project weeks, school fayres, cooking experiences and on school trips. These wonderful people offer insights into different ways of life that, without them, we could not possibly understand as well as we do.

All children need to see that, while they are different in some ways, their life is normal, and they should celebrate their identity both within our school and as a member of their community. We further encourage this by nurturing an open dialogue with children and their families to ensure that in our school, diversity is always seen as a strength and that we ask questions before making judgements. As a teacher, I have learned that for children to view diversity positively, I myself must set a positive example. I ensure that I show children in my class and around school that I might still be learning about their race, culture or religion, when it differs from my own, but I respect them and will always ask questions to show them I value them and want to learn all about their life and the similarities and differences it has to my own life. While scary at first, the joy I see on the children's faces as they light up with pride and excitement to tell me all about their experiences is truly magnificent. Not only have I learned a great deal from working at Wollescote, but I truly believe the lives of all children who attend our school are enriched by such diverse surroundings. They gain first-hand experience of things other children may only learn about in school lessons, books, films or the media.

Reflective questions ⑦

» Gemma talks about being a good role model, asking questions in order to avoid making assumptions. Make a list of some positive and open questions that you could ask a child or family in order to find out about a culture, race or religion you know little about.

» How valuable do you think it is for children to be surrounded by diversity? If you are working in a setting that has little or no diversity among its population, how could you provide children and young people with these experiences?

» What can you learn from the example set by this school?

Diverse teams

As well as having a diverse community of children, there are many benefits of having a diverse staff team. Lave and Wenger (1991) coined the term *'community of practice'* to describe a group of people with a common goal. A staff team at a school, a nursery, a hospital department, a class of students, a social work team, etc is a community of practice. Lave and Wenger (1991) describe how powerful the community can be: *'it is through the process of sharing information and experiences with the group that members learn from each other and have an opportunity to develop personally and professionally'*. The sharing of information and experiences among people with diverse backgrounds is instructive and enlightening. In an inclusive society, having a diverse staff team is valuable. Rock and Grant's (2016) research demonstrates that diverse teams:

- focus more on facts;
- process facts more carefully;
- are more innovative.

They conclude: *'working with people who are different from you may challenge your brain to overcome its stale ways of thinking and sharpen its performance'* (p 109).

Research by Iskhacova and Ott (2020) indicates that working in culturally diverse teams develops the team's motivation, performance and CQ (cultural intelligence). CQ is the ability to recognise and adapt to cultural differences, making it a very useful skill. Deady (2017) describes a situation where a class was planning an overnight trip, a sleepover. One child, a Syrian refugee, did not return the permission slip, repeatedly saying he had forgotten it. After several reminders, the teacher phoned the child's mother, who said she was not giving permission for the trip. The teacher was disappointed for the child, but if she had been more culturally aware, she may have realised that the last time this family were separated from each other was at a traumatic time when they were displaced at a refugee camp in Syria. If the teacher had been more aware of families like this, if she had learned about refugee families through her interactions with others, she would have been more sensitive to the child and family's feelings about the trip. Looking back at the case study by Gemma we can see how powerful this *'learning through interaction'* is. But we must not forget to do this with staff too, learning about their lives so that we better understand them as people with talents and strengths.

Reflective questions ⑦

Team diversity audit

Reflecting on your staff team, answer the questions in Table 10.3 honestly.

Table 10.3 *Team diversity audit (questions adapted from Croft, 2021)*

1. Is your organisation's vision, mission statement or motto inclusive?	
2. Are your workplace policies inclusive and flexible?	
3. Is there any bias in the recruitment of staff? (open or hidden)	
4. Do all employees feel valued?	
5. Is leadership and management empathetic towards employees?	
6. Are cultural differences celebrated?	
7. Are there leadership development opportunities for everyone?	
8. Do staff listen to each other?	
9. Is your workplace a safe space?	
10. Now reflect on any of these areas that you think could be improved. How could they be improved?	

Chapter summary 📖

In this chapter, themes of diversity and anti-discriminatory practice have been analysed, in relation to a range of *differences*. The sequence of stereotypes, prejudices and discrimination outlines the consequences of making assumptions about people based on one characteristic. Ahzan's case study shows how something as crucial as mispronouncing a child's name can impact a child. However, anti-discriminatory practice is not sufficient; in strength-based practice, we aim to truly celebrate diversity, rather than seeing difference as a barrier. Gemma's case study outlines good practice in celebrating all children's lives, sharing the lives of the children at the school rather than the tokenistic practice that is still so often adopted. In the UK, we live in a diverse culture in many ways, and this is a strength of our society. Learning about each other inspires interest in, and celebration of, each other.

Further reading 📖

- Cultural Competence Learning Institute (2020) Group Activities. [online] Available at: https://community.astc.org/ccli/resources-for-action/group-activities (accessed 19 June 2023).

- This website has some useful activities that can be used with groups of people in order to help people to engage with, and reflect on, values. The intention is to increase cultural competence.

- Stonewall (2022) www.stonewall.org.uk (accessed 19 June 2023).

- There are hundreds of resources on this website to support all sorts of settings to fight discrimination of the LGBTQ+ community. There are good practice guides, letter and policy templates, and activities and documents which support inclusion.

References

Bettez, S (2017) Flipping the Script from Talking to Teens about 'Celebrating Diversity' to Promoting Equity through Embracing Vulnerability and Enacting Courage. *Multicultural Perspectives*, 19(2): 90–7.

Care Quality Commission (CQC) (2013) Equality Counts: Equality Information for CQC in 2013. [online] Available at: www.cqc.org.uk/sites/default/files/documents/edhr_annual_report_january_2014final.pdf (accessed 30 June 2023).

Croft, A (2021) How to Build & Lead a Diverse Team? [online] Available at: https://everhour.com/blog/diverse-team/#7_Celebrate_cultural_differences (accessed 19 June 2023).

Deady, K (2017) Why Culturally Responsive Teaching Matters Now More Than Ever. [online] Available at: www.teachaway.com/blog/why-culturally-responsive-teaching-matters-now-more-ever (accessed 19 June 2023).

Devarakonda, C (2020) *Promoting Inclusion and Diversity in Early Years Settings: A Professional Guide to Ethnicity, Religion, Culture and Language.* London: Jessica Kingsley Publishers.

Equality Act (2010) [online] Available at: www.legislation.gov.uk/ukpga/2010/15/contents (accessed 19 June 2023).

Gannon, M (2016) Race Is a Social Construct, Scientists Argue: Racial Categories Are Weak Proxies for Genetic Diversity and Need to Be Phased Out. *Scientific American*, 5 February. [online] Available at: www.scientificamerican.com/article/race-is-a-social-construct-scientists-argue/ (accessed 19 June 2023).

Iskhacova, M and Ott, D (2020) Working in Culturally Diverse Teams: Team-level Cultural Intelligence (CQ), Development and Team Performance. *Journal of International Education in Business*, 13(1): 37–54.

Jensen, R (2020) Mustard-tasting, Calligraphy and a Dragon in the Library: Celebrating Culture and Diversity. *The School Librarian*, 68(2): 72–4.

Kampen, M (2020) *7 Ways to Support Diversity in the Classroom.* University of Rhode Island. [online] Available at: www.prodigygame.com/main-en/blog/diversity-in-the-classroom/ (accessed 19 June 2023).

Lave, J and Wenger, E (1991) *Situated Learning: Legitimate Peripheral Participation.* Cambridge: Cambridge University Press.

Mohammed, N (2021) *Avoiding Tokenism in Multicultural Education.* [online] Available at: http://blog.tesol.org/avoiding-tokenism-in-multicultural-education-7-strategies/ (accessed 19 June 2023).

National Storytelling Network (2012) *Sikh Woman Balpreet Kaur Turns Cyber Bullying Incident into Inspiration.* [online] Available at: https://storynet.org/sikh-woman-balpreet-kaur-turns-cyber-bullying-incident-into-inspiration/ (accessed 19 June 2023).

Ofsted (2023) *Equality Objectives Progress Review 2020 to 2021: Updated 31 May 2023*. [online] Available at: www.gov.uk/government/publications/ofsteds-equality-objectives-2020-to-2022/equality-objectives-progress-review-2020-to-2021 (accessed 28 July 2023).

Prowle, A and Hodgkins, A (2020) *Making a Difference with Children and Families: Re-imagining the Role of the Practitioner*. London: Red Globe Books, Bloomsbury.

Rock, D and Grant, H (2016) *Why Diverse Teams are Smarter*. [online] Available at: https://hbr.org/2016/11/why-diverse-teams-are-smarter (accessed 19 June 2023).

Stonewall (2014) *The Teachers' Report: A First-hand Look at the Experiences of Teachers Tackling Homophobic Bullying at School*. [online] Available at: www.stonewall.org.uk/resources/teachers-report-2014-0 (accessed 28 July 2023).

Stonewall (2022a) *Getting Started: A Toolkit for Preventing and Tackling Homophobic, Biphobic and Transphobic Bullying in Primary Schools*. [online] Available at: www.stonewall.org.uk/resources/getting-started-toolkit-primary-schools (accessed 19 June 2023).

Stonewall (2022b) *Ten Steps to Tackling Homophobic, Biphobic and Transphobic Language in Your School*. [online] Available at: www.stonewall.org.uk/system/files/10_steps_to_tackling_hbt_language-march2022_-_final_edited.pdf (accessed 19 June 2023).

Sullivan, J, Wilton, L and Apfelbaum, E (2020) Adults Delay Conversations About Race Because They Underestimate Children's Processing of Race. *Journal of Experimental Psychology: General*, 150(2): 395–400.

Thompson, N (2021) *Anti-discriminatory Practice, Practical Social Work Series Produced in Association with BASW*, 7th ed. London: Bloomsbury Academic.

White, A and Wanless, S (2019) PRIDE: Positive Racial Identity Development in Early Education. *Journal of Curriculum, Teaching, Learning and Leadership in Education*, 4(2): 73–84.

11 Strength-based leadership

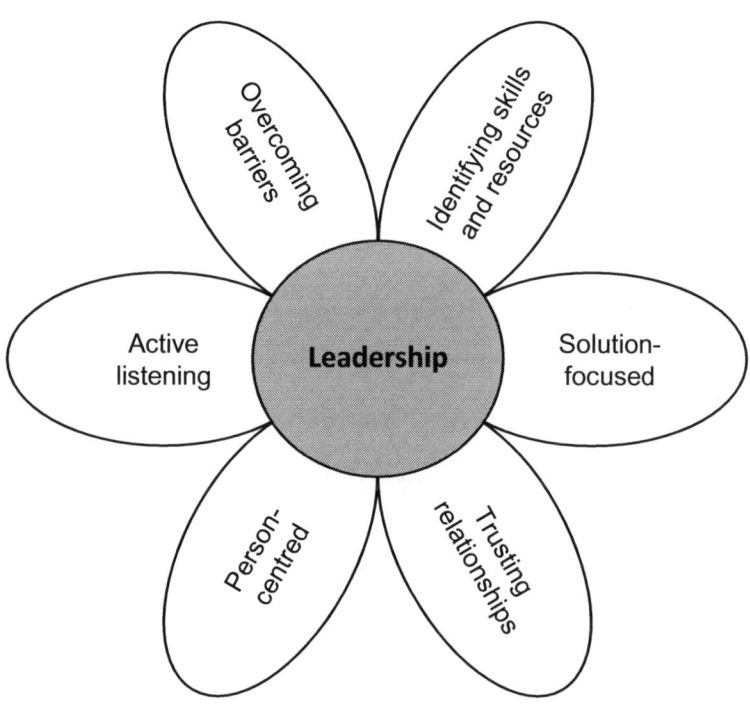

Chapter objectives ◎

This chapter:

- provides definitions of leadership in the context of services for children and families;
- explores the importance of leadership in a challenging professional landscape and a changing world;
- considers how a focus on strength-based working can transform leadership;
- encourages readers to reflect upon how they can apply strength-based working in their roles and organisations.

Introduction

Leadership is challenging. It is about having and achieving a vision, creating an ethos, getting the best out of the people and resources around you, and ultimately improving outcomes for children and families. Most people who enter the children and families' workforce do so because they want to make a positive difference in children's lives; however, sometimes the organisational systems and culture around us can make this difficult to achieve. While it is now far more widespread to hear mention of strength-based direct work with children and families, it is less common to find organisations applying this ethos to their own staff and organisation. This chapter focuses upon what we mean by strength-based leadership and shows we can strive towards it at all levels in our organisations. We consider what it means to be a strength-focused leader, and how this may differ from traditional conceptions of leadership. Through case studies, we also explore the experiences of some inspirational leaders who are using this philosophy to transform practice and create strength-based services in which children can be appropriately supported to flourish and meet their potential. Finally, we reflect upon how we can become strength-based leaders and make a positive difference to the lives of those we work with and for.

Reflective questions ⑦

»   Before we begin our exploration of leadership, take a few moments to identify four or five people you consider to be, or have been, great leaders.

»   Think about what makes them a good leader.

»   Do these individuals have anything in common?

What is leadership?

There are many definitions of leadership, which range from a person with followers (Peter Drucker) to one who can empower others (Bill Gates). One of the most helpful definitions of leadership comes from Kevin Kruse, author of *Great Leaders Have No Rules* (2019). Kruse (2013) says,

> *Leadership is a process of social influence, which maximizes the efforts of others, towards the achievement of a goal.*

This threefold definition is helpful as it incorporates the leader's ability to make visible a desirable end goal and then motivate and inspire others to help achieve that goal.

Harvard professor John Kotter (1990) provides a point that leadership is not the same as management. Leadership and management are two distinct but complementary skill sets. He argues that leadership is fundamentally about dealing with change, while management is more about imposing order on complexity. Hence, according to Kotter's model, leaders create a vision and inspire and empower others to help make that vision a reality. Managers help to achieve that vision through ensuring that processes, such as budgeting, staffing and day-to-day running, are operating effectively and consistently.

Of course, this distinction of the role is not absolute, and there is a lot of crossover between the two skill sets. Managers can demonstrate leadership within their roles by looking for and implementing changes. Similarly, leaders may need to undertake managerial tasks. For a service or project to run effectively both skill sets need to work in tandem, and both are equally important. Many modern roles will expect both leadership and management to be undertaken by the same person. Indeed, referring to the children and families' sector specifically, Pound (2008) suggests that staff often move seamlessly between leadership, management and teamwork as they undertake their roles. Figure 11.1 below explores the distinctions between leadership and management in more detail.

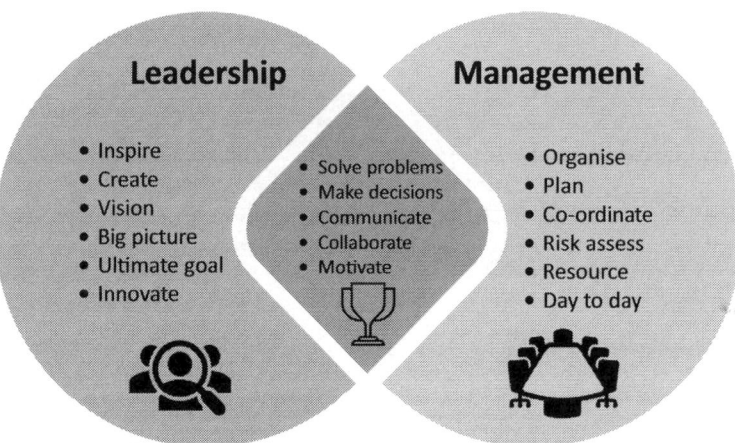

Figure 11.1 *The relationship between leadership and management*

Hence leadership is concerned with the big picture and long-term visioning, while management focuses more on the detail and the day-to-day running of a service or project. However, certain skills such as the ability to communicate and collaborate with others is crucial to both roles. This chapter focuses on leadership while recognising that there is an overlap with management (as shown in Sarah's case study).

Towards a strength-based model of leadership

In the past, leadership was often defined in relation to the character traits shared by those considered good leaders (Zaccaro, Kemp and Bader, 2004). Under this model, leaders were often conceptualised as strong, dominant and certain, and often with charismatic personalities. Such traits were seen as innate (Galton, 1869) and could not be learned or coached. In other words, leaders were born, not made. Fortunately, leadership theory has moved on, and it is now widely recognised that leadership is highly situational (Hersey and Blanchard, 1969) and that we need different leaders for different situations.

Recognising that leadership is collaborative in nature and that achieving lasting change requires a buy-in from all those affected can lead to transformational leadership (Burns, 1978), where leaders and followers can together raise each other to new heights of achievement and imagining of a better world. Bass (1985) said that such leaders prioritise the following aspects of practice shown in Figure 11.2 below.

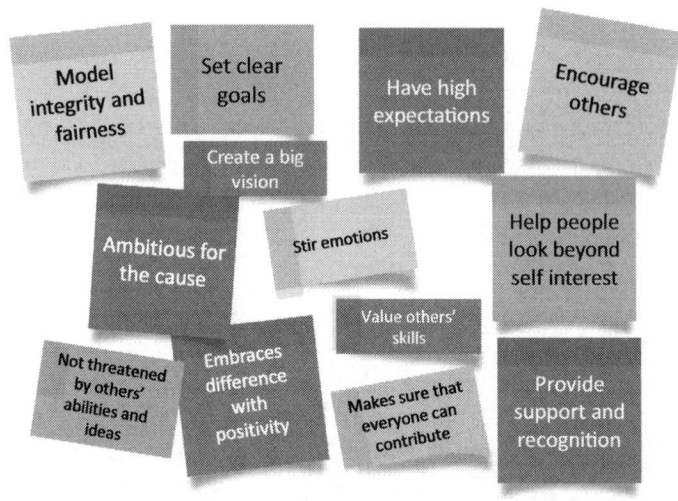

Figure 11.2 *Transformational leaders*

Another helpful model of leadership is the idea of the leader as a servant (Greenleaf, 1977). A servant leader focuses on the needs of others, particularly staff and those who use the service. They acknowledge others' feelings and perspectives and lead through example and through getting involved and building a sense of community; being '*in it together*'. Such leaders are very democratic and are excellent at building trust and engagement in teams. Mary Whalley (2011), writing in the context of early years, highlights that leadership is all about community and relationships, recognising the connections between staff, children, parents/carers and partner agencies as well as the wider society.

A final model that is helpful is that of leadership through practice. McDowall Clark (2012) argues that those working on the ground with children and families are in a perfect position to lead and inspire change. Making a difference in this way is not dependent upon a position of power. However, to enable this kind of leadership the whole culture of the organisation needs to be collaborative and participative.

Overcoming challenges in leadership

Leadership is not easy, and certainly comes with its own challenges. Many within the children and families' workforce will be dealing with limited resources while also possibly seeing an increase in demand and need within their services. At the same time, it may be difficult to recruit and retain staff, source affordable training, and align government directions with your own vision. While outward challenges may be difficult to navigate, there may be internal barriers too. Figure 11.3 gives just some examples.

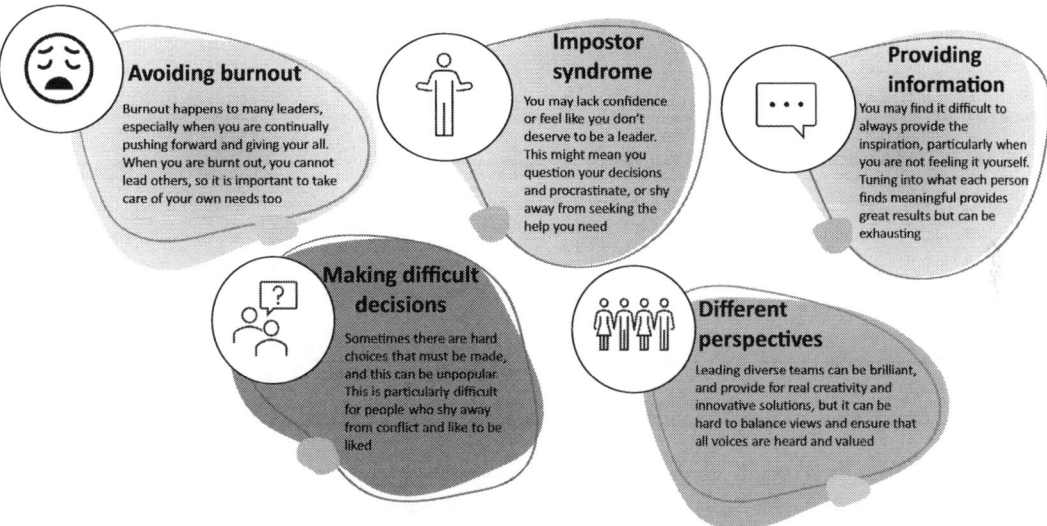

Figure 11.3 *Challenges of leadership*

Self-care is important for leaders, both for your own sake and to model appropriate boundaries to staff and those who use the service. There are many ways to take care of yourself as a leader. Figure 11.4 shows just a few.

Figure 11.4 *Effective self-care for leaders*

Dealing with change

Change is all around us. Sometimes changes are external to our organisation, like large-scale societal changes. Sometimes they are closer to home, as in the example of staff changes. Some changes are imposed, for example government directives and policy agendas. Some are identified by us as a way of improving services. Some happen swiftly, for example Covid lockdowns. Others, such as technological changes, happen over time. However, there is much evidence that human beings are hardwired to find change difficult and resist it when they can (Beckhard, 1969).

Psychiatrist Elisabeth Kübler-Ross first introduced the Change Curve Model in 1969 in the context of loss and change. It outlines five stages of grief, namely:

1. denial,

2. anger,

3. bargaining,

4. depression; and

5. acceptance.

(Kübler-Ross, 1969, p 36)

The theory suggests that when faced with change, people naturally go through these stages. While the original work focused on bereavement, many have argued that it is equally applicable to organisational change. For many, the cycle of change, while helpful, does not fully capture the range, intensity and unpredictability of emotions when encountering change. For them, it is more like a whirlpool or a set of rapids where there is no defined order in which one encounters the emotions. For any leader, understanding change and change resistance is crucial when change is needed in a service. It is important that leaders acknowledge the resistance, create a vision and rationale for the change and engage people within the change process if the change is to be successful.

Sarah Savage is an experienced social worker and team manager for a 0–25 disability service. She has successfully led her team through not one but two service reorganisations. In this case study, she talks about how she adopted a strength-based approach to support both staff and those using the service through an ambitious programme of change.

CASE STUDY ☉

Sarah Savage

About six years ago, the local authority decided to move from separate children's disability and adults' services into one unified cradle to grave provision. It was a huge change and involved creating a whole new team from two disparate services, aligning approaches and procedures, and helping everyone move to new ways of working. It was a long and arduous process but there was so much learning. We had really improved the whole transition from children to adult services, making the process much smoother and more transparent for both young people and their careers. We were also finding ways to build on the aspirations of young people and the whole service was much more outcomes focused. Hence, the new model had much to commend it, but an external evaluation highlighted that without additional resources the current model would not be sustainable. Unfortunately, we are working in a time of financial austerity and resources are tight, so there was no possibility for additional resources for the team. It was decided that we would move to a model of 0–25 provision, which would protect the improvements we had made in transition and outcomes focus but also be sustainable within existing resources. So, it was all changed for us as a service once again.

Once the decision had been made, the change happened quickly, and this was important for staff morale and well-being as well as for the families. Uncertainty is very hard for people, so I thought 'OK, this is where we are going, let's just get on with it!' There were lots of emotions involved, for me as well as the staff, and acknowledging these emotions was important in helping us move forward. Our first priority was to work with each member of the team to find out where their interests and aspirations lay. We needed some staff to move over to other teams along with over 25 caseloads. Fortunately, everyone got their first choice of role. I was able to work with the managers of the other teams to make the transition to the new service smooth and also so that we could provide support to the staff who in turn could provide continuity for those service users.

Alongside mourning what we had lost, I was also keen to identify the strengths of the new model. With more capacity, we would have a real opportunity to undertake development work and introduce new projects to help the young people become independent and to build on their aspirations. We could also further strengthen the good practice around transition and move from specific transition workers to all staff sharing this expertise. It was a great development opportunity for the staff to pool good practice, learn from one another and expand their skill sets. So, selling the benefits to overcome resistance to change was important, as well as ensuring everyone's voice was heard in the design of the new service.

As we have moved on together, it has been important to help the team to celebrate success and to use positive praise as a motivator, giving them freedom and ownership to run with new ideas and to think creatively outside the box. Formal and informal case supervision is so important, allowing staff quality time for reflection, sharing concerns and proactive problem solving. It is so important that their manager shows an interest in their work and ideas, and staff are seen as individuals with lives outside work. So as a leader, I see myself more as an enabler or facilitator, providing a conducive environment for staff growth, development and excellent service delivery. I certainly don't micro-manage every aspect of the team's work. Managing the staff in this way leads to better outcomes for the families.

As for my own strengths, I suppose there is a recognition that I need others and can't do everything alone. I love seeing staff blossom and grow in this enabling environment. I think I have a positive outlook and can-do attitude. I am resilient and can always see the

→

opportunities, even when things are tough. I have a passion for the work and improving outcomes for young people. This job is unique. It is a privilege; we can make a real difference for children and help them to have positive futures. I guess that brings me to the point that our biggest strength as a team is the young people themselves, so I am passionate about helping them to develop a strong voice, a purpose and a hope. Then there is a ripple effect from that empowerment into families and communities. I suppose ultimately it is all about having passion and a strong value base and collaborating with others at all levels to get the best outcomes. In a nutshell, that's me as a leader.

Reflective questions ⑦

»   Using the leadership theory explored in this chapter, how would you describe Sarah's approach to leadership?

»   How did Sarah use a strength-based approach to leading change?

»   Think about some of the changes you are facing within your life or job role. Learning from this case study, how could you apply a strength-based approach?

The strength-based leader

Linley (2008, p 8) defines a strength as a

> *pre-existing capacity for a particular way of behaving, thinking, or feeling that is authentic and energising to the user, and enables optimal functioning, development and performance.*

Being good at something does not constitute a strength; it must be actively employed as one to be maximised. '*Playing to your strengths*' is more than just a mantra but can be a recipe for very successful leadership. However, before we can activate and maximise our strengths, we first need to identify what they are. This question can form the basis of a helpful professional reflective conversation with a trusted colleague, as sometimes our strengths are more visible to others than they are to us. Benefits of identifying our strengths may include increased self-efficacy, productivity and motivation as well as improved understanding of our goals and how to reach them (Peterson and Seligman, 2004). It is worth thinking creatively when attempting to identify our strengths and including attributes not just from the work context but from our life. Also, think about how difficulties can be re-framed as strengths.

Seligman et al (2005) talk about the importance of identifying our own signature strengths, the character strengths that are essential to who we are. Peterson and Seligman (2004) categorised these character strengths into six virtues (*Wisdom and Knowledge, Humanity, Justice, Courage, Temperance, Transcendence*). These virtues are then translated into 24 signature strengths as shown in Table 11.1.

Table 11.1 *Positive psychology's six virtues*

Positive psychology's six virtues and associated signature strengths					
Wisdom and Knowledge	**Humanity**	**Justice**	**Courage**	**Temperance**	**Transcendence**
creativity curiosity open-mindedness love of learning perspective	love kindness social intelligence	teamwork fairness leadership	bravery perseverance integrity zest and enthusiasm	self-control humility prudence forgiveness teamwork fairness leadership	appreciation of beauty gratitude hope and optimism humour connection

Knowing and utilising our own signature strengths can help us to adopt a style of leadership that is unique to us and congruent with our own value base and way of being.

Creating a strength-based culture

It is essential that strength-based leadership operates in a culture that is equally positive and valuing of strengths. This is much easier when building a service from scratch, as we saw with the Supporting Change team in Chapter 9. However, it is more difficult in a culture which is used to working within a deficit model and perhaps managing staff in a less positive and more punitive way. Changing a culture, getting people on board with a vision and helping them become empowered to take that vision forward is difficult and painstaking work and change does not happen overnight. The next case study considers a person who took it upon himself to try to change the whole culture of education.

This case study with Mark Escott (MBE) is presented as a reflective conversation. Mark is the founder and chief executive officer of The Life Chance Group, an award-winning organisation supporting children who have experienced trauma. Life Chance is based around four pillars.

1.   Education – therapeutic education for children who struggle in mainstream schools.

2.   Training – specialist trauma-informed sessions for professionals working with children and young people.

3. Care – assessments for children with social, emotional and mental health difficulties.

4. Trust – a charitable fund, providing access to grants, mentorship, training, and support for young people aged 16–25.

Here, Mark talks about his own leadership journey from being a young person who was failed by the systems around him, to developing a cutting-edge education service and inspiring children and young people to flourish and achieve on their own terms.

CASE STUDY ⊖

A leadership journey

Alison   *Mark, I've read your book (see Further reading) and I know that your early relationship with the education system was not very positive. Can you tell me more?*

Mark   *I was born in 1972 to my mum who was 19 years old at the time, and sadly my Gran died the same day. We lived with my dad in an area that in those days was quite rough. My parents split up and I've had three different stepfathers. There was physical, emotional and sexual abuse that went on in my younger years into my teens. School wasn't that great for me. I didn't really enjoy school. I remember liking it a little bit when I was younger, but as soon as it moved beyond play, it became a real struggle for me. I also had to move schools when my mum got divorced. I got excluded a few times and by then I was taking drugs. I was smoking, I was drinking alcohol, smoking cannabis and sniffing glue as well. At the age of 14 they tested me in a new school and found out I was dyslexic, and I had word blindness. So, in a way that helped but they put me in a class with younger children and I got teased and called a dunce. One day I was asked to answer some questions on the computer and ended up hacking the computer and doing the entire year's work! That's when I started to realise that maybe I was more intelligent than I'd been told or thought I was. I left school with no qualifications; the only thing I ever got from school was a 50-metre swimming badge! Looking back now, I can see why I was so angry and upset. I could see how taking drugs and alcohol helped to numb my feelings.*

Alison   *That must have been so tough. So how did things turn around for you?*

Mark   *Well, I ended up in the criminal justice system. By the time I was 19, I was living in a hostel for young men on probation, serving two years of a suspended sentence. I had a probation officer and one day he asked me what I wanted to do next. I told my probation officer that I wanted to do his job because he was rubbish. I told him I wanted to be a translator and he asked, 'what do you mean?' I said, 'well, I can learn to speak your language, but you can't learn to speak mine'. My career started with a big chip on my shoulder. I had to do some voluntary work and ended up working with young people with disability. I met some amazing people who took me under their wing and mentored me. I met a man called Fred Ehresmann who was a psychiatric nurse and he saw something in me. He said, 'I can see you've put up some armour around yourself, Mark', and he could see through this. When I dropped this armour of this aggressive boy, there was this kind, caring man underneath. And I think working with young people with disability really brought that out of me. I really started to enjoy the caring side of that and what it felt like to look after people. So, I continued that path, and I trained as a youth worker in my early 20s. As I got to my mid-20s, I was still using quite a lot of drugs myself. It was like a pendulum; wanting to progress my career and make a difference, but then craving that numbness that drugs gave me. Eventually I went into drug recovery, but the thing that really made a difference was starting to see a psychotherapist and doing a self-development course.*

Alison   *Tell me about that.*

Mark   *They mentioned the word integrity. I didn't understand, but then I realised how important it was. I needed to get my integrity back, so I was working with a coach, and I handed myself in to the police for all the crimes I had committed. I was interviewed and filled up six sheets of paper and was looking at a sentence of 8–10 years. The next day I got a letter asking me to meet the chief of police. I explained my story to him and he said, 'I understand how important integrity and authenticity is to you'. I said, 'yeah, it's transformed my life doing this. I want to go on to help more young people who have lived experiences like me. I want to work in youth work. I think I can connect with these young people'. He asked me to make him a promise inside my world of integrity. He said I was more used to society outside prison. So, I gave my word that I would fulfil my mission. That was it. I was going to become an unstoppable stand for the transformation of the education system.*

Alison   *What did you mean by that, Mark?*

Mark   *It's one of these moments, I don't know where it came from. I stood up in front of 100+ people and declared myself as an unstoppable stand for the transformation of the education system. When I say I want to be an unstoppable stand, I see it in my mind's eye as, I am 12ft tall with 6ft of me being underground and the other 6ft sticking out of the ground. So, nothing can move me. I'm an unstoppable stand!*

Alison   *And after that?*

Mark   *Well, as a youth worker, I worked with young people who were excluded. Then I worked in Child and Adolescent Mental Health Services (CAMHS) and, quite by fluke, we ended up renting a space in a school, co-located with social workers, play therapists and voluntary sector workers. It was a multi-disciplinary team and I thought 'yes, this is what we need!' That was the vision and it led to me*

→

becoming co-founder of the Life Chance Group, an organisation that is committed to transforming the life chances of young people and families by helping to heal our own and our collective trauma.

Alison   Wow. What a journey! Tell me more about Life Chance.

Mark   It is based around four pillars:

Pillar 1 is Life Chance Education and that runs our schools, called School for Inspiring Talents. It has a multidisciplinary team, we work with young people from five to 16 years old with complex life histories, including severe abuse and neglect. Pillar 2 is Life Chance Training, where we train other professionals to respond in a trauma-informed way. Pillar 3 is Life Chance Care where we provide an outreach service for families and schools. Pillar 4 is The Life Chance Trust which we introduced to provide grants and mentorship to young people post-16.

My multidisciplinary team consists of speech and language therapists, occupational therapists and mental health workers. We have our own trauma recovery practitioners. We have family practitioners. We have access to a consultant. Clinical psychologist. And play therapists and drama therapists as well. So that's in a nutshell, the last 50 years of my life!

Alison   Incredible! Can you tell me about how you work in a strength-based way? How does it identify and build on the strengths of the children and young people? Part of your story is about people identifying something in you that weren't even aware of yourself and seeing that potential. It is powerful.

Mark   For me, it is about being authentic and realising that respect is earned not given by virtue of position. Listening to children. There is a lot of student voice and that is crucial. Listen to what they need and what they want, because even though we're experts, we can still miss important stuff. I have lots of people who are inspired by my story, but I've realised that you need enough ego to believe you can transform the world, and enough humility to realise you can't do it on your own. And that my work around my strength-based approach is I have continuously tried to find people who are better than me to take on my roles.

Alison   I guess that's about recognising strengths in other people as well, isn't it?

Mark   Yes. Some of my staff, like me, have lots of lived experience that they now use as a strength, but others bring different experiences and skill sets. It's really all about the value base and a passion for the work – all staff go through a children's panel at interview, and they can tell if this person is not genuine.

We recently had an Ofsted inspection, and the inspector was amazed. He said 'so you're telling me there was a consultant clinical psychologist, a mental health worker, a teacher and two teaching assistants in that room?' He said, 'I couldn't *tell you who was who'. There is no hierarchy, no standing on titles. We are all equal. We are one unit in that building, working together to cause transformation of their lives and it's a two-way street; the young people teach us as much as we teach them!*

Alison   *What about the strengths of the young people?*

Mark   *Yes, we must help them spot and reframe their strengths. Take me, I'm an entrepreneur, but I use the same skills I used as a drug dealer when I was younger. I used to be called a 'blagger' but now I'm a 'very highly skilled communicator'! We need to look differently at the strengths that can help us succeed.*

Alison   *Any top leadership tips, Mark?*

Mark   *We must really get into those young people's worlds, into their shoes. We must be alongside them and help hold them safe and be the emotionally available adult for them. So, I think authentic supervision is important, and reflection where you must look inwards at yourself.*

Alison   *What advice would you give to other leaders?*

Mark   *Do you really want to cause transformation in these young people's lives? Are you just going to aim for them to get through to 16 and pass their exams? Or do you see further afield? You know that phrase I used earlier about having enough ego to believe you can cause transformation, and enough humility to know you can't do it alone? One of the biggest things from being a leader is that it's OK not to know. Ask questions. When you don't know something, ask the team around you for advice. One thing we share a lot at School for Inspiring Talents and Life Chances is that we are not a finished product. We are perfectly imperfect. We get things wrong. Own it. Say sorry. It comes back to that integrity really!*

Alison   *Thank you, Mark. You have given us so much to think about!*

Reflective questions ⑦

»   How does Mark's lived experience contribute to his vision for a transformed education system?

»   In what ways does Mark's journey into leadership challenge conventional leadership theory?

»   What leadership qualities does Mark demonstrate? How might these relate to his signature strengths?

→

> » Mark says that leaders need enough ego to believe that they can make a difference and enough humility to realise they can't do it alone. Do you agree? Is this a difficult balance to achieve?
>
> » As a strength-based leader Mark recognises his own strengths as well as the strengths of his staff and the young people. He points out that, sometimes, things that have been seen as problems or difficulties can be reframed as strengths. What strengths do you have that could be helpful to you as a leader?

Chapter summary

This chapter has considered a range of issues connected to strength-based leadership. Strong, strength-based leadership is positioned as crucial for creating and delivering a vision for services that improve children's life chances. We have explored the importance of looking beyond traditional models of leadership and considering the scope for leaders to work collaboratively and creatively with others to bring about positive change. Sarah's case study demonstrated that a focus on strengths can enable teams to navigate their way through difficult situations. Mark's case study demonstrates that unlikely leaders can achieve incredible results when vision, humility and integrity are prioritised. As the children and families sector moves forward to faces new challenges in an ever-changing world, we need leaders with the passion, commitment and willingness to challenge the status quo, put children first and help all children to succeed.

Further reading

• To read more about Mark Escott's extraordinary personal journey to transformational leadership, read his biography. Escott, M (2022) *One More Life Chance: How to Support the Journey from Trauma to Transformation*, 2nd ed. Great Yarmouth: Rethink Press.

• Prowle, A and Hodgkins, A (2020) *Making a Difference with Children and Families – Re-imagining the Role of the Practitioner*. London: Red Globe Books, Bloomsbury.

  Chapter 5 of this book, *The practitioner as leader and agent of change*, provides a useful overview of leadership. In particular, the case study with Emma Davis, the then manager of a thriving preschool, which had previously been deemed inadequate, demonstrates how one individual identified her own previously unacknowledged leadership skills and was able to lead her setting on a strength-based journey to outstanding.

References

Bass, B M (1985) *Leadership and Performance Beyond Expectations*. New York: Free Press.

Beckhard, R (1969) *Organization Development: Strategies and Models*. Reading, MA: Addison-Wesley.

Burns, J M (1978) *Leadership*. New York: Harper & Row.

Galton, F (1869) *Hereditary Genius*. New York: Appleton.

Greenleaf, R K (1977) *Servant Leadership: A Journey into the Nature of Legitimate Power and Greatness*. Ellicott City, MD: Paulist Press.

Hersey, P and Blanchard, K H (1969) Life Cycle Theory of Leadership. *Training & Development Journal*, 33(6): 94–100.

Kotter, J P (1990) *A Force for Change*. New York: Free Press.

Kruse, K (2019) *Great Leaders Have No Rules: Contrarian Leadership Principles to Transform Your Team and Business*. Pennsylvania: Rodale Books.

Kruse, K (2013) *What is Leadership*? [online] Available at: www.forbes.com/sites/kevinkruse/2013/04/09/what-is-leadership/?sh=22d83305b90c (accessed 19 June 2023).

Kubler-Ross, E (1969) *On Death and Dying*. New York: Macmillan.

Linley, A (2008) *Average to A+: Realising Strengths in Yourself and Others*. Coventry: CAPP Press.

McDowall Clark, R (2012) 'I've never thought of myself as a leader but …': The Early Years Professional and Catalytic Leadership. *European Early Childhood Education Research Journal*, 20(3): 391–401.

Peterson, C and Seligman, M E P (2004) *Character Strengths and Virtues: A Handbook and Classification*. Washington, DC: American Psychological Association.

Pound, L (2008) Leadership in the Early Years. In Cable, C and Miller, L (eds) *Professionalism in the Early Years* (pp 75–84). London: Hodder Education.

Seligman, M E P, Steen, T A, Park, N and Peterson, C (2005) Positive Psychology Progress: Empirical Validation of Interventions. *American Psychologist*, 60: 410–21.

Whalley, M E (ed) (2011) *Leading and Managing in the Early Years*. London: Sage.

Zaccaro, S J, Kemp, C and Bader, P (2004) *Leader Traits and Attributes. The Nature of Leadership*. Thousand Oaks, CA: Sage.

12 Looking to the future with hope

Chapter objectives

This chapter:

- discusses the strength of the practitioner as an architect of hope;
- outlines the psychology of hope;
- stresses the importance of practitioner self-care in working with children and families;
- identifies key messages from the chapters in this book;
- analyses the importance of hope in an uncertain world.

Introduction

The chapter summarises and concludes some of the themes from this book. In this final chapter, we discuss the practitioner as an '*architect of hope*' (Prowle and Hodgkins, 2020). Hope has been a key theme throughout this book, and consequently, we examine a range of theoretical ideas about hope from different disciplines (Figure 12.1).

Working with children and families can be stressful and emotional; in this chapter, we highlight the importance of self-care for practitioners and offer advice on ways of coping with the emotional demands of practice. It is essential that practitioners care for themselves before providing care and support for others, so building your own strength and resilience is essential.

Each chapter in this book has taken a distinct area of working with children and families' practice and we have examined each of these through a strength-based lens. In this final chapter, we identify key messages from each of the chapters to conclude our primary thoughts. To conclude the chapter, we identify some of the challenges in practice today and offer our fundamental advice for a hopeful and positive future.

Theories and ideas about hope

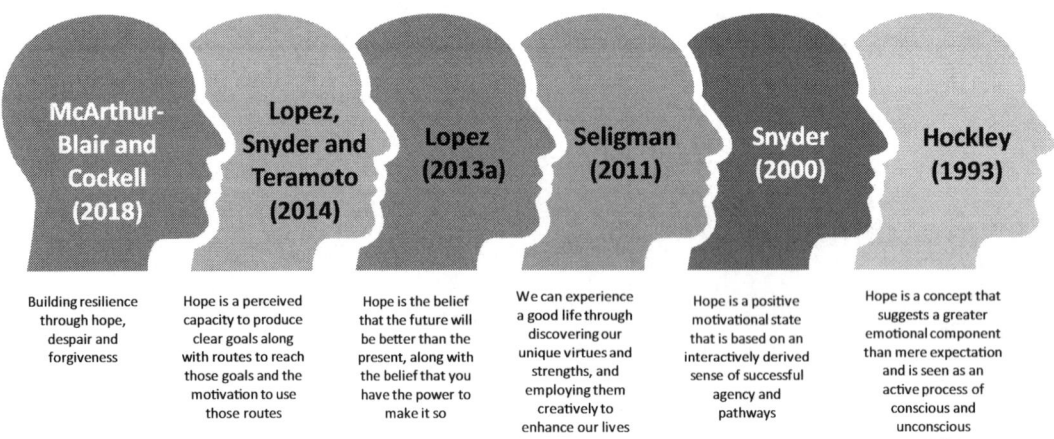

McArthur-Blair and Cockell (2018)	Lopez, Snyder and Teramoto (2014)	Lopez (2013a)	Seligman (2011)	Snyder (2000)	Hockley (1993)
Building resilience through hope, despair and forgiveness	Hope is a perceived capacity to produce clear goals along with routes to reach those goals and the motivation to use those routes	Hope is the belief that the future will be better than the present, along with the belief that you have the power to make it so	We can experience a good life through discovering our unique virtues and strengths, and employing them creatively to enhance our lives	Hope is a positive motivational state that is based on an interactively derived sense of successful agency and pathways	Hope is a concept that suggests a greater emotional component than mere expectation and is seen as an active process of conscious and unconscious reasoning

Figure 12.1 *Theories and ideas about hope*

If we ask a member of the general public to define '*hope*', they are likely to say something like '*wanting something to happen*'. However, the Cambridge Dictionary (2023) goes a little further than this and defines hope as '*to want something to happen or to be true, **and** usually have a good reason to think that it might*'. This is interesting, as Hockley (1993, pp 181–6) made the point that hope is more than wanting something to happen, it is '*a greater emotional component than mere expectation*'. Hockley's work was in palliative care, and she discusses the importance of hope in people who are seriously ill, the '*will to live*' being the ultimate expression of personal hope.

Snyder is one of the most prolific writers on the subject of hope; in Snyder's (2000) Hope Theory, he identifies three components that people need:

1.   **Goals** – focused thought to identify goals in life.

2.   **Pathways** – strategies developed in order to achieve goals.

3.   **Agency** – self-belief and motivation to make the effort required to reach these goals.

Snyder believes that hopeful people are those who can establish their own clear goals, devise ways to meet these goals and are able to persevere, even when things become difficult. If one of these three components is missing, then a person will lose their sense of hope (Table 12.1).

Table 12.1 Reflective activity based on Snyder's Hope Theory (2000)

Goals	Identify one or two goals for yourself. They can be long or short term, but they need to be achievable.	*My goals:*
Pathways	Identify ways of achieving each of your goals. List things you will need to do to make them happen and create a contingency plan in case of problems.	*My plans:*
Agency	Decide how you will make sure you stay on track; how will you develop good habits? How will you remind yourself what you are aiming for? How will you stay motivated?	*My motivations:*

Reflective questions ⑦

» Consider a personal objective and identify your own three components – goals, plans and motivations. You might choose to do this for your personal life or for your professional setting. Here's an example based on a personal objective:

My goals: to be fitter and healthier, to be able to walk the dog without struggling for breath, to have more energy.

Pathways: shop for healthier food, cook more instead of buying takeaways, increase exercise a little every week.

Agency: include other members of the family so we can keep each other going, reward myself with new walking shoes after staying on track for a month.

» Try using Table 12.1 with a work group. Draw up a plan together with colleagues.

Seligman (1975) is a pioneer of '*positive psychology*', a term originating with Maslow which explores human potential. Much of Seligman's work is about the pursuit of happiness, hope for the future being an important aspect of happiness in the present. Seligman identified strengths as the key to happiness. Two terms originating from Seligman's research are '*learned helplessness*' and '*learned optimism*'. The first term originated from (thankfully no longer used) experiments on dogs and rats. Seligman and colleagues were able to show that animals could be conditioned to believe that they had no power and thus were helpless. This happened when they repeatedly experienced stress. In humans, learned helplessness can lead to low self-esteem and depression. An example of learned helplessness in real life today is domestic abuse. Abusers subject their victims to violence and cruelty over time, until the victim believes that they have no power and are helpless. Hearing about a woman whose husband has been abusing her, people may say '*why didn't she just leave?*', but the likelihood is that she feels helpless and powerless to change anything. This is called '*cyclic abuse*' (Walker, 2017) and it involves four stages:

1. tensions build – external stressors, frustration and dissatisfaction intensify over time;

2. incidents of abuse or violence – the abuser gains power and control;

3. reconciliation – tensions fade, leading to a honeymoon stage of kindness and gifts;

4. calm – apologies, denial, justifying the behaviour.

Children can experience learned helplessness if their needs are not met, because of neglect or abuse. If a child has a learning disability, this can also lead to learned helplessness if the child feels they can never succeed, and that achievement is out of their control. Learned helplessness in children can lead to anxiety or depression. However, there are ways of counteracting this in children. Seligman (2011) realised that training in resilience could reverse the effects on people and could lead to '*learned optimism*'. Dweck's (2006) '*growth mindset*' theory indicates that children can learn to believe in their ability to develop and succeed. Figure 12.2 presents some of the ways this can be done.

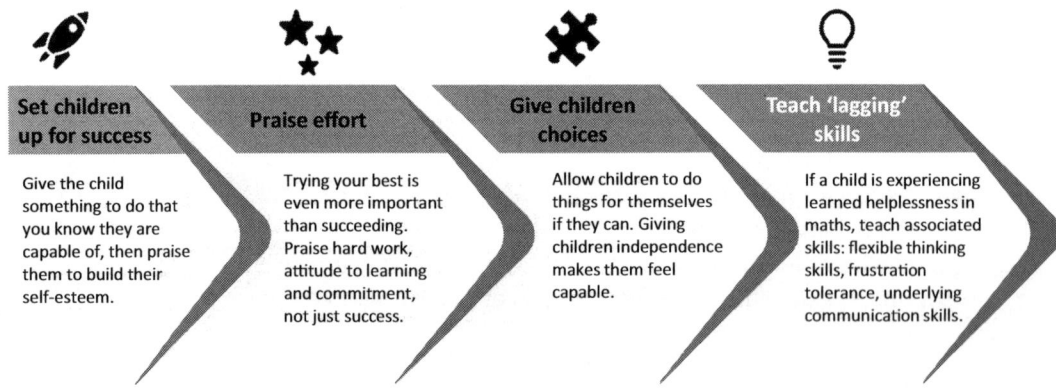

Figure 12.2 *Learned hopefulness/growth mindset activities*

Lopez' work on hope (2014) was related to teaching, the premise being that hopeful students are more successful in school. Lopez (2013a) identified three characteristics that make hopeful children more successful. He claimed that hopeful students are more excited about the future, they are more likely to go to school and they are engaged at school. Lopez claimed that getting children to identify goals for themselves motivates them to feel hopeful about their future; '*When students see a direct connection between the future they want and their attitudes and behaviors today, their commitment and effort soar*' (Lopez, 2013b, p 22).

McArthur-Blair and Cockell are two of the most recent writers on the subject of hope, building resilience and creating positive futures. Their view of hope is that '*Hope is not a simple concept. It is not about being joyful or optimistic all the time*' (McArthur-Blair and Cockell, 2018, p 7). For them, hope is the belief that the future will open new possibilities. They advocate use of Appreciative Inquiry (AI) to identify what is working well, a cornerstone of strength-based practice. They believe that resilience, the ability to '*bounce back*' from adversity, is a skill that can be learned and practised. Dvorsky et al (2019) explain the five C's of resilience taken from the Positive Youth Development movement (Figure 12.3).

Competence
• children need opportunities to develop skills and to be seen succeeding

Confidence
• children should be nurtured in experiencing success through age-appropriate activities

Connection
• children need to feel the security of being part of a group or community so they know they are not alone

Character
• children need an understanding of right and wrong and the capacity to make ethical decisions

Caring
• helping others makes it easier for children to ask for help if they need it; asking for help is important in developing resilience

Figure 12.3 *The five C's of resilience, adapted from Dvorsky et al (2019)*

The practitioner as an architect of hope

Given the importance of hope for achieving positive outcomes, it is crucial that the practitioner recognises their role in fostering and sustaining hope. Deegan (1996) suggests that practitioners should always model hope, offering opportunities for those they are working with to envisage a good outcome and imagine positive possibilities. Even when previous solutions and suggestions have been rejected, we should continue to offer support and choices. In this way, practitioners become 'Hopeful Helpers' (Sælør et al, 2015) in recognition that having someone who believes in you is one of the most important factors in developing resilience and working through challenges. Weingarten (2000) similarly suggests that hope should not be left to the individual, but is an entirely collaborative venture. In other words, practitioners need to scaffold and support hope, particularly when the individual is experiencing setbacks. The scenarios below explore how practitioners could help inspire hope in difficult circumstances.

Reflective questions ⑦

Read the following practice scenarios and explore the reflective questions.

Andy is a Learning Support Assistant, working one to one with Josh, a *13 year-old* boy who has missed lots of school due to a long-term, life-limiting illness. Josh loves technology and would like to be a programmer. However, his confidence is very low, and his health outcomes are very uncertain. Josh often gets very frustrated and is also having CAMHS support for depression and anxiety.

Becca is the recently appointed manager of an early years setting which has just received a disappointing Ofsted judgement. The team, who work very hard and are committed to their roles, are feeling very demotivated. The local newspaper ran an article about the Ofsted inspection, and this has left parents very concerned and unsettled.

Ranya works for a small voluntary organisation as a family support worker. She has recently received a referral for the Russell family. Susie is a young mum with three children under five, one of whom has additional needs. Her partner, Chris, is serving a five-year custodial sentence for aggravated burglary. Susie is very isolated and has little support around her. She often feels overwhelmed. Despite this, she takes good care of her children, and their relationships are very loving.

» Why is hope important in each of these situations?

» How can the practitioners help inspire hope in these challenging scenarios?

» What practice situations are you facing, where inspiring hope may be in ~~rt~~ nt?

Practitioner self-care

As we have seen, practitioners have an important role in fostering and sustaining hope in the children and families they work with. They also have a crucial role in identifying strengths and maintaining a positive mindset. This role can be challenging for practitioners because of the emotional labour involved. Emotional labour is a term coined by Hochschild (2012) to describe the management or suppression of emotions seen as inappropriate and the introduction of *'feeling rules'* (p 50). Figure 12.4 shows some of the *'feeling rules'* you may be expected to follow when working with children and families.

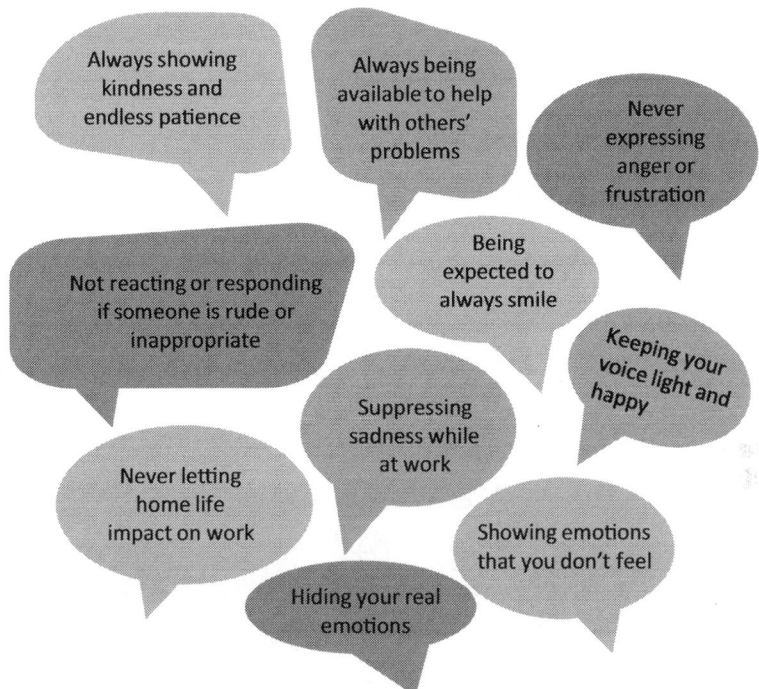

Figure 12.4 *Emotional labour 'feeling rules'*

The irony here is that practitioners working with children and families encourage children to express their feelings, as they know this is a healthy way to develop socially and emotionally, yet they are expected not to do this themselves. Working with children and families is hard work and can be emotionally as well as physically draining. Demonstrating empathy and compassion and prioritising children's needs above one's own can be exhausting. In the children and families sector, people also often feel that the profession is undervalued, and this, too, can lead to negative outcomes.

Compassion fatigue and burnout

The emotional load in working with children and families can result in 'compassion fatigue' or emotional distress (Taggart, 2011; Elfer et al, 2018). Compassion fatigue occurs when someone experiences stress as a result of helping others, especially when working with people who are experiencing trauma. Working in the child protection field, for example, is likely to expose workers to stories of trauma; when these experiences become overwhelming for the worker, this is compassion fatigue. Although compassion fatigue is widely reported as being a symptom of trauma work, the emotions of others do not need to be severe in order to create stress for practitioners. Being present for the normal reactions of young children at times of transition, for example, can be very emotional. Datler, Datler and Funder (2010, p 82) researched transitions and studied a young child starting nursery, observing his emotions and the reactions of staff. They concluded,

> *How hard and disturbing it is to be confronted so intimately with the primitive and often catastrophic emotions of very young children during their process of transition from home care to out-of-home care.*

Witnessing distress in children or families causes an emotional reaction in most practitioners and, if not recognised and managed, compassion fatigue can evolve into the more serious condition of burnout. At this stage, physical health can be affected, and practitioners may withdraw from the situation to protect themselves from suffering (Table 12.2).

Table 12.2 *Compassion fatigue and burnout*

	Compassion fatigue	**Burnout**
Affects	Unique to those working in caring or emotional support professions	Affects those working intensively without sufficient rest or relaxation
Causes	Caused by repeated exposure to others' stress, adversity or trauma	Caused by job-related stress, excessive workload
Signs	Insomnia, irritability, headaches, sore muscles, tiredness, feeling *'drained'*, negative thoughts, anxiety, relationship issues, self-blame, disconnection, self-medication, substance abuse	As for signs of compassion fatigue PLUS potential physical problems (weakened immune system, heart disease, high blood pressure, type 2 diabetes) Work-related feelings of inadequacy Lack of enjoyment at work
Appearance	Occurs suddenly	Develops over time
Effects	Can lead to burnout or depression if not managed Easier to manage than burnout	Withdrawal, hopelessness, isolation Emotions can become duller Long recovery process
Needs	Emotional support Training in stress management Work/life balance Prioritising self-care Take a break Set boundaries Mindfulness	Flexibility Time off work Work/life balance Regular exercise, healthy diet, good sleep habits Communication with others Mindfulness and meditation Professional help services

The Buddha once said, '*if your compassion does not include yourself, it is incomplete*' (Kornfield, 1996, p 5). It is vital that practitioners develop self-awareness so they can assess their own mental state. Feeling happy, being productive and realising our potential are all important aspects of mental well-being and this is essential to enable us to cope with the daily stresses of life. Figure 12.5 illustrates just some of the ways that practitioners can take care of their own mental health. Different things will work for different people; for some, spring cleaning the house provides a feeling of happiness and well-being; for others, a long hot bath will be the best option. Considering self-care from a strength-based perspective means awareness of your own triggers and appropriate self-care.

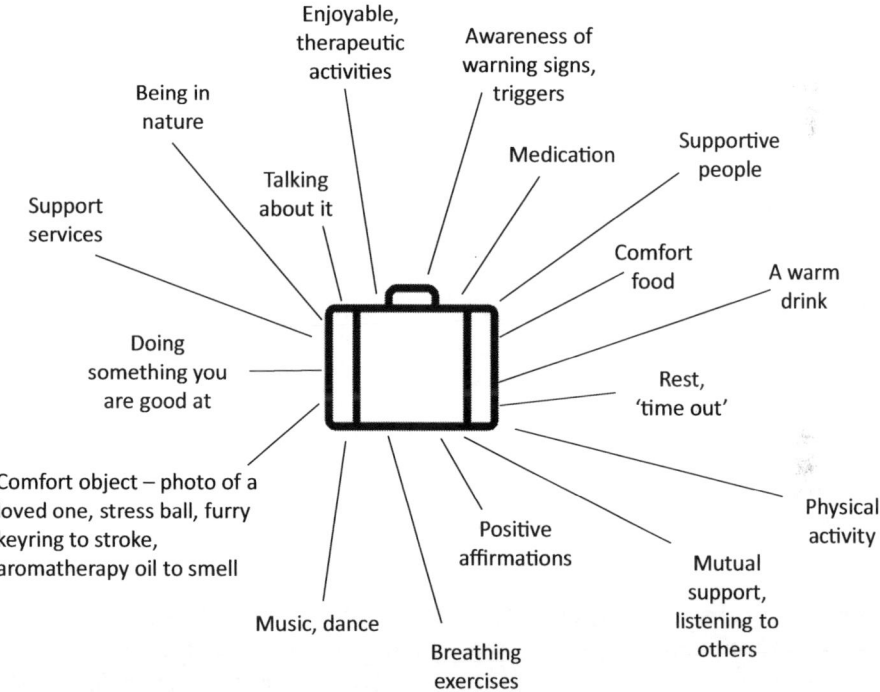

Figure 12.5 *Mental health toolkit (Prowle and Hodgkins, 2020)*

Compassion satisfaction

Compassion fatigue, as previously discussed, can be a result of working with others who are upset, suffering or traumatised, within a caring profession. However, a contrasting concept, '*compassion satisfaction*' may be the key to coping with such fatigue. The view that compassion and emotion work can have a positive effect on people has been the subject of recent research (eg Stamm, 2013; Singer et al, 2020). Stamm studied people working in a range of caring professions including carers, rape crisis workers, mental health workers and victim support counsellors. Stamm concluded that '*a person could be at high risk for experiencing compassion fatigue and, at the same time, still experience high compassion satisfaction*' (2013, p 113). In a recent research project examining empathy and compassion in the early years (Hodgkins, 2022), practitioners identified these five examples of satisfaction within the role (Figure 12.6). Practitioners taking part in the research reported having lots of fun with children and one participant said it was the best job in the world. Compassion satisfaction is indeed a strength, one that can mitigate the negative effects of compassion fatigue.

Figure 12.6 *Compassion satisfaction themes*

Key messages from the chapters of this book

Each of the chapters in this book has focused on one area of practice with children, young people and families and we have discussed many aspects of strength-based practice throughout. Here, we summarise a key message from each of the Chapters 2–11 (Figure 12.7).

- **Chapter 2** – Chapter 2 explored strength-based approaches to working with very young children, from before birth through the first few months of life. The key message from this chapter was about expectations and the reframing of negative perceptions of people.

- **Chapter 3** – in Chapter 3, the practice of '*strength-spotting*' was introduced, in relation to the care and education of young children in early childhood. Spotting and emphasising a child's strengths is a good way to instil confidence and self-esteem.

- **Chapter 4** – this chapter explored the amazing opportunities that middle childhood presents for identifying and building upon children's strengths. During this period, children are beginning to explore their world more independently, making friendships outside the home and discovering their preferences and interests. This is a time for playfulness, creativity and adventuring, all of which the practitioner can support and scaffold.

- **Chapter 5** – in Chapter 5, we considered the importance of young people's participation in decision making, both individually, in relation to matters that directly affect their lives, and collectively, in relation to public life and civic spaces. Youth work was presented as an essentially strength-based and person-centred process that could provide a helpful model for practice in other disciplines.

- **Chapter 6** – in Chapter 6, the emphasis was on acceptance of difference in relation to ability and learning. The multiple intelligences theory is the key message here, celebrating all types of intelligence and finding children's talents.

- **Chapter 7** – in this chapter, the focus was upon supporting strong relationships within the family and particularly between parents/carers and children. The concept of good enough parenting was introduced to dispel the myth of parental perfection and to support parents' confidence in their ability to provide nurturing environments for children.

- **Chapter 8** – this chapter explored the importance of a strength-based approach when working with children and families who are experiencing multiple adversities. The key message here was that, even in very challenging circumstances, there will be resilience factors that have enabled the individual or family to survive this far. These aspects can be harnessed as strengths for the present and future. The importance of challenging deterministic thinking was also explored; sensitive intervention and effective support can contribute to positive outcomes.

- **Chapter 9** – in Chapter 9, a strength-based approach was associated with child protection and safeguarding in the widest sense of the term. The key message in all aspects of safeguarding is listening to the voice of the child and acting on the child's voice.

- **Chapter 10** – in Chapter 10, diversity was examined, and difference considered as a strength to be celebrated. The key message for practitioners is the importance of positive representation, so that all children and families feel seen and heard.

- **Chapter 11** – in Chapter 11, we considered strength-based leadership as a way of harnessing your own potential as well as that of your team and your environment, to effect positive change. Leadership was reconceptualised as essentially collaborative and enabling rather than dependent on a strong charismatic personality.

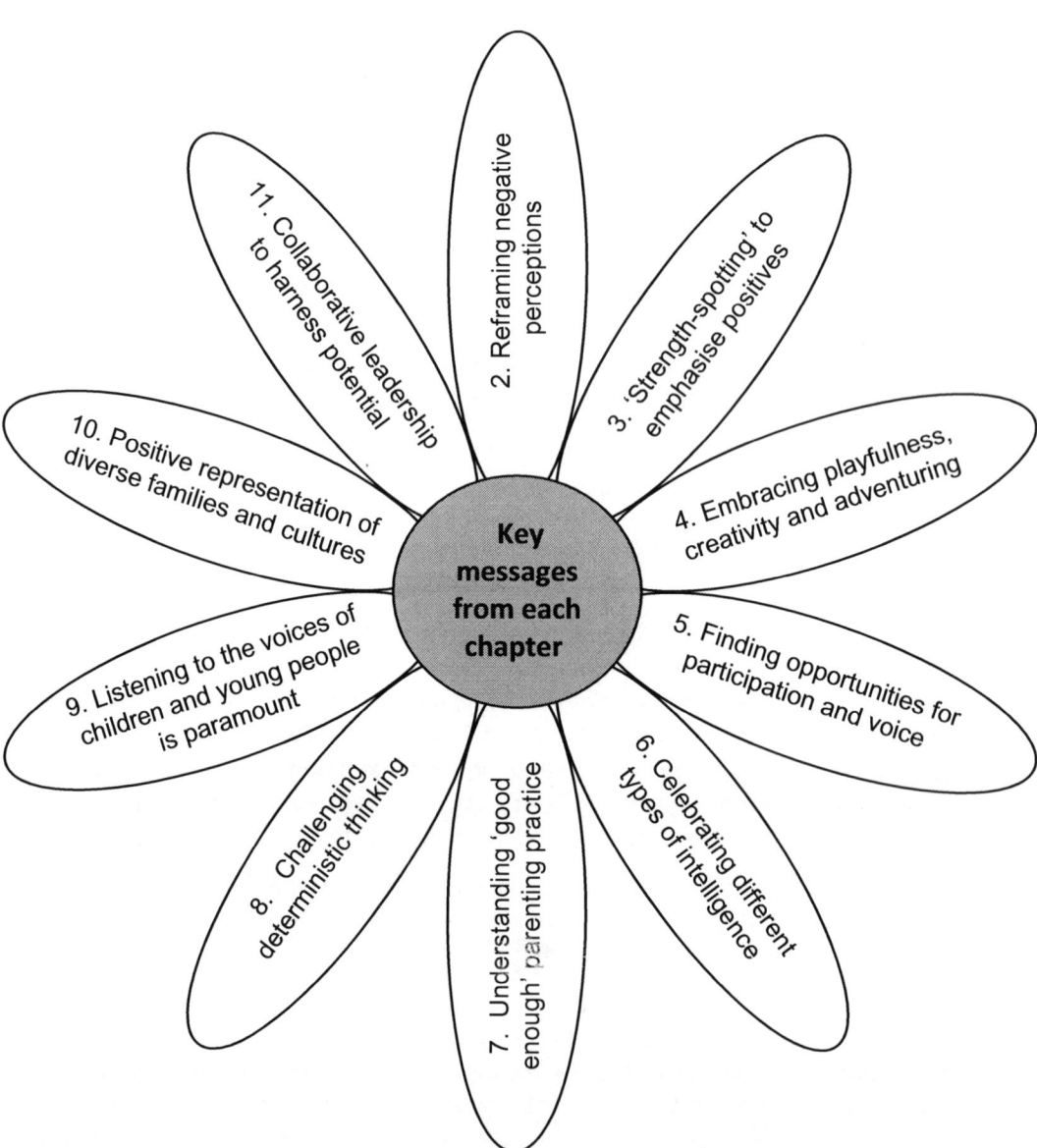

Figure 12.7 *Key messages from each chapter*

Cultivating hope in an uncertain world

We live in uncertain times. Climate emergency, war in Europe and the recent Covid-19 pandemic have all served to show us how tentative and unknowable our futures are. For many individuals, as Jensen (2022) points out, hopefulness in this context is more important than ever and encapsulates the twin aspects of being able to imagine a plausible, better future, and believing you have the tools to achieve it. In order to start cultivating hope, Mattis (2021) states that action is imperative, identifying key strategies:

- start with goals;

- move beyond wishing into imagining and action;

- harness the power of uncertainty and think about those aspects that are under your control;

- manage your attention through focus;

- seek community with others and enlist their support.

Hardy (2020) proposes eight evidence-based ways for cultivating hope. These are shown in Figure 12.8 below.

Figure 12.8 *Ways to increase hope (adapted from Hardy, 2020)*

Other strategies, like keeping a hope journal, can also be helpful in enabling individuals to sustain hope.

Chapter summary

In this chapter, we have explored the importance of hope in a rapidly changing and unpredictable practice landscape. Sometimes, a reason for hope is not immediately visible, so practitioners need to actively seek out opportunities for hope and optimism, especially in challenging circumstances. They can then model hopeful solutions and collaborate with those who use their services to envisage and then work towards positive outcomes. However, it is equally important for practitioners to be aware of and to work on their own strengths. Self-care is a crucial aspect of practice necessary to avoid compassion fatigue and burnout. Finally, we have identified some key messages from the book to support strength-based approaches to practice.

Further reading 📖

- Helman, C (nd) *The Science of Power and Hope*. TED talk. [online] Available at: www.ted.com/talks/chan_hellman_the_science_and_power_of_hope (accessed 19 June 2023).

  This TED talk by Dr Chan Helman explores the science of hope and how hope can be harnessed by individuals to help them achieve positive change.

- Hochschild, A (2012) *The Managed Heart – Commercialization of Human Feeling*, 3rd ed. California: University of California Press.

  A very interesting book about emotional labour. Hochschild's work began with aeroplane cabin crew, a group of professionals expected to display particular emotions at work. They are expected to smile and to be calm at all times, regardless of the way they feel and the way they are treated by customers.

- Houston, E (2019) What is Hope in Psychology? 7 Exercises & Worksheets. [online] Available at: https://positivepsychology.com/hope-therapy/ (accessed 19 June 2023).

  An excellent resource on the importance of hope is found on the Positive Psychology website. The resource contains explanations, activities and signposts to further resources.

References 📚

Cambridge Dictionary (2023) *Hope*. [online] Available at: https://dictionary.cambridge.org/dictionary/english/hope (accessed 19 June 2023).

Datler, W, Datler, M and Funder, A (2010) Struggling Against a Feeling of Becoming Lost: A Young Boy's Painful Transition to Day Care. *Infant Observation*, 13(1): 65–87.

Deegan, P (1996) Recovery as a Journey of the Heart. *Psychiatric Rehabilitation Journal*, 19(3): 91–7.

Dvorsky, M R et al (2019) Factor Structure and Criterion Validity of the Five Cs Model of Positive Youth Development in a Multi-University Sample of College Students. *Journal of Youth and Adolescence*, 48(3): 537–53.

Dweck, C (2006) *Mindset: The New Psychology of Success*. London: Random House.

Elfer, P, Greenfield, S, Robson, S, Wilson, D and Zachariou, A (2018) Love, Satisfaction and Exhaustion in the Nursery: Methodological Issues in Evaluating the Impact of Work Discussion Groups in the Nursery. *Early Child Development and Care*, 188(7): 892–904.

Hardy, B (2020) 8 Science-backed Ways to Increase your Hope. *Forge* [online] Available at: https://forge.medium.com/10-science-based-ways-to-increase-your-hope-430892caacb2 (accessed 19 June 2023).

Hockley, J (1993) The Concept of Hope and the Will to Live. *Palliative Medicine* 7(3).

Hodgkins, A (2022) Exploring Early Childhood Practitioners' Perceptions of Empathy with Children and Families: Initial Findings. *Educational Review* (Birmingham), ahead-of-print(ahead-of-print), 1–19.

Jensen, D (2022) Sustaining Hope in Uncertain Times. *The Harvard Business Review* [online] Available at: https://hbr.org/2022/03/sustaining-hope-in-uncertain-times (accessed 19 June 2023).

Kornfield, J (1996) *Buddha's Little Instruction Book*. Chicago: Ebury Publishing.

Lopez, S (2013a) *Making Hope Happen: Create the Future You Want for Yourself and Others*. New York: Simon & Shuster.

Lopez, S J (2013b) Making Hope Happen in the Classroom. *Phi Delta Kappan*, 95(2): 19–22.

Lopez, J, Snyder, C and Teramoto, J (2014) *Positive Psychology: The Scientific and Practical Explorations of Human Strengths*, 3rd ed. Thousand Oaks, CA: Sage.

Mattis, E (2021) 5 Strategies for Cultivating Hope this Year. *The Conversation*. [online] Available at: https://theconversation.com/5-strategies-for-cultivating-hope-this-year-152523 (accessed 19 June 2023).

McArthur-Blair, J and Cockell, J (2018) *Building Resilience with Appreciative Inquiry*. Oakland, CA: Berrett-Koehler Publishers.

Prowle, A and Hodgkins, A (2020) Chapter 10: The Inclusive, Hope-inspiring Practitioner. In *Making a Difference with Children, Young People and Families* (pp 137–52). London: Red Globe Books, Bloomsbury.

Sælør, K, Ness, O, Borg, M and Biong, S (2015) You Never Know What's Around the Next Corner: Exploring Practitioners' Hope Inspiring Practices. *Advances of Dual Diagnosis*, 8: 141–52.

Seligman, M E P (1975) *Helplessness: On Depression, Development, and Death*. London: W H Freeman/Times Books/ Henry Holt & Co.

Seligman, M E P (2011) *Flourish: A New Understanding of Happiness and Well-Being - and How to Achieve Them*. London: Nicholas Brearley Publishing.

Snyder, C R (2000) *Handbook of Hope: Theory, Measures & Applications*. San Diego, CA: Academic Press.

Stamm, H (2013) Chapter 5: Measuring Compassion Satisfaction as Well as Fatigue: Developmental History of the Compassion Satisfaction and Fatigue Test. In *Treating Compassion Fatigue* (2nd ed. New York: Routledge.

Taggart, G (2011) Don't We Care? The Ethics and Emotional Labour of Early Years Professionalism. *Early Years*, 31(1): 85–95.

Walker, L E (2017) *The Battered Woman Syndrome*, 4th ed. New York: Springer Publishing.

Weingarten, K (2000) Witnessing, Wonder and Hope. *Family Process*, 39(4): 389–402.

Index